HOMO SAPIENS

The history of humans and the development of civilization

WILLIAM POTTER

ARCTURUS

ARCTURUS

This edition published in 2023 by Arcturus Publishing Limited
26/27 Bickels Yard, 151–153 Bermondsey Street,
London SE1 3HA

Copyright © Arcturus Holdings Limited

ISBN: 978-1-78828-091-4
AD005827UK

Printed in Malaysia

HOMO SAPIENS

CONTENTS – HOMO SAPIENS

INTRODUCTION

Approximately 12,000 generations separate us from the first *Homo sapiens*. Over 300,000 years we have worked together to build civilizations, to record our ideas and experiences through language, art and music, looked deep into time and space, and begun to understand the building blocks of nature. We are creatures capable of wonders. This is the story of humankind.

The human journey is rich with astonishing achievements, cultural peaks and remarkable discoveries. From hunter-gatherers to an agrarian society, farmsteads to cities, adventurers to astronauts, it is a story of progress and spirit against adversity.

The adventure begins with the ancestors of our species, *Homo sapiens,* and the great spread of humankind across the globe. The first attempts to domesticate plants and animals lead to regular harvests that allow communities to grow and artisans to flourish. From stone to clay, painted and chiselled records of our ancient past survive to tell us something of early beliefs and customs.

The invention of the written word provides deeper insight into the path of humanity, with hierarchies, laws and wars, as well as attempts through religion to understand our purpose on Earth. Cultures spring up on separate continents and contact is made with neighbours through travel and trade. Philosophies and inventions follow merchants and armies; pandemics, too. Civilizations rise and fall, knowledge is lost, then rediscovered.

Human history is marked out by revolutions in agriculture, industry, the humanities, politics and science. Nations have united in struggles against dictatorships, inequality and climate change to reach the present day. We are now part of a global network of enquiring minds, sharing passions and ideas over the internet as our ancestors would have done by crossing country borders.

Petroglyphs on Newspaper Rock, Utah, USA.

Astronauts Joe Acaba and Rick Arnold outside the International Space Station, 2009.

History is never a fixed thing. It is constantly being updated thanks to new science and new discoveries, such as fossils that push back the date of humankind's emergence ever further. Newly developed DNA analysis can recognize the source of pollen found beside hominin bones. Even the word *hominin* is a recent choice, to distinguish early and modern humans from our ape cousins. *Homo sapiens'* path from Africa continues to be diverted, and diverting.

History changes due to perspective, too. Ancient rulers used archaeology to confirm their status among revered bygone kings (see panel). Modern regimes can be selective about how they treat historical records, wishing to be seen in a positive light and diminishing the achievements of rivals. Twenty-first-century sensibilities also colour our perception of the past. The reputation and behaviour of conquerors, explorers, trading companies and empires are continually being reassessed. Heroes become villains; villains, heroes. Non-Eurocentric stories are sought out. The roles of indigenous people and black, brown and female participants are rightly given greater prominence.

EARLY EXCAVATIONS

Discovering the buried past often occurs by accident, when laying the foundations of new buildings. The first recorded archaeological excavations came about in Mesopotamia, with the last of the Neo-Babylonian kings ordering that the foundations of former temples be traced to guide new constructions. The final king, Nabonidus (556–539 BCE), made efforts to date the uncovered ruins and artefacts, and tried to legitimize his rule by linking his own with the earlier Akkadian Empire.

Early archaeological digs were haphazard treasure hunts rather than serious scientific studies. Dating discoveries involved guesswork. Historic sites were explored to confirm what was already assumed from Classical texts and legend, and to support the pedigree of rulers and collectors keen to display their taste and to emphasize their lineage.

The so-called Grand Tours of the 17th to 19th century saw wealthy Europeans travelling to Italy for a cultural education, collecting Classical antiquities to display back home. Some private collections became so extensive they provided the cornerstone for museums.

History is dynamic and illuminating. It provides lessons for the present and the future. It reminds us of what we have achieved and what we could continue to achieve. The chipped flint tool in our ancestors' hands is now an infrared telescope in solar orbit, peering back to the dawn of the universe. *Homo sapiens* looks back in order to better understand the future.

Bison depicted in the cave art at Altamira, Spain, from approximately 30,000 years ago.

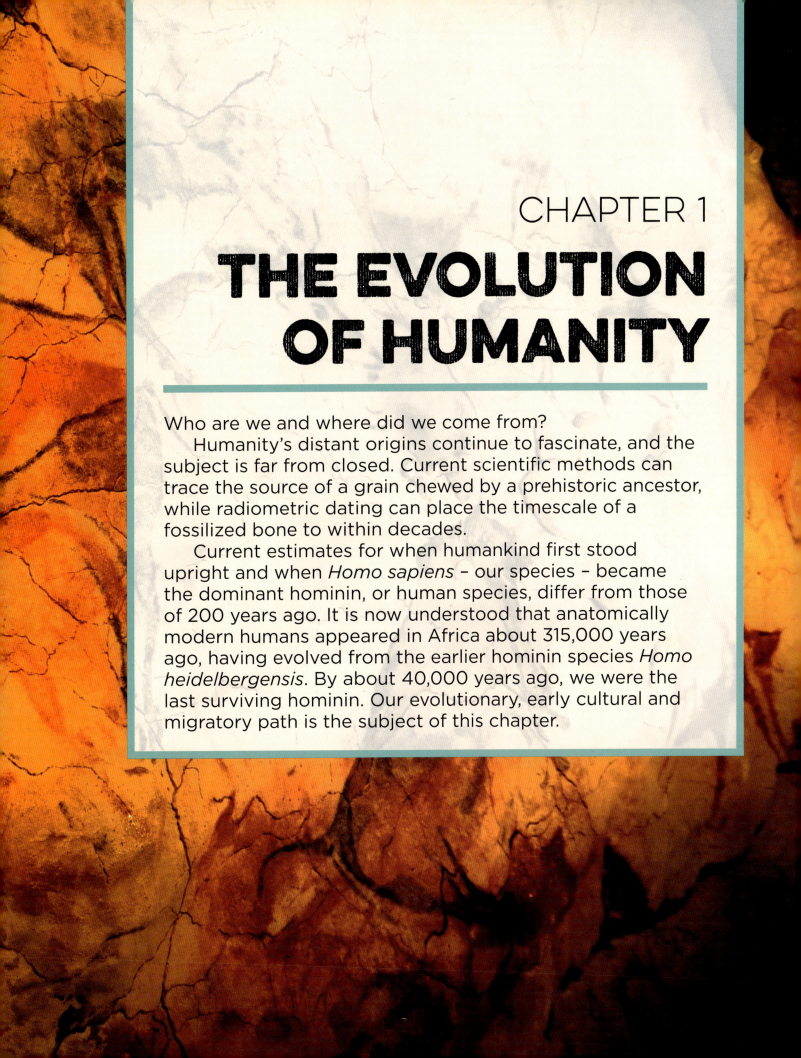

CHAPTER 1
THE EVOLUTION OF HUMANITY

Who are we and where did we come from?

Humanity's distant origins continue to fascinate, and the subject is far from closed. Current scientific methods can trace the source of a grain chewed by a prehistoric ancestor, while radiometric dating can place the timescale of a fossilized bone to within decades.

Current estimates for when humankind first stood upright and when *Homo sapiens* – our species – became the dominant hominin, or human species, differ from those of 200 years ago. It is now understood that anatomically modern humans appeared in Africa about 315,000 years ago, having evolved from the earlier hominin species *Homo heidelbergensis*. By about 40,000 years ago, we were the last surviving hominin. Our evolutionary, early cultural and migratory path is the subject of this chapter.

TIMELINE OF HUMAN EVOLUTION

The evolution of humankind can be tracked back millions of years to our early primate ancestors that dwelt in the trees. Bipeds arrived about six million years ago, but it would be another 5.5 million years before the first *Homo sapiens* appeared.

mya = million years ago
ya = years ago

55 MYA
First lemur-like primates evolve, probably in Asia, according to fossil records

~10 MYA
Gorillas and human evolutionary lines split

~8 MYA
Chimpanzee and human evolutionary lines split

7–6 MYA
Sahelanthropus tchadensis, early hominin, in Central Africa

6.2–5.8 MYA
Orrinin tugenensis, possible first hominin to walk on two legs, in East Africa

700,000–200,000 YA
Homo heidelbergensis lives in Africa and Europe. Has a brain similar in size to modern humans. Last probable ancestor of *Homo neanderthalensis* (Neanderthals), and *Homo sapiens* ('wise man')

1.8 MYA
Homo erectus ('upright man'), lives in Africa, Europe and Asia

2.3 MYA
Possible first 'Homo', the large-brained hominin *Homo habilis* ('handyman'), appears

1.9 MYA
Homo ergaster ('working man'), lives in East Africa

3.6 MYA
Australopithecus afarensis leaves footprints in volcanic ash in Laetoli, northern Tanzania

4.2 MYA
Australopithecines, small hominins with chimp-sized skulls, appear in East Africa

3.3 MYA
Oldest-known stone tools made in Lomekwi, Kenya

3.2 MYA
Australopithecus afarensis 'Lucy' lives in Ethiopia

3–2 MYA
Hominins lose body hair

190,000 YA

1 m (3 ft) tall *Homo floresiensis* (colloquially known as 'hobbits') live in Indonesia

130,000–115,000 YA

First migration of *Homo sapiens* from Africa to the Middle East

115,000 YA

Last glacial period of Pleistocene Ice Age begins

110,000 YA

Oldest-known jewellery, made from seashells

300,000 YA

Fire commonly used

315,000 YA

Homo sapiens lives in Morocco

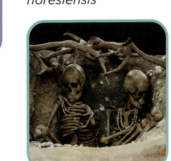

70,000 YA

Second migration of *Homo sapiens* from Africa to the rest of the world

50,000 YA

First burials, clothes manufacture, improved hunting techniques. Extinction of *Homo floresiensis*

335,000–236,000 YA

Homo naledi lives in southern Africa

45,000 YA

Earliest known musical instrument, a bone flute in North Africa. *Homo sapiens* arrives in Australia

430,000 YA

Earliest evidence of *Homo neanderthalensis*, Spain

400,000 YA

Oldest-known wooden spears found in Schöningen, Germany

40,000 YA

Red-dot cave art, El Castillo, Spain. Last evidence of Neanderthals in Europe. *Homo sapiens* becomes the sole surviving hominin

16,000 YA

Homo sapiens reaches America

500,000 YA

Oldest known graphic mark, left by *Homo erectus* on a shell in Trinil, Java

12,000 YA

Beginning of the Agricultural Revolution

450,000 YA

Neanderthal and Denisovan lines split. Neanderthals evolve in Europe, Denisovans in Asia

11,700 YA

End of the last interglacial, cold phase

THE SEARCH FOR HUMAN ANCESTORS

Until the middle of the 19th century, it was understood by many that humankind had appeared on Earth just a few thousand years ago (on 23 October 4004 BCE, to be precise, according to one widely circulated calculation based on the Bible). A series of archaeological finds in Europe would stretch that timescale by almost a hundredfold.

A customs official by day, Jacques Boucher de Perthes spent his free time as an amateur archaeologist, surveying gravel quarries in the Somme Valley. Around 1830, he uncovered flint stones that he suspected had been worked by human hands and carefully chipped into useful cutting tools. The discovery of ancient stone tools was not extraordinary on its own; it was what de Perthes found alongside them that would revolutionize our understanding of human development. The flint hand axes were positioned in layers of rock alongside elephant and woolly rhinoceros remains, animals that had been extinct in the region for 10,000 years. Similar finds had been made by others in southern France and Britain, but few experts accepted the idea that the long-dead animals and hominins were contemporaries.

De Perthes' research was finally vindicated in 1859, placing humankind in the Late Pleistocene age that ended 11,700 years ago. Researchers had a new era for the study of humankind: prehistory. We now know the tools that de Perthes uncovered belonged not to modern humans but to *Homo neanderthalensis*, or Neanderthals, that populated the area at least half a million years earlier. The publication of Charles Darwin's *On the Origin of Species* in the same year that de Perthes' theories were accepted provided a new context for this 'Antiquity of Man'. The idea that our ancestors had descended from apes and existed for millions of years led scientists to re-examine fossils and seek to build a family tree that linked apes to modern humans. Over 20 hominin species have now been identified as existing over the last 3.5 million years.

HUMAN REMAINS

Paleoanthropology, the scientific study of ancient human remains, became a serious endeavour from the late 19th century. The discovery of 18 anatomically modern human skeletons among flint tools in a cave in Aurignac and in a rock shelter in Cro-Magnon, France, proved our species, *Homo sapiens*, existed between 10,000 and 35,000 years ago.

The family tree that led to our species separated from apes about 8 million years ago (mya) with short, early upright-walking hominins, Australopithi-

Two flint hand axes discovered by Jacques Boucher de Perthes in the Somme Valley.

cines found in Africa from 4.2 mya. The first known example of the genus Homo was *Homo habilis* ('handyman'), from about 2.3 mya, though lack of fossil evidence has raised debate on the nature of this species. *Homo habilis* had a brain about 40 per cent larger than a chimpanzee and was able to wield stones as simple tools. The species survived in Africa for about 650,000 years.

The Homo genus includes several species that came to a dead end, but *Homo ergaster* ('working man') from 1.9 mya was one that survived to become our direct ancestor. From Ergaster came *Homo heidelbergensis* between 700,000 and 200,000 years ago, the final predecessor of both *Homo neanderthalensis* and our species, *Homo sapiens*.

As more ancient human remains are discovered and dated by new accurate scientific means, details of the age and path of *Homo sapiens* are sure to be updated. As recently as 2017, skeletal fragments and stone tools were discovered in Jebel Irhoud, Morocco, that predated the previous record holder from Ethiopia by 150,000 years. Currently, Sapiens is considered to have emerged about 315,000 years ago with the coming together of groups from eastern and southern Africa.

WHAT ARE FOSSILS?

When a living creature dies, the soft parts of its body rot away, leaving the bones. In rare circumstances, the body is buried under layers of sediment which compress the skeleton. The bones slowly dissolve as water permeates the rock. Minerals in the water replace the bone, leaving behind a rock replica: a fossil. Not all fossils are the remains of a living creature or plant. Some, known as trace fossils, are evidence of actions, such as footprints or excavations.

THE CRADLE OF HUMANITY

In 1924, the Australian anthropologist Raymond Dart made a discovery that would answer questions about the origin of humankind. Quarrymen in Taung, South Africa, unearthed the skull of an ape-like human that Dart recognized as belonging to a human ancestor. Dart named it *Australopithecus africanus* for 'southern ape from Africa', and so located the 'cradle of humanity' in Africa.

This origin was further confirmed in 1974 by the discovery of 'Lucy' in Hadar, Ethiopia, by Donald Johanson and Maurice Taieb. Lucy was the name given to the fossilized bones of a female hominin that lived 3.2 million years ago. At the time, her remains were the earliest evidence of upright-walking hominin life on Earth. Lucy was one of a species called *Australopithecus afarensis*. Footprints from others of her species have since been found in Laetoli, northern Tanzania, and dated to 3.66 million years ago.

Named after a Beatles song, 'Lucy' is the fossilized skeleton of a young female Australopithecus afarensis, *found in the Afar region of Ethiopia in 1974. She stood about 1–1.6 m (3–5 ft) tall and weighed about 30 kg (66 lbs). Her remains are reckoned to be 3.2 million years old.*

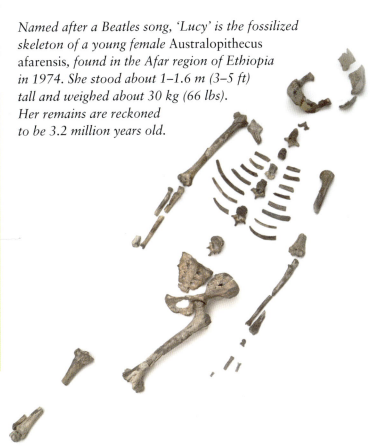

UNEARTHING THE PAST

Tracing the path of our human ancestors and determining their way of life requires the work of prehistorians. By analyzing fossilized hominin remains and the fragments of tools, their age and position, we have been able to understand something of the millions of years before the written record began (around 6,000 years ago).

Formal methods for exploring sites were pioneered at the end of the 18th century, with excavations marked out with string grids. Finds were recorded with sketches before they were transported for study. William Smith's development of stratigraphy (see panel) in the 19th century led to more accurate dating of discoveries, matching finds with those in other locations based on their position within layers of rock.

In the present day, work at an archaeological site involves many disciplines. Geophysicists map beneath the surface with 3D sensors; sedimentologists investigate the soil and rocks; palynologists research the historic climate by examining pollen and spores; paleontologists study fossilized bones.

With most organic matter (flesh and wood) long decayed, experts must make deductions from fossilized remains. Complete skeletons are rare. Often all that is left are the stone elements of tools and pieces of bone or teeth, but these can reveal much about the past. Careful recording of position can help experts reconstruct a jigsaw of broken bone fragments at a later date. Tooth size, decay and wear can indicate an individual's age, health and diet.

Modern technology unlocks the secrets of fossils and artefacts back in a lab. Radioactive dating (see panel) can ascertain the age of a find; chemical analysis can detect traces of foods; the source of raw materials used by ancient humans can be located; electron microscopes can identify bacteria and individual species of pollen; DNA samples can be extracted from fossilized bones to determine the relationship between populations.

While modern archaeology uses aerial photography and LIDAR scanning (which creates a 3D map using lasers), the trusty trowel and brush have remained part of an archaeologist's toolkit for more than a hundred years.

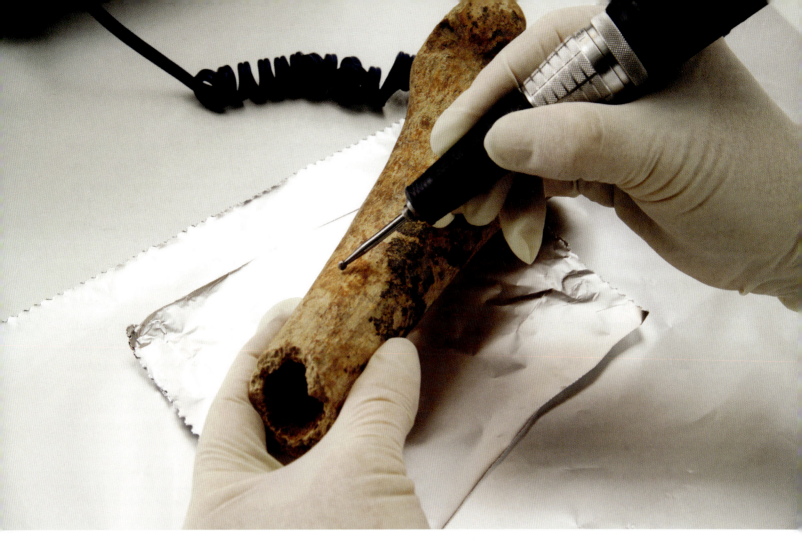

Bone tissue includes naturally occurring radioactive isotopes of carbon. When the tissue dies, one isotope decays at a constant rate. By comparing the samples of carbon isotopes in ancient bones, scientists can calculate the date that the tissue died.

SETTING A DATE

Over millions of years layers of rock, lava, ash and sediment have built up over the earth, burying the past. Like the rings in a tree trunk, layers of rocks mark periods of Earth's history. Igneous rocks are formed when molten rock cools; sedimentary rocks are the result of compressed sediment. Layers may be separated by thin lines of ash, identifying periods of great volcanic activity.

The timescale for these different layers, or strata, was first mapped by the English geologist William Smith in 1840 using fossils found in each of 32 layers as key identifiers for each era. Knowing when a fossilized creature existed allowed Smith to date other fossils found in the same strata. Smith's dates provided archaeologists with a guide to dating the remains of early hominins. Since then, newer, more accurate methods have been invented that can pinpoint the age of a find.

Radiometric dating was invented in 1907. It works by measuring the decay of naturally occurring radioactive isotopes in materials such as carbon or rocks. While its accuracy can be affected by contamination, random tests from different laboratories have confirmed its effectiveness.

EVOLUTION OF THE BRAIN

Hominins evolved from primates, walking taller and developing new skills, using simple tools and working in groups, but it was the evolution of the human brain that set us apart from our ancestors. How did this come about, and was size all that mattered?

Early hominins had brains equivalent in size to those of modern apes. Brain volume is not a good measure for intelligence; many animals have brains much larger than humans. A better comparison is between brain size and body mass.

By measuring skull capacity, scientists have been able to estimate the brain size of our ancestors. Over millions of years brain size increased compared to body mass, from 1.2 per cent for *Australopithecus afarensis* (3.7–3 mya) to 1.46 per cent for *Homo erectus* (1.8–0.03 mya), then to 2.75 per cent for *Homo sapiens*.

The increase in brain volume for hominins was not uniform. There was little change in brain size for Australopithecus, the early hominins that roamed Africa between 4.4 and 1.4 mya. Their brains remained about 35 per cent the size of *Homo sapiens*, comparable with those of the chimpanzee. However, evidence found in *Australopithecus sediba*, a hominin discovered near Johannesburg, South Africa, in 2008, suggests that the hominin brain was changing shape. The neocortex had begun to expand, allowing the brain to focus less on visual processing and more on other areas. Australopithecus and later hominins were able to deal with new challenges, such as climate change.

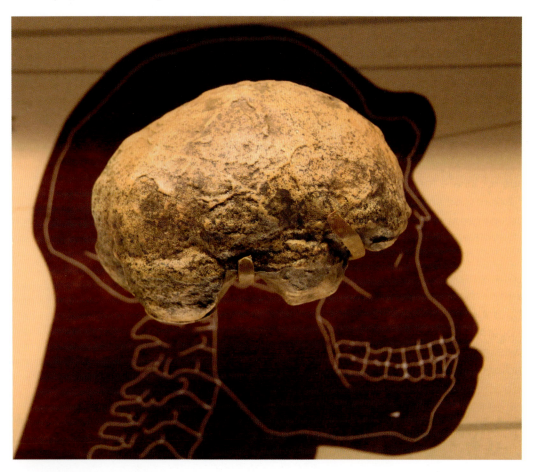

This endocast – a model of the brain made by using the imprints left by its blood vessels and the brain itself on the skull – shows how the brain fitted within the skull of a Homo erectus.

BRAIN POWER

Human brains require a lot of a body's energy. Despite being just 4 per cent of the body's volume, human brains demand as much as 20 per cent of our energy, even at rest. This compares to 8 per cent for apes. As hominins turned to a more carnivorous diet, and enjoyed omega 3-rich seafood 2 million years ago, the extra calories would have helped fuel and build the brain. Once fire was adopted and archaic humans began to cook food, they would have found it easier to digest, requiring less energy and smaller guts. This freed up more resources for brain development in Neanderthals and Sapiens. A trade-off in focusing on increased brain power was a reduction in physical strength. Smaller muscles require less fuel.

Related to this, primates with strong jaw muscles bring into play a force across the whole skull, which limits brain growth. With food becoming easier to digest, hominins were able to survive with weaker bites and provide space for brain growth.

Size of brain was clearly not everything. Neanderthals had slightly larger brains than *Homo sapiens* yet they were pushed back from their territory and eventually became extinct, while Sapiens dominated. It seems that *Homo sapiens* had better cognitive abilities than their predecessors and were able to outsmart them and communicate better.

BEING UNDERSTOOD

The brain was key to the development of speech. The growth of part of the brain's frontal lobe called Broca's area helped *Homo sapiens* to make more varied sounds. Broca's area helps control complex movements for both the hands and tongue. Chimpanzees have similar anatomy to humans but different nasal cavities, higher larynxes and less adaptable lips and tongues that prevent them from mastering a complex range of sounds that could be understood as language.

HEAD SPACE

With a larger brain came a larger cranium, which presented a fresh problem. The size of the hominin pelvic girdle is restricted by the need for females to walk upright. This limits the width of the birth canal and the size of a baby's head that a mother can give birth to. The solution for hominins was, in effect, to give birth prematurely. This means a newborn human child is dependent on its parents for many months while its brain almost doubles in size in the first year. No other primate requires her baby to go through as many twists and turns during birth before emerging so undeveloped. While there are risks in giving birth to a helpless child – and there were many dangers for early hominins, including predators – our species thrived by providing a quality of care for infants who were vulnerable but quick to learn.

Subtle differences in chimpanzee anatomy prevents them from vocalizing in as complex a manner as humans.

THE FIRST TOOLS

The ability to fashion and utilize tools was a major advance for humankind, aiding the hunt for food, its preparation and the production of warmer clothing.

The first evidence of tool use dates back 3.3 million years, to East Africa's *Australopithecus afarensis*, about a million years before the genus Homo appeared. Fossil remains show stones were used to break animal bones to access the fatty marrow inside. Such bones would have been left behind by predators unable to crunch the large bones of the kill in their jaws.

Homo habilis, a human ancestor from 2.3–1.65 million years ago, shaped stones to create cutting edges. Flint was a useful stone to work with. It easily chips, leaving sharp finishes. When struck against pyrite it can sometimes produce a spark sizable enough to light kindling.

Improvements in stone-tool manufacture were prolonged, over millions of years. Around 250,000 years ago archaic humans mastered the Levallois technique, which involved chipping flakes from the edge of flint in an organized way to produce a rounded sharp stone like a tortoise shell. Eventually, the sharp cutting stones were attached or embedded in wood handles. *Homo neanderthalensis* worked out how to use heated birch-tree pitch to glue stone points to spear shafts. Meat then became the primary source of nutrition for Neanderthals. Spears were used for hunting big game, such as woolly rhinoceros, red deer and bison, while blades were used to scrape hides, strip carcasses and divide portions between members of a group.

This Stone-Age hand axe was crafted in the Lower Paleolithic era (300,000–50,000 years ago).

CUTTING EDGE

By the Upper Paleolithic (50,000–12,000 years ago) *Homo sapiens* were employing stone, bone and wooden tools for hunting, hammering, cutting and drilling.

Bone fishhooks, harpoons and barbed spears were carved from reindeer antlers by northern hunters. About 20,000 years ago, the Cro-Magnons (early European *Homo sapiens*) designed the throwing stick, or atlatl. At its most basic, this was a hooked stick used to propel a spear further through the air than was otherwise possible by arm and hand power alone. With greater range, hunters could surprise prey and risk attacking large animals, such as the mammoth. Other weapons employed around this time include the harpoon, javelin and boomerang. Hunters also worked out how to set traps, including snares for small animals, such as rabbits and boar.

BOW AND ARROW

Arrowheads have been discovered dating back more than 60,000 years, but the earliest confirmed appearance of both bows and arrows as hunting tools is from 48,000 years ago, found in the Fa Hien Cave in Sri Lanka. Game hunted with this early bow and arrow could have included monkeys and squirrels.

The early wooden bow was strung with stretchy animal sinews and used to fire wooden arrows tipped with stone or bone. Later, the arrowheads were cut into barbed shapes to keep them fixed in their intended target. Hunting with a bow and arrow required target practice and the patient ability to stalk and approach prey without disturbing it.

Ivory and bone tools dated to between 30,000 and 18,000 years ago, including a tool to make needles, a needle, a harpoon head, a barbed point and two carved heads.

NEEDLECRAFT

Whittling bone, antlers and ivory into tools was explored from about 30,000 years ago. The needle was one early and revolutionary invention. Fine needles were crafted by rounding one end of the material, then scraping the other end to a fine point. The needle was then polished with abrasive sandstone before an eye was drilled into the round end with a sharp point of flint.

Animal sinews, dried, sliced and then chewed to make them flexible were used for thread. Garments could then be sewn together using softened animal pelts. One example of clothing from the Upper Paleolithic era was a child's tunic made of squirrel fur, unearthed in Grimaldi, northern Italy.

These better-fitting and warmer clothes helped humans survive in the colder temperatures of the Eurasian steppes or the northern land route into the Americas. The needle and thread was also used to construct tents. Much later, about 4,000 years ago, Inuits threaded together stretched seal hides over a framework of branches or whalebone to build their kayaks.

STONE AGE CULTURE

Through cave painting, sculpture and personal adornment, the people of the Stone Age left descriptions of their lives for future generations. What do we know of their rituals and culture?

Without a written record, much of our knowledge of *Homo sapiens* during the Stone Age period (2.5 mya to 2,000 BCE) comes from their buried remains, artefacts and DNA investigations. While these can give us an idea of ancient human distribution, health and activity, there is another historical record that brings the period to life: art.

Most prehistoric rock art has been discovered in cave shelters where the work has survived millennia of weather erosion. These early traces show humans doing more than surviving; they are finding ways to express ideas about themselves and recording their way of life. After hours hunting, foraging and feasting, there would have been time left for groups to socialize, groom themselves and produce decorations.

The Cueva de las Manos (Cave of the Hands) in Santa Cruz, Argentina, is decorated with ancient hand stencils added to the rock walls over different periods from about 7,300 years ago.

The earliest examples of expressive marks have been found in the Blombos cave, South Africa. Among discarded spearpoints are stones notched with repeated diagonal patterns. Similar, faint geometrical markings painted in ochre on rock fragments have been dated to 73,000 years ago. There are also pierced shells which would have been strung to form beads for personal adornment.

Pigments used to decorate cave walls and ceilings include red and yellow ochre, charcoal, hematite and manganese oxide. Among the earliest images found is a red hand stencil reckoned to have been left by a Neanderthal in a Spanish cave more than 64,000 years ago. Depictions of pig hunting in Indonesian caves date back over 43,000 years. Early daubed images of humans and animals could be describing a typical hunt, or they could have been painted as part of a ritual, with the art serving a religious function.

Some of the most spectacular examples of cave art date from between 28,000 and 13,000 years ago, when populations moved south during the Ice Age. Fine images of deer, aurochs (large Eurasian oxen), horses and bison survive in caves in Spain and southwestern France, notably those in Lascaux. These appear along with images of men and women, and stencils left by blowing pigment over splayed hands. One cave in Gargas in the French Pyrenees boasts over 200 such negative human handprints, dating from around 27,000 years ago. Similar displays have been found in Australia, Brazil and in California in the USA. Clearly, there was an appetite for early *Homo sapiens* to leave its mark.

Cave painting was later aided by the light provided by hearth fires and oil lamps. Stone lamps appeared 20,000 years ago. In Europe, gouged limestone would have been filled with animal fat or resin, which was then set alight to illuminate shelters after dark. In the Middle East, large shells were used as oil receptacles.

FEMALE FORM

Around 25,000 years ago, stone figurines began to appear. A popular subject was the female form, often exaggerated, perhaps inspired by fertility worship. More than 200 rounded 'Venus figurines' have been unearthed in sites across Europe. Carved from soft stones (limestone, calcite or steatite), bone or ivory, or shaped in clay and fired, these voluptuous figures often lack hands and feet. The faces are vague or absent, though hair fashions may be detailed.

This so-called Venus figurine was discovered in a cave in Willendorf, Austria, in 1908. The 11 cm (4.3 in) piece was carved from limestone around 25,000 years ago.

CUPULES

The earliest known prehistoric art does not depict any animal or human form. Cupules are cup-like indentations in vertical rocks that appear to have no purpose other than as decoration or symbolism. There may be thousands of such hollows arranged in a single location, each 1.5–10 cm (0.6–4 in) in diameter. The indentations would have required numerous percussive blows with handheld hammer-stones. Cupules predate cave painting by thousands of years. Among the oldest examples are cupules found in caves in the Madhya Pradesh region of central India, dating from between 290,000 and 700,000 BCE.

SOCIAL LIFE

The existence of hearths in rock shelters and the traces of many footprints suggest *Homo neanderthalensis* lived in social groups of about 10 to 30 individuals that gathered around a warm fire in the evenings. Children would have learned survival techniques from their forebears by watching and copying. Groups tended to travel between familiar resting spots as they followed the migration of prey, such as deer, and foraged locally. The remains of fires have been found in different layers in rock shelters, proving that archaic humans would set up camp in one spot many times. The soot deposits measured at the Mandrin Cave in southern France reveal up to 80 visits by Neanderthal groups.

Away from caves, Neanderthals also built simple windproof shelters, by hanging pelts and threading branches between posts. The evidence for this is found in La Folie, France, where traces of a riverside camp have been detected from around 60,000 years ago. There are holes for wooden posts, supported by stones, arranged in a circle. A padded sleeping area would have been placed at the rear of the enclosure, opposite the entrance.

MYSTERY IN THE DARK

A most curious Neanderthal construction was discovered in 1990, behind a rock fall, 300 m (1,000 ft) deep within a cave near Bruniquel, France. What first appeared to be random piles of broken stalagmites was eventually revealed to be two intentional circular arrangements, with many stalagmites balanced against each other. There is also evidence of charring within the circles. The construction has been dated to about 176,000 years ago – long before *Homo sapiens* reached Europe – identifying it as the work of Neanderthals. As Neanderthals tended to camp by the entrances of caves, venturing so deep would have required firelight and much commitment to lifting two tonnes of stalagmites. The purpose of the construction remains unknown.

BURIAL RITES

There is much debate over whether or not Neanderthals buried their dead. What appears to be a deliberately dug grave could instead be an existing pit where a body fell and was covered by natural rock fall or sediment. If it did occur, deliberate burial may have been for purposes of hygiene or to keep scavengers away, but it could also suggest a belief in an afterlife. Mass Neanderthal graves have been found in Spain, Croatia and France, but there is no conclusive evidence that the bodies were placed there in any thoughtful way. However, they may still indicate that Neanderthals did designate places for the dead.

One supposed Neanderthal grave in a rock shelter in Shanidar, Iraq, was found to contain pollen. This raised conjecture that the deceased was buried with flowers. While this funerary offering is disputed, other graves in the site provide better evidence of ritual burial, with possible artificial pits and bodies lying on their sides in a foetal position.

Certainly, *Homo sapiens* went to the trouble of burying its dead. The earliest agreed examples of human burial date from around 100,000 years ago in Israel. The remains of 15 individuals found in a cave in Qafzeh are interred in pits along with stone tools and stained with red ochre. The bones of one ten-year-old boy feature a set of deer antlers lying across his chest. They may once have been held in his hands.

These fossilized bones of a Homo sapiens *mother and child date from 90,000–100,000 years ago. Found in a cave in Qafzeh, Israel, they are one of the earliest examples of the ritual burial of an anatomically modern human.*

A SHARED EARTH

While *Homo sapiens* was the eventual sole survivor in the evolution of hominins, we shared the planet with our predecessors and other evolutionary branches for a time. But how did we become the last humans standing?

Neanderthals are typically imagined as the archetypal 'caveman', somehow subhuman, but they shared many traits with *Homo sapiens*. Recent archaeological finds have revealed both physical and cultural similarities between the two species. *Homo neanderthalensis* reached a similar average height, had a slightly larger brain, wore clothes and may have employed limited speech in a higher pitch than *Homo sapiens*.

The first fossil hominin to be discovered, in Belgium in 1829, was finally identified as an archaic human in 1857 and called *Homo neanderthalensis*. Named after the location of one fossil's discovery in the Neander Tal (Valley) in Germany, *Homo neanderthalensis* remains have since been found across Europe, from southern Spain to Siberia and southwest Asia. Neanderthals occupied these areas for more than 200,000 years, a huge time period in hominin history.

Homo neanderthalensis differed from modern humans in having a larger, barrel chest, stronger arms, and stubbier fingers. Their jaws were wide but lacked a chin. Neanderthals were slightly shorter but stockier than *Homo sapiens*, which could have helped them survive in colder Ice Age environments. Despite their sturdiness, Neanderthals lived somewhat brutal lives, threatened by the climate and predatory animals. Most lived for an average of 40 years.

The remains of a Neanderthal man with few remaining teeth and evidence of arthritis suggests that *Homo neanderthalensis* provided support for its weaker members and may have also buried its dead. Neanderthals were able to fashion composite tools using adhesive made from birch bark tar, build shelters, and hunt deer, birds and fish. They may also have ingested certain plants for their medicinal properties. Along with *Homo sapiens* and *Homo erectus*, *Homo neanderthalensis* regularly lit fires for warmth and cooking. These were no simple cave-people.

Another contemporary of *Homo sapiens* was identified through DNA samples in 2008. *Homo denisova* evolved from the same branch of hominins as Neanderthals but, while Neanderthals settled in Europe, the larger-toothed Denisovans migrated to Asia.

CONFRONTATION

Homo sapiens' initial attempt to move into the Middle East from East Africa between 130,000 and 115,000 years ago failed, perhaps due to an uncomfortable climate or aggression from Neanderthals. Thirty thousand years later they tried again and managed to cross into the Arabian Peninsula and Eurasia. Here they encountered the established Neanderthals, but was the meeting fierce or friendly? Evidence suggests both. In 2010, scientists successfully mapped the Neanderthal genome and compared it with modern humans. The results revealed that 1–4 per cent of European and Middle Eastern DNA is Neanderthal, confirming that some interbreeding took place between the species. Later tests proved that modern Melanesians and Aboriginal Australians have 6 per cent DNA from Denisovan ancestors.

While relationships between the species, consensual or not, appear to have taken place, overall, the result of *Homo sapiens*' spread was the demise of their hominin competitors. There were probably only about 100,000 Neanderthals living in Eurasia in total, and these existed in small groups. *Homo sapiens* were better hunters, having fashioned spears that could be thrown at prey and they were more able to cooperate. Unable to compete with a wave of *Homo sapiens* moving into their lands, hunting and gathering the same food, and possibly affected by pathogens transported by *Homo sapiens* from Africa, Neanderthals went into retreat.

Over a period of 20,000 years, the hominin species that shared the planet with *Homo sapiens* disappeared; *Homo soloensis, Homo denisova* and *Homo floresiensis* (see panel) became extinct about 50,000 years ago, and *Homo neanderthalensis* 40,000 years ago. With their passing, *Homo sapiens* became the only surviving human species.

Neanderthals and Homo sapiens *certainly encountered each other, but were their meetings harmonious or violent?*

Hobbit humans

One group of pre-*Homo sapiens* hominins remained unknown to archaeologists until 2003. Found on the island of Flores in Indonesia, *Homo floresiensis* was quickly nicknamed 'hobbit', after the diminutive characters in J.R.R. Tolkien's *The Lord of the Rings*. The skull and bones of an adult female, along with bone fragments from several other individuals, were unearthed. The fully-grown female would only have stood 1.1 m (3 ft 6 in) tall. Although *Homo floresiensis* had a small brain in proportion with her body, she was able to use tools and fire. Probably not unrelated, this dwarfish archaic human became extinct around the same time *Homo sapiens* found its way to Flores, 50,000 years ago.

HUMANITY COLONIZES THE WORLD

Homo sapiens was not the first evolution of humans to step beyond their place of origin to occupy new lands, but their success at adapting to new environments led our ancestors to become the dominant species on Earth.

It was never a sure thing that *Homo sapiens* would emerge as the sole hominin survivor. Indeed, the species came close to extinction outside Africa on more than one occasion.

These upright-walking and large-brained hominins occupied Africa for hundreds of thousands of years. They began to migrate towards the Middle East 130,000–115,000 years ago but few, if any, managed to reach beyond the eastern Mediterranean. (There is debate over dental evidence that some reached China.) Later attempts at migration may have been held back by an Ice Age and a catastrophic volcanic explosion from Toba in modern-day Sumatra, Indonesia, that may have been responsible for major weather disruption and reducing Earth's hominin population to just a few thousand individuals 70,000 years ago. Cold and dry conditions over much of the migration route across the Middle East made it uninhabitable and, thus, impassible for millennia.

Human remains and stone tools found at Jebel Irhoud in Morocco are estimated to be around 315,000 years old, making them the earliest evidence of Homo sapiens.

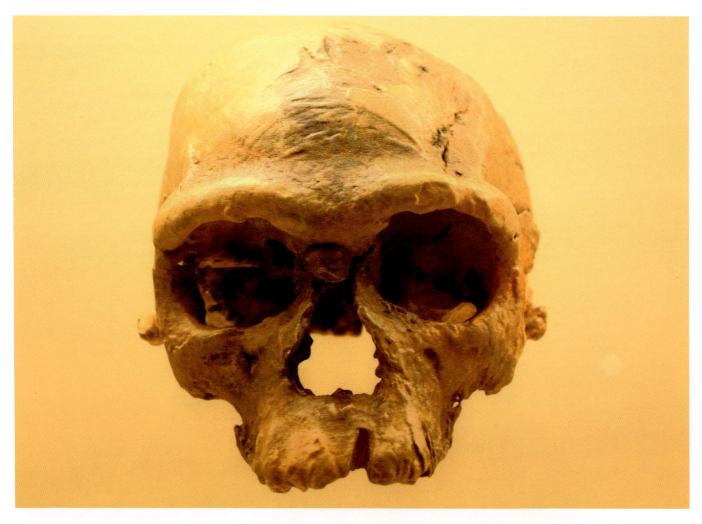

THE RECENT DISPERSAL

Between 70,000 and 50,000 years ago, however, another relocation of *Homo sapiens* made far greater progress. With much water held as ice at the poles, lower sea levels allowed our ancestors to cross the Arabian Peninsula. This successful migration would have been helped by Sapiens getting to grips with more-defined stone tools, improving their hunting and fishing abilities with barbed spears and therefore improving their chances of surviving for longer. A population boom and confidence in new skills could then have led groups to divide and spread outwards to find new homes. This time they spread north and eastwards, following the southern coast of Asia and Oceania, and finding their way to Europe about 40,000 years ago.

There is evidence that *Homo sapiens* encountered other branches of humanity en route, such as Neanderthals and Denisovans that had left Africa for Eurasia 350,000 years ago (page 24). Whether through conflict, competition for food, or disease, the Neanderthals were extinct by 40,000 years ago. *Homo sapiens* now ruled. In the European forests, they hunted reindeer, bison and woolly rhinoceros, fished, and foraged for nuts and berries. These anatomically modern humans worked out how to use the bow and arrow to hunt dangerous and skittish animals from afar and to carve bones into fishhooks. They could craft bone needles and fashion clothes from animal skins, to help them to survive winters and venture into colder lands.

Over 5,000 years, the initial exodus of what was likely just a few hundred individuals led *Homo sapiens* as far as Australia. At that time, the continent was accessible via a relatively short sea crossing of 90 km (55 miles). Other Sapiens branches headed to the furthest eastern corner of Asia, eventually crossing the land bridge between today's Siberia and Alaska, to occupy North America.

It would be much later before these wanderers constructed reliable rafts and boats, and gained the confidence to strike out across open waters and discover Micronesia and remote islands such as the Philippines, Tahiti and Hawaii. By about 16,000 years ago *Homo sapiens*, the last survivor of the Homo genus, occupied most of the planet.

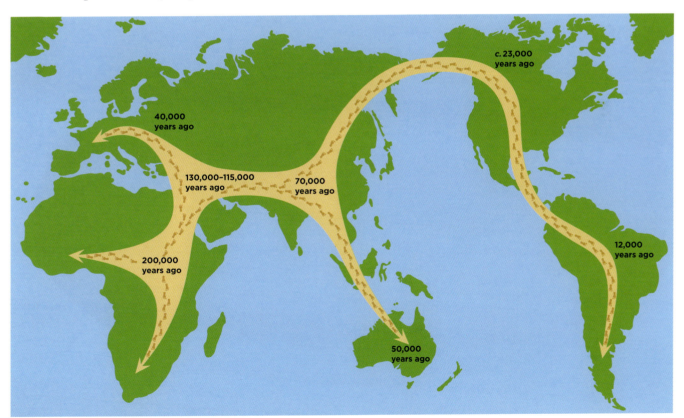

After an initial foray into the Middle East 130,000–115,000 years ago, Homo sapiens *migrated into Europe, Asia and beyond from 70,000 years ago, finding its way into northern Australia and the Americas over 50,000 years of exploration.*

ICE AGES AND CLIMATE

Earth has endured several periods of freezing followed by warmer phases over millions of years. Early humankind had to cope with climate change, just as we do today.

There is geological evidence that five major Ice Ages have affected Earth, with the last, the Great Ice Age, beginning about 115,000 years ago. These dramatic changes in Earth's surface temperature were caused by subtle shifts in the planet's tilt towards the sun and atmospheric changes. The Great Ice Age was a long glacial period that lasted until about 11,700 years ago. The period coincided with the migration of *Homo sapiens* from Africa into Eurasia (page 26).

The Last Glacial Maximum (when ice sheets spread to their greatest extent across Earth before receding) occurred between 26,500 and 19,000 years ago, and *Homo sapiens* may have been forced to move south from its new home in the northern hemisphere, to follow the herds it hunted, as much as to avoid freezing temperatures. Ice sheets would have covered much of Northern Europe, North America and Asia, and for many miles south of the glaciers the land was barren from nine-month-long winters. The average temperature of the planet would have been several degrees cooler than it is today and the climate would have been drier, with resulting droughts and the spread of deserts.

The movement of *Homo sapiens* into Europe may have been delayed as the migrants adjusted to the colder climes. Warmer shelter and clothing were needed. Here, the invention of cutting tools and the needle and thread would have helped them sew clothing from pelts (page 19).

The sea level is estimated to have been 125 m (410 ft) lower than it is today, with much water locked into vast ice sheets. Between 90,000–12,000 years ago, it was possible for early humankind to walk from Siberia to Alaska via a land known as Beringia.

The last glacial period from 115,000–11,700 years ago saw ice covering about a third of Earth's land mass at its peak accompanied by a dip in sea levels. Extended coastlines are marked here in yellow.

THE BIG THAW

The big thaw, when it came, was much swifter than the cooling. Over about 6,000 years from 17,000 years ago, the ice sheets withdrew northwards. Land bridges disappeared, with the meltwaters causing a huge and permanent rise in sea levels. Up to 40 per cent of the coastline was submerged. The Bering Strait between Asia and the Americas was formed; Britain was separated from the European continent by the English Channel; Spain split from Africa at the Straits of Gibraltar; the Mediterranean opened to the Atlantic Ocean; Sri Lanka, Japan, the Philippines and Taiwan became islands. With warmer temperatures and more ground water to evaporate and form clouds, rainfall also increased. Prairies and forests began to replace the frozen tundra. What is now the Sahara Desert became a fertile land of grasses, lakes and rivers. From 12,000 years ago, Earth's great rivers, the Nile, Ganges, Indus, Yellow, Tigris and Euphrates, were in full flow.

Once again, *Homo sapiens* had to adapt. People moved into the lush new habitats and began to hunt smaller mammals, such as deer, cattle and wild boar, to fish and to gather shellfish. The changing environment and spread of *Homo sapiens* hunters spelled the end for many large species in Eurasia. The woolly rhinoceros, steppe bison and mastodon were all gone by 10,000 years ago, with isolated populations of woolly mammoth surviving for a few thousand years longer.

With a lack of trees for wood, ancient Siberians used mammoth bones as building materials.

ADAPTATION

As Homo sapiens spread into new lands, our species learnt to cope with extremes of temperature and altitude, become familiar with new foods and discover new opportunities to hunt. There is evidence that *Homo sapiens* lived in the northern extremes of Siberia and the Arctic Circle 40,000 years ago. Just as today, these lands were often frozen, with few plants for food and wood. The people that lived there at first hunted mammoth, building huts from their bones and tusks. Over millennia, their bodies adapted, becoming more compact and resistant to the cold.

From here, people moved to the Tibetan plateau, around 4 km (2.5 mi) above sea level, where oxygen levels are halved. Again, humanity adapted, with modern-day Tibetans and Andean Indians able to take in higher levels of oxygen than their lower-living relatives, thriving in a challenging environment.

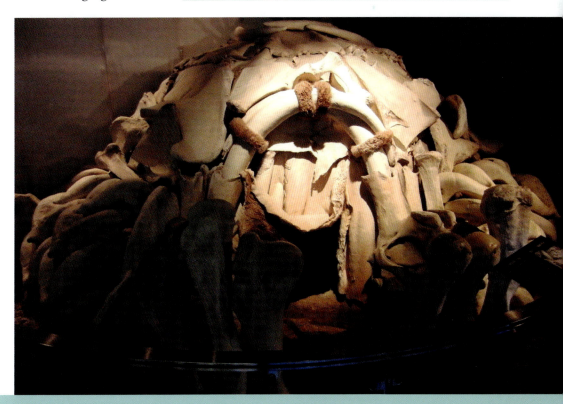

HUNTER-GATHERERS

Early humans lived a nomadic lifestyle, following the migratory routes of deer and where seasonal fruits and nuts could be found.

With the retreat of glaciers in the northern hemisphere, *Homo sapiens* was able to exploit new territory and food resources.

Early *Homo sapiens* was a forager who moved with migrating species and the seasons to make the most of food resources. As deer herds travelled from uplands in summer to lowland pastures in winter, so did groups of early humans, gathering plants and picking off individual deer as needed.

We know much about the diet of early humankind from the debris they left in rock shelters. This includes animal bones, seeds, and nut and mollusc shells. We also know that our ancestors sought out honey from wild bee nests from depictions in Spanish cave paintings. Among the food sources that humans exploited were fruit trees and bushes, mushrooms, termite nests and roots. Diets were varied, disease was rare and some humans were now living into their sixties.

As early humans hunted, they learnt to set traps for their prey. In some areas, fishing nets were woven from plant fibres. Pits were dug to catch large animals, while snares were set for rabbits and wild boar. A more elaborate set-up which required collaboration in the group was the game drive lane. Herds, such as gazelle, were chased through these lanes, sometimes built from piled-up stone, into dead ends or to cliff edges, where the animals were killed.

HOME AND AWAY

Prehistoric hunter-gatherers tended to live outside densely wooded areas, near water sources, for drinking and fishing. They built temporary shelters along their circular routes tracking game and fruit. During summer, they might camp for months. One such camp, found on the archaeological site Ohalo II in Israel, is dated to 21,000 BCE. It comprised six oval dwellings built from branches and brushwood, with hearths outside. There is even evidence of early plant cultivation, with the seeds of 100 species of wild cereals and fruits, plus grinding stones and sickles uncovered. Groups in the Pacific coast of North America set up permanent homes in reach of abundant salmon and seafood.

For those on the move, a nomadic lifestyle meant keeping possessions to a minimum. Useful items for the journey included basic tools for hunting, fishing and cutting. These included spears and the bow and arrow. Some decorations were kept, crafted from shells, bones and antlers, sometimes sewn into clothing.

Stone-age archers used a range of arrows, depending on the hunt. Some arrowheads were cut to a fine point; some had fine cutting edges; others were barbed. To bring down birds and small mammals, a blunt club-like arrowhead would be used to stun the prey. This stun-arrow is still used by Inuit today.

DIVISION OF WORK

A division of roles may have taken place, as it does in hunter-gathering groups today, with men hunting the big game while women gathered plants and small animals. Toolmaking could have been a male activity, while the crafting and weaving of pots and baskets was looked after by women, who were also responsible for bringing up infants. Group size was likely between 10 and 100 individuals. The population remained fairly stable; a nomadic lifestyle and the need to nurse infants made it difficult for women to bear and care for more than one child at a time.

Foraging did not just mean food; *Homo sapiens* also gathered the materials it needed for tools: flint and wood. Over time, groups would memorize a map of their territory, remembering the best places for supplies, plus the fruiting seasons and migratory routes. Without calendars, they would have had to recognize seasonal signals, such as weather patterns and blooms. This intimate knowledge of the land, the weather and wild food is generally lost today, except among the few rural groups that still rely on foraging and hunting for sustenance.

BEST FRIEND

The first animal to be domesticated by humans was the dog. Descended from ancient wolves, the dog would have been attracted to human camps by cooking smells and carcasses. The remains of dogs, as companions to humans, have been dated to 14,200 years ago, with the buried remains of a human couple and dog discovered in Bonn-Oberkassal, Germany, but they may have lived together for thousands of years more. Certainly, dogs were domesticated long before farm animals.

The Temple of Ggantija on the island of Gozo in Malta, built c.3600 BCE. In the Neolithic era, megalithic monuments sprung up across Europe.

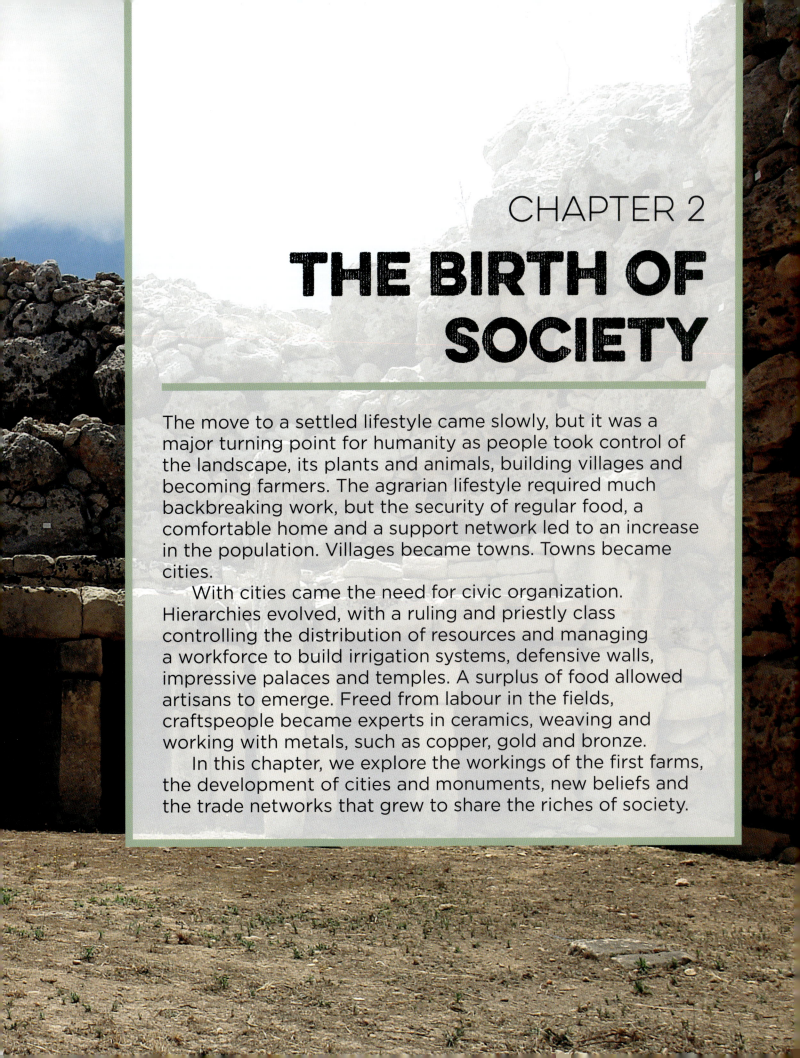

CHAPTER 2
THE BIRTH OF SOCIETY

The move to a settled lifestyle came slowly, but it was a major turning point for humanity as people took control of the landscape, its plants and animals, building villages and becoming farmers. The agrarian lifestyle required much backbreaking work, but the security of regular food, a comfortable home and a support network led to an increase in the population. Villages became towns. Towns became cities.

With cities came the need for civic organization. Hierarchies evolved, with a ruling and priestly class controlling the distribution of resources and managing a workforce to build irrigation systems, defensive walls, impressive palaces and temples. A surplus of food allowed artisans to emerge. Freed from labour in the fields, craftspeople became experts in ceramics, weaving and working with metals, such as copper, gold and bronze.

In this chapter, we explore the workings of the first farms, the development of cities and monuments, new beliefs and the trade networks that grew to share the riches of society.

THE AGRICULTURAL REVOLUTION

Among the first wild plants to be gathered and deliberately sown were species of wild wheat and barley.

The move from nomadic foraging to raising crops and settling in one place was one of the most significant developments in the story of humankind.

What has been described as an 'agricultural revolution' was not an overnight change to *Homo sapiens'* circumstances. The revolution was a gradual swing from foraging to farming over about 8,000 years, and was a major adaptation which still governs our way of life today.

Not all people built villages to settle beside fields of crops; some retained their nomadic ways while cultivating crops in certain areas; others built homes but continued to forage. There is evidence of cereal seed harvesting dating from 23,000 years ago at the Israeli archaeological site Ohalo II (page 31), but the point at which settlements and agriculture became the prevailing trend is considered to be about 10,000 years ago.

By 9000 BCE, the human population had grown to 5–6 million from an estimated 50,000 at the time of *Homo sapiens'* spread from Africa (page 26). Larger populations competed for the same food resources, and the changes in climate following the retreat of glaciers in the north meant relocation for many. With less water trapped in ice, rainfall increased and plant life thrived. Grasses and fruit trees reclaimed formerly frozen and dry lands. As animals frequented oases and riverbanks, so did humans. The need to travel to find food decreased as wildlife returned to the same spots. Humans put down roots. Some groups moved to the coasts, which were now much further inland since sea levels had risen dramatically; some groups moved to the land revealed by the ice melt; others turned to herding and planting.

SETTLING DOWN

The process of becoming gardeners and farmers would have been unhurried. A forager gathering seeds from wild grasses would have accidentally dropped some close to their camp. Some of these seeds would have sprouted into healthy plants. Before long, the relationship between seed and plant would have been recognized. Deliberate gathering of plump seeds for planting near a settlement followed. To sow and maintain crops, soil needed to be prepared and water provided during periods of low rainfall. Where rainfall was sporadic, early farmers delivered water to their plants using irrigation, digging trenches to redirect downpours and river flow to crop fields. The earliest discovered example of this occurred 8,000 years ago in Khuzistan, in present-day Iran.

People planned for the future, building dry stores for grain that could be planted or processed at a later date. Simple containers were fashioned from clay. And, as local food resources increased, so did the population. Staying in one place allowed women to give birth more often. Nomadic tribes typically planned one child about every four years, to allow time to raise a baby that could walk with the group rather than be carried. This was no longer a concern.

The earliest-known farming village dates from around 8000 BCE in the Palestinian West Bank. At least 800 people lived there in mud-brick homes by a lake. They supplemented their diet of gazelle and wild sheep by growing figs, barley and wheat, harvested with flint sickles. A typical hunter-gatherer would require a territory of about 26 square km (10 square mi) to satisfy his needs; 2.6 square km (1 square mi) of cultivated land could provide grains and vegetables to support a community of 50. While some people continued to live a hunter-gatherer lifestyle – notably in isolated Australia – the agricultural revolution was a point of no return for most of humankind.

THE FERTILE CRESCENT

Agriculture is understood to have first begun in an area called the Fertile Crescent, or the Levantine Corridor. Now an arid zone, 10,000 years ago this was a verdant, wooded area rich with game. The foothills of the Zagros mountains were ideal for wild wheat and barley. Residents could live there all year round and forage the grains to support their diet of hunted gazelle and sheep.

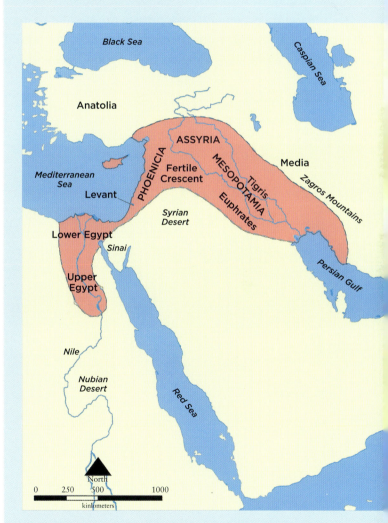

The Fertile Crescent was an arc of land that curved north-east of modern-day Jordan and Israel, south of Turkey and Syria's borders to the edge of Iran and Iraq.

ANIMAL AND PLANT DOMESTICATION

Ten thousand years ago, the first farmers began cultivating the local wild plants that would become our modern-day staples. They also tamed the wild beasts they used to hunt, making them docile and easy to raise.

The move to farming did not occur in one place but in several disconnected locations around the world, according to the latest evidence. An agrarian lifestyle apparently began independently in the Middle Eastern Fertile Crescent from around 8000 BCE, in central China, along the Yangtze and Yellow rivers from

Einkorn is an ancient species of wheat that grew wild in the Fertile Crescent before being cultivated.

6500 BCE, Central America around 3000 BCE, South America around 2500 BCE and in southern Africa from 2000 BCE. With different climates, landscape and native flora in each territory, farming had a distinct character for these separated people.

Plants growing wild in the Fertile Crescent that were adopted by farmers include the wild grasses emmer and einkorn wheat and barley, along with pulses, lentils and chickpeas. Wild cereals have small, husked seeds which fall easily from the plant when ripe. While this suits the plant in the natural world, farmers need a seed that stays in place for harvesting, and preferably one without a husk that needs to be removed. Over generations of selection and cultivation, farmers developed varieties of cereal that worked for them but which would not reproduce without human intervention.

Cereals, once chewed raw, were now threshed and winnowed to separate the grains from the chaff and ground into flour. Mixing the flour with water produced a simple porridge, or gruel. Spread and baked on hot stones, gruel was also used to make flatbreads.

RICE, MILLET AND MAIZE

The people living in the wetland valleys of China's Yangtze river were subjected to heavy rains. The native cereal here was rice, which thrived in damp conditions. There is evidence of rice harvesting from about 11,000 years ago. Over time, farmers learnt how to plant rice seedlings in flooded areas with retaining walls, known as paddy fields.

Around 650 km (400 mi) north of the nascent rice fields, in a much colder and drier climate, settlers along the Yellow river were making the most of their local cereal crop, millet, adding it to their diet of fish and deer. Eventually, the two Chinese cultures met and both rice and millet began to be grown in neighbouring plots.

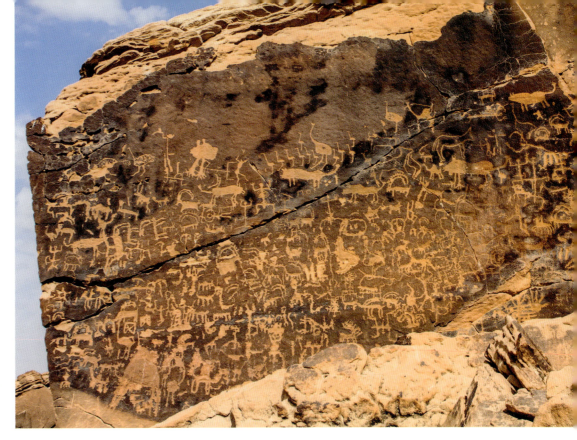

The Musayqirah petroglyphs – rock carvings – from Saudi Arabia show a range of animals that were hunted during the Neolithic period.

This 8,000-year-old millstone and grinding stone were discovered in a Neolithic settlement in Cyprus. Much of the laborious work in preparing grains for flour with such tools was likely done by women.

Ten thousand years ago, in the highlands of New Guinea, the large island north of Australia, people were cultivating taro and banana. By 4500 BCE they were clearing land, preparing plots for sugar cane and developing irrigation.

Between 9,000 and 7,000 years ago, in what is now Mexico, settlers began what would become an extensive domestication of maize (or corn), turning a variant of teosinte, a plant that bore one thumb-sized inedible ear of corn, into a tall, leafy plant that sprouted numerous cobs of sweet kernels. As well as being enjoyed for its cooked kernels, maize could be dried and ground into flour. Early Mexicans also enjoyed a diet of squash, beans, avocado, papaya and guava.

Further south, in what is now Peru and Bolivia, potatoes and quinoa were grown more than 7,000 years ago. Potatoes contain a toxin that can cause sickness when eaten raw, but are a starch-filled staple when cooked. The seed of the flowering quinoa plant provides a gluten-free source of protein, fibre and minerals. It was first grown for animal feed before being enjoyed for human consumption about 4,000 years ago.

THE DOWNSIDE

The move to agriculture and settling down was not necessarily a good thing. The hunter-gatherer lifestyle required fewer hours of work and no back-breaking digging. Grinding grains was strenuous and meant hours of toil in crouched positions. Studies of human bones have revealed the onset of osteoporosis as bones became lighter. Life in settlements meant people walked shorter distances. Remaining in one place, with livestock, also increased the spread of diseases such as smallpox, influenza and measles, all of which originated in animals.

Reliance on one main food crop was a big risk. Should the harvest fail, due to bad weather, plant disease or pests, starvation was a concern. Diet became less varied and higher in carbohydrates. Cooking cereals turns the starch in the grains into sugars. While this made digestion easy, it encouraged tooth decay. Despite these adverse effects on health, populations did slowly rise.

TAMING THE BEASTS

Alongside the wild plants that humankind cultivated were the wild animals they succeeded in domesticating. The dog, a descendant of an ancient wolf, was the first beast to be brought into the human community (page 31), but it was kept as a guard and a hunting companion rather than a source of food.

The first farmers in the Fertile Crescent had three grazing animals to choose from, all fairly docile and easily corralled. These were the sheep, the goat and taurine cattle (a Near Eastern and European species of cattle, as opposed to indicine, or Indian, cattle). All three accepted containment and simple foods, were kept within a herd, did not threaten their human owners and bred fast. Domestication probably began with people following, then controlling, the movements of a herd before leading them into purpose-built pens. Once a herd had been claimed, the most passive and largest providers of meat and milk would have been selected and nurtured. Most males were slaughtered for meat, with a select few kept as studs. Females were useful for producing milk and young.

Of the three domestic animals, the cow was the most challenging to control. Its ancestor was the auroch, a long-horned beast measuring about 1.8 m (6 ft) high at the shoulder. Wild cattle still had the potential to gore or trample humans, but they would congregate and feed on grass. Sheep, descended from the wild Asiatic mouflon breed, and goats, from the bezoar goat of west Asia, ate most kinds of foliage. Sheep were kept for meat, but later became appreciated for their wool and milk.

At first, cows only produced enough milk to feed their calves. The ability to produce high yields of milk that could be consumed by humans came through selective breeding. It also took centuries for humans to comfortably accept dairy into their diet. In parts of Asia, with little or no history of breeding cattle, lactose intolerance is common. As well as meat and milk, kept animals provided skin and hair for clothes, rope and nets. Dung was used for fertilizer and fuel, as it burns more slowly than wood.

In central China, the pig, descended from the wild boar, was most easily domesticated. The pig happily fed on refuse. The domesticated water buffalo was useful not only for its meat but also for its milk and for working in the fields. Once the meat of the animal was consumed, the buffalo's shoulder blade provided a conveniently shaped spade. In northern China, the pig was supplemented by chickens.

Not every animal took to domestication; consider the zebra, an untamable relative of the horse. Overall, only 13 large mammals over 50 kg (110 lbs) have been successfully tamed for farming. As well as the above, these include reindeer, horses, yaks and llamas.

Approximate dates for domestication

 Ass
4000 BCE

 Bactrian camel
3500 BCE

 Cattle
8500 BCE

 Chicken
6000 BCE

 Dog
12,000 BCE

 Dromedary camel
3000 BCE

 Goat
8000 BCE

 Goose
1500 BCE

 Horse
3600 BCE

 Llama
4500 BCE

 Pig
9000 BCE

 Reindeer
1000 BCE

 Sheep
8500 BCE

 Turkey
0 BCE

 Water buffalo
4300 BCE

 Yak
5000 BCE

 Banana
5000 BCE

 Barley
8500 BCE

 Cassava
6000 BCE

 Cocoa
3000 BCE

 Date
5000 BCE

 Maize/Corn
7000 BCE

 Olive
5000 BCE

 Potato
6000 BCE

 Rice
8000 BCE

 Sorghum
3000 BCE

 Sweet potato
2500 BCE

 Tomato
5000 BCE

 Wheat
9000 BCE

TOWNS AND CITIES

Agricultural settlements expanded, a surplus of food became available, and birth rates increased. Before long, small farming villages became towns, then cities.

While the effort to plant and harvest crops was greater than foraging, having the security of local food and water meant that human communities could grow. There was no longer the need to relocate with all of one's belongings to follow herds and fruiting seasons. Young children were less of a burden, and families grew in size. Homes were now permanent structures of stone or plastered mud-brick. Clay granaries were constructed to safely store the harvest to see settlements through the year.

Among the earliest-known towns was Jericho, in Palestine. Sited beside a natural spring, Jericho was first used as a campsite for hunter-gatherers. Occupation

The clay figures unearthed at 'Ain Ghazal are the oldest-known large human statues ever found.

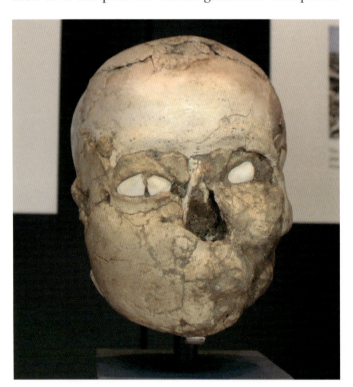

This human skull, found in Jericho and dating from between 8,500–6,000 BCE, was covered with plaster, with eyes made from shells, to resemble a living person. The skull had been buried with many others in a pit.

periods gradually extended, and from 9000 to 7000 BCE Jericho expanded from a village to a 40,000 square m (430,000 square ft) settlement. The town was made up of clusters of 5 m (16 ft)-wide circular dwellings of sun-dried clay and straw bricks cemented with mud. Inside, floors were plastered and many homes included an oven and an outside yard. The town was surrounded by a huge stone wall more than 3.6 m (12 ft) in height, with 8.5 m (28 ft)-tall towers. The wall was probably built as much as a defence against flooding as attacks from outside. At least 300 people lived there, feeding on harvests of figs, wheat and two types of barley, while hunting wild sheep and gazelle.

'Ain Ghazal is a 14 ha (35 acre) site uncovered in the 1980s and 1990s near Amman, in Jordan. The town was populated by farmers around 7000 BCE. The peo-

This image painted on to a plastered wall in Çatalhöyük is thought to show a vulture removing the heads (or souls) of the deceased. Griffon vultures may have been allowed to strip the flesh from the dead before the bones were buried indoors.

ple that lived here subsisted on crops of wheat, barley, peas and lentils, along with the meat from domesticated goats. They also hunted gazelle and deer. The site is notable for the discovery of large sculptures of cattle and humans – the oldest-known large human figures to have been found. The painted statues are formed of plaster over a reed frame.

The town was made up of rectangular living quarters built with mud-brick on stone foundations. Walls and floors were plastered and re-covered every few years. To make the plaster required the burning of limestone at temperatures up to 850°C (1,560°F). A consequence of this was the degradation of the environment, with trees cut down and burned over a 3 km (1.9 mi) radius. After 700 years of continuous planting, the soil in the area was also seriously degraded and no longer useful for agriculture. Most of the community was forced to relocate from 6500 BCE.

MUD-BRICK MAZE

One of the earliest-recognized cities is Çatalhöyük, in modern Turkey. An average of 5,000 people lived in this settlement between 7400 and 6200 BCE. The 13 ha (32 acre) site consisted of a maze of mud-brick domestic buildings butted up against each other. Some are grander than others, but there is no obvious public space as you might expect for such a large complex. Access to the buildings was by ladder or stairs, through holes in the ceilings. There are few public pathways between the homes. This may have been a defensive arrangement.

Living in the town was not entirely pleasant. Animals were kept indoors with families, and refuse, including human waste, was dumped between houses, inviting vermin.

Decorating the inside of the buildings are paintings of deer and leopards, and there are large horned auroch skulls plastered and positioned on the walls. Among the finds on the site is a notable example of a terracotta fertility figure. This voluptuous woman is giving birth on a throne with armrests shaped like leopards. While the idea that early societies were ruled by women has been generally dismissed, the popularity of these 'Venus figurines' in Neolithic societies suggests that fertility continued to be of significance.

The towns and small cities that arose in and around the Fertile Crescent were not isolated. The presence of obsidian – a rare volcanic glass only found in eastern Anatolia, Turkey – confirms that exchanges took place between communities from modern-day Turkey to Israel. Knowledge of farming methods would also have been shared not just across the land but across the sea to Europe, too.

Imported seeds and animals, plus significant building in Crete and Cyprus in this pre-pottery Neolithic period, suggests that navigation over the Mediterranean was possible at the time. The earliest-known Neolithic site in Europe dates from around 7000 BCE. It was discovered under the palace of King Minos in Knossos in Crete (page 76). Agriculture and permanent settlements continued to arise further westward, appearing in Egypt in the 6th millennium BCE.

HIERARCHIES

Early farmers suffered from occasional poor harvests due to drought and disease but, generally, they were able to put aside surpluses from plentiful harvests for leaner months. The use of draught animals and irrigation made it possible for harder and more arid land to be turned over to crop plantation. More people could be fed and towns could expand. Communities

A terracotta mother goddess figurine from Turkey.

did not need to focus all their efforts on farming and new roles were taken. Individuals could practise and become proficient at toolmaking and building, while being fed with the surplus in exchange for their skills. This list of tradespeople would later include potters, weavers, painters, sculptors and metalworkers. Crop fields and stores required protecting, so some people would train to guard the town's resources from wild animals or rival communities.

As agricultural settlements expanded, towns became cities. Societies were able to focus on community projects that required organization and leadership. In this way, hierarchies were born. Major town properties, such as temples, irrigation systems and defences, required managers to guide teams in their construction and to provide food for those kept away from the fields. Social hierarchies developed with leaders, priests, administrators and record-keepers held in higher esteem, potentially claiming more of the community's labour and output. It would have been easy for chiefs to control and divide a community's store of food as they wished.

Women also found new roles in the growing towns and cities. An increasing burden of childcare, food production and preparation saw them spending more time in the home and in monogamous relationships.

Several rooms in the 8,000-year-old complex of Çatalhöyük, modern Turkey, are decorated with the horns of auroch, extinct giant cattle.

Cereal threshing, grinding and baking was arduous work, and it is likely women spent time digging and planting in the fields, too. The evidence for a male/female division of roles is found in burial sites, with men increasingly bearing arrow wounds, and buried with weaponry, while women were interred with ceramics and the tools for working animal skins. These roles were of importance in settled communities, but women often found themselves excluded from leadership roles.

ANCESTOR WORSHIP

Respect for the dead was a common theme in early Neolithic towns, with burials taking place within the home. Bodies were tightly folded into foetal positions, wrapped in mats, and interred beneath raised sleeping areas. Almost every home in Çatalhöyük had skeletal remains under the floor. People were literally sleeping above their ancestors. Some skeletal remains had their skulls removed, possibly for rituals. A number of skulls had been plastered and painted with ochre, to resemble the living.

MONUMENTS

With large communities came shared beliefs and the construction of monuments celebrating spirits and the seasons, with rituals that remain a mystery.

Plentiful food, an available workforce and regional leadership allowed early communities to combine resources to build large stone structures known as megaliths for rituals and seasonal celebrations. These buildings included large-scale tombs and meeting places, the purpose of which is lost in time.

Impressive monuments were erected across Western Europe and the Mediterranean from about 4500 BCE. The alignment of these structures suggests a fascination with the movement of the sun, moon and stars, while carvings and remains at the sites indicate celebrations of ancestors.

The stone structures that arose during the early Neolithic period may have been positioned to mark a group's territory. Structures include monumental graves called long barrows, wooden or stone burial chambers covered in mounds of earth and stone, with passageways to the tombs. The gravesites were likely to have been shared with the local community, possibly indicating territory. The effort involved in constructing these structures and moving large amounts of rubble required large, coordinated teams freed from the responsibility of hunting or farming.

The passage grave at Newgrange in County Meath, Ireland, from 3200 BCE, is not only enormous in scale – covered with an estimated 200,000 metric tonnes (196,841 tons) of rubble and turf – but it is aligned with the seasons. A small opening above the entrance is positioned so that the midwinter solstice sun of 5,000 years ago would have shone directly along the passageway to light the main burial chamber. The chambers contained human bones, some of which were burned, along with various offerings. The larger stones are carved with spirals and diamond patterns. A similar construction in Maes Howe, in the Scottish Orkneys, from 4,800 years ago, is also aligned with the winter sun.

COMMUNITY EFFORT

Later structures were purely for meetings and ceremonies. Large circular arrangements of stones, often surrounded by ditches, began cropping up across Western Europe from 3000 BCE. These 'henges' required an even greater workforce to construct than long bar-

The huge blue stones used for Stonehenge were transported from west Wales to southwest England for positioning 5,000 years ago.

rows. One estimate is that 300 people working for a whole year would be needed to transport the large stones and erect a typical henge.

One of the largest monoliths, the 'Grand Menhir', in Locmariaquer, Brittany, France, weighs 348 metric tonnes (342 tons) and was dragged from its origin site several kilometres away.

The best known of these monuments is England's Stonehenge. It was originally built as a wooden circle of 56 posts in 2800 BCE before several huge bluestones were transported with enormous effort, probably over wooden rollers, from more than 217 km (135 mi) away in Wales. It is assumed the builders believed the stones possessed magical powers. About 100 years after they were erected, the bluestones were surrounded by a wider ring of 30 sarsen stones with lintels.

Stonehenge was just part of a huge mapping of the English southwestern landscape in Neolithic times, with monuments, burial sites and long, parallel ditches, called cursuses, which could stretch for many kilometres. The communities that constructed these monuments must have shared some religious faith that convinced them to put in the immense effort to build them, many of which, from a modern perspective, appear to have no functional purpose.

THE FIRST TEMPLE?

Among the earliest and most curious constructions to be found in the Fertile Crescent is Göbekli Tepe, in Turkey. The settlement is dated to between 9500 and 8000 BCE, in the Neolithic period, before there was knowledge of metalwork and pottery. The deepest remains of the town include the world's oldest known megaliths arranged in a circular design supported on decorated T-shaped pillars, some 2 m (7 ft) tall. Construction would have required a considerable workforce, to source the stone, transport it and put it in place. At the time it was built, humans were still hunter-gatherers. What persuaded them to band together and build such a monument? Was it for a shared ritual, or as a site for processing wheat?

Of particular interest are the decorations on the pillars and statuettes found inside the town. These depict animals such as foxes, boars, snakes, wild sheep and gazelle. Some experts have described this site as the 'world's first temple', which suggests that groups living in the area found food plentiful enough to devote time to building structures for ceremonies.

Located in the foothills of the Taurus mountains, Göbekli Tepe would have been surrounded by abundant wild cereals (that were processed for porridge and beer) and grazing animals. It appears the 'temple' predates the settlement that grew around it. This was a sophisticated setup for the time, but its purpose remains a mystery.

To position the huge monolithic stones in Göbekli Tepe, Turkey, would have required the cooperation and coordination of several groups of hunter-gatherers.

BELIEFS

As humanity sought reassurance about harvests and answers about an afterlife, religions and rituals became part of community life.

Neolithic monuments raised across Europe and the Middle East (page 44) and artefacts found within them reveal something of human society's early religious beliefs. One of humanity's defining traits is our ability to wonder about the universe and to question the purpose of our existence. Religions contributed answers to the mysteries of the ancient world and offered comfort by mapping the unknown. They could also provide solace for those experiencing loss. Shared beliefs brought communities together for rituals and celebrations, and recommended a way of living that encouraged people to consider the needs and wants of others.

Ancient art and burial practices provide clues to early religious ideas. Death seems to have been understood as a bridge to another existence. The inclusion of precious objects and weaponry with bodies suggests people believed their ancestors would continue to play a role in some other realm. The close presence of burial sites to homes, even beneath the floors of houses in the Fertile Crescent, connected the living with their ancestors and may have given them a feeling of continuation and security.

Animism was an early belief that all animals, plants and places have awareness and can communicate with people, and could be addressed, sometimes through song or dance. Hunters could respect their prey and thank it for its sacrifice, for example. Deep connections with the natural world are described in Neolithic artwork, and this bond continued, particularly in Native American beliefs in spirit animals, and the Australian Aboriginal Dreamtime that connects the supernatural with the landscape. Following the domestication of livestock and the later Agricultural Revolution, however, people began to see animals differently, as property and as commodities. Humanity lost some of its rapport with the natural world.

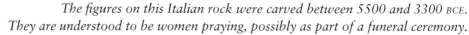

The figures on this Italian rock were carved between 5500 and 3300 BCE. They are understood to be women praying, possibly as part of a funeral ceremony.

PRIESTLY ELITE

Ancient rotund female statuettes (page 21) have been interpreted as objects used in fertility rites. Certainly, the productivity of crop fields and families would have been a major concern for communities. Fear of drought and disease led people to invent rituals and to pray for the health of the harvest and of kinfolk. A priestly class followed, one that convinced the populace that they had a direct connection to the spirits in control of the weather and fate. Priests could offer practical advice, observing the heavens and recommending the best times to sow or harvest crops. They would also be sought out to conduct official blessings.

The priestly elite were not involved in earthly matters, such as farming and construction, but they would be fed and maintained by the community, and could demand surplus food as offerings to the gods.

The megalithic sites of Western Europe and the Mediterranean were used for repeated ceremonies. The position of monuments such as Stonehenge (page 45) and their relationship with other sites and geological features described a sacred landscape. At special times of the year, such as the solstices, communities from different towns gathered together in these places, united in their common beliefs.

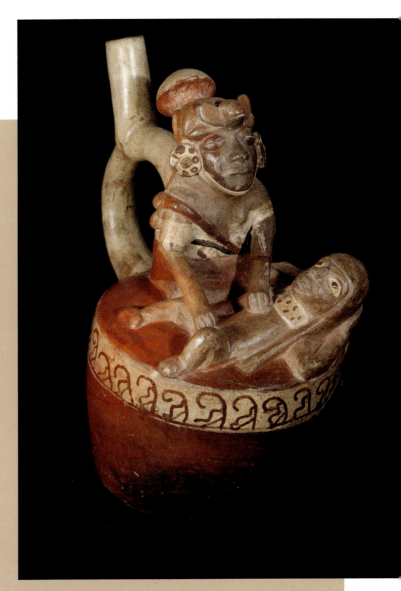

This ceramic from the Moche culture, 100–700 CE, found near Trujillo, Peru depicts a shaman treating a patient.

SHAMANS

As in some hunter-gatherer societies today, thousands of years ago people may have elected shamans as intermediaries with the spirit world. Through art, music and incantation, shamans were trusted to communicate with ancestors, to share the myths and legends of the people, and to offer answers and judgements on community dilemmas. Hallucinogenic substances were sometimes used to induce a trance-like state. Shamans would provide help to the sick, using their specialist knowledge of herbal medicines. Sickness might be understood as originating in a spirit realm, with the banishing of the illness pursued by a supernatural act. A shaman's secret knowledge and perceived close connection with spirits often led to him living apart from a community in fear and awe of his powers. The tomb of what is believed to be a Neolithic shaman was uncovered in Xishuipo in Henan, China, in 1987. Dating from around 4000 BCE, the grave included a male figure placed next to the bodies of three children, and shell mosaics of tiger and dragon spirit animals.

CLAY, CLOTH AND SONG

People developed artisanal skills during the Neolithic period, crafting pots and weaving fabrics that were functional and showed artistic flair.

Improved agriculture and the foundation of towns and cities provided support for an artisan class, crafting tools, jewellery, pottery, musical instruments and fabrics. Much of this was utilitarian, but some fine examples were designed for higher status individuals.

Nomadic groups stored food in holes in the ground or in woven baskets. This did not protect it from insects or thieving animals, nor did it keep the food fresh. Clay pots, however, did both. While clay figurines were initially created more than 30,000 years ago, the first clay pots date from about 19,000 years ago, in China, with evidence discovered in the Xianrendong Cave in Jiangxi province.

Sophisticated examples of pottery in Japan date from about 16,500 years ago. The people of the country's Jōmon era, which began around 14,000 BCE, became particularly adept at design, pressing rope against the wet clay to create patterns. The Jōmon people shaped pots for cooking as much as for storage and for transport. They fished and hunted, and then warmed up their catch in pots above a fire, in soups and stews. Independently, pots were being made in sub-Saharan Africa, in what is now Mali, in 9400 BCE, for use in collecting wild cereals, and in South America and the Nile Valley from about 400 years later.

Clay pots were generally shaped by pinching large lumps of clay or built up from coils to form leakproof vessels. The pots were hardened by leaving them to dry in the sun or by placing them in a pit fire, where extremely high temperatures could be reached. Pots

This Neolithic Jōmon pot was decorated with impressions made by cord. It was discovered in Japan in the 19th century. A gold leaf interior and wooden lid were added later.

often bore geometric designs painted with natural pigments or repeated marks made by pressing objects into the soft clay. The invention of the potter's wheel, possibly in Sumer in 3129 BCE, allowed new radial designs to be created. The patterns used in ancient pottery help archaeologists identify their origins and the cultures they came from.

WEAVING

The weaving of plant fibres to make baskets was a skill already known by Neolithic farmers. Using hemp, flax and animal wools to weave fabrics for clothes was a natural development. Hemp fibres have been used for materials for 50,000 years, with the first known example found in China. Linen comes from the flax plant and may have been used for weaving fabrics for more than 30,000 years. The woody parts of its stems had to be removed first to extract the fibres. In Peru, evidence of the early use of cotton for fabrics has been found dating from 6000 BCE.

Wool came from camels, goats and sheep, and had to be washed and untangled by hand before dying and weaving. It was a job that required patience and dexterity, and was likely to have been taken on by women. The first hand loom was probably built around 4400 BCE. This helped weavers create more regular patterns in their cloth. The quality of clothing and jewellery worn by an individual could denote their status in a community.

This reconstruction shows what a loom used in the Neolithic period may have looked like.

SOUNDS OF THE PAST

Early human communities were able to express themselves with song and dance. Remains of simple musical instruments found in archaeological sites include drums made with clay and alligator skin from 5500 BCE, and fragments of 30 flutes found in graves in Jiahu, China, dating from 7000 BCE. The flutes, made from the bones of the red-crowned crane, have between five and eight holes and can produce a sophisticated range of notes.

By piecing together the remains of this ancient bone flute, or gǔdí, scientists have been able to recreate the sounds played 9,000 years ago.

MASTERS OF METAL

The Neolithic period of wood, stone and soft metals was superseded by the discovery and production of bronze. A new era of durable tools and weapons had arrived.

Before the ability to produce bronze and then iron, humans worked with the metals they found in rocks. Shiny copper and gold could be easily extracted. Both were soft and malleable, ideal for ornamental work but not useful for crafting into weapons or shields.

The first copper artefact dates from 8700 BCE and was found in the Middle East, with a pendant discovered in northern Iraq. Initially, naturally occurring copper was hammered into shape with stones, to form beads and basic axe heads. The more that copper is struck, the harder it becomes. Copper was not very hardy when used for blades and hatchets but, once the cutting edge became blunt, the metal could be melted down and reused.

Smelting – heating copper ore using charcoal to extract purer copper – and the use of casts with molten copper came later, with evidence of the practice dating from around 7500 BCE in modern-day Serbia and Turkey. Gold, silver and lead were also used around this time. Copper mines from the 5th millennium BCE have been uncovered in Ain Buna in Bulgaria and Rudna Glava in Serbia. Gold did not need to be mined as nuggets were relatively easy to find in alluvial soils and streams. Well-crafted copper and gold trinkets were valued for trade between towns, with areas around Turkey and Iran particularly rich in deposits.

AGE OF BRONZE

A major breakthrough came around 3500 BCE, in Mesopotamia in the Near East, when it was discovered that a combination of copper and tin, another easily mined soft metal, made the much more resilient alloy, bronze. This was the beginning of the Bronze Age.

The Trundholm sun chariot is a Bronze Age treasure. Made in Denmark around 1400 BCE, using the lost-wax method, the 25 cm (9.8 in) disk on the chariot bears exquisite gilding. The sculpture also dates the use of spoked wheels to more than 3,000 years ago.

A ceremonial vessel from Shang dynasty China, 1300–1050 BCE.

The techniques for smelting and working with bronze spread far and wide. The lost-wax process – making clay moulds around wax models, for molten bronze to be poured into – resulted in an artistic boom. Countries with copper and tin mines fared well and new cities and trade routes opened. City armouries, such as those in Ur, forged vast numbers of bronze weapons for the Sumerian king and his army, and through greater military strength and conquest, the city of Ur became the centre of an empire (page 56).

GOLDEN YEAR

The earliest-known gold treasure was discovered in 1972, at the Varna Necropolis in Bulgaria. Dating from 4500–4200 BCE, items found in 294 graves included a pair of gold appliqué bulls, a miniature crown, fine beaded gold necklaces, bangles and rings, as well as copper axe heads and decorated pottery.

A single grave in Bulgaria's Varna Necropolis contained more gold than had ever been found in the entire world for the same time period.

Bronze was a much superior material than copper in many ways. It did not form air bubbles during casting, which made it stronger than copper, had a lower melting point, was much more durable and could be re-forged if damaged or bent. The first bronze was made with a mix of copper and arsenic, a metalloid that releases toxic fumes when heated. Mixing copper and tin was much safer. Both tin and copper were widely available in the Caucasus region between the Black Sea and the Caspian Sea, and it was probably here that copper-tin bronze was first smelted.

The Bronze Age covers different periods in the world, depending on when it was in use as the most important material for making tools and weapons. In the Middle East, the Bronze Age is considered as the period 3000–1200 BCE. For China, 1600–1100 BCE. The use of bronze in China is of particular note. Under China's second ancient dynasty, the Shang (page 72), bronze mining and manufacture was taken to an industrial level. Ornate ceremonial objects and vessels were made by uniting parts from several casts.

TRADE AND WAR

The demand for metals and crafted artefacts led to new trade networks. But along with stronger bronze weaponry came rivalries and conflict.

Demand for metals for bronze production, rare stones and fine artisanal wares meant great opportunities for the cultures ruling lands rich in those materials, and the opening up of trade routes over land and sea.

To produce bronze, metalworkers needed to combine copper and tin, but neither metal was widely found across Europe and Asia. Copper mines were dug in Cyprus (the word 'copper' comes from the Greek name for the island, Kupros), Bulgaria and Serbia. Tin was sourced on the German/Czech border, southwest England, the Iberian Peninsula and Brittany, France. Large deposits of copper and tin in China led to a booming production of bronze tools and ritual objects there. The demand for these useful metals raised the status of many towns and created a new trade network across Eurasia and the Middle East.

Trade had existed between towns and villages for centuries, with grain and stone being bartered. Gift offerings forged new relationships between communities. Rare materials, such as the volcanic glass obsidian, changed hands in 12,000 BCE, with some pieces discovered 900 km (560 mi) away from their origin in Anatolia. The ancient town of Çatalhöyük (pages 41 and 43) was a major hub for the obsidian trade.

Improvements in boat building and navigation turned the Mediterranean into a major commercial route. The ancient Egyptians were able to sail to the coast of Crete by around 3000 BCE. The copper of Cyprus was transported by sea to the Near East and Egypt throughout the 2nd millennium BCE.

Trade routes in Bronze Age Europe around 2000 BCE showing the movement of copper, tin and amber.

By around 2000 BCE, a vast trading network had formed, stretching from Afghanistan – the source of the rare blue rock lapis lazuli – west to the islands of Sicily and Sardinia, and to Spain, as well as north to the shores of the Baltic Sea and Cornwall in southwest England, where tin was mined.

Portuguese potters and metalworkers, from what is known as the Bell Beaker culture, for the shape of the cups they made, shared their skills and wares across the whole of Europe from 2800–1900 BCE. Along with products, trading links also passed on new techniques for making pottery, religious beliefs and burial practices. Alliances between different communities were sometimes sealed with marriages.

More detailed accounts of international trade would appear with the rise of the Sumerian Empire around 4500 BCE and the creation of written accounts. Many early writings record the financial transactions between merchants.

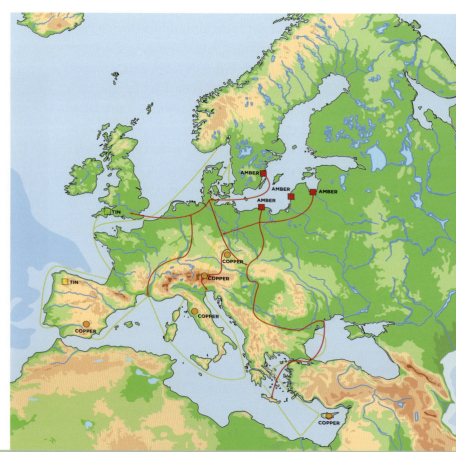

CULTURES CLASH

Not all encounters between cultures were amicable. Competition over resources or the desire to claim greater territory led to warfare between some towns and cities. The evidence for conflict is found in the graves of what appear to be warriors, interred with weapons, their bodies showing signs of violent death.

The ruins of a city in Mersin, Anatolia, dating from 4300 BCE, include fortifications and soldiers' quarters. Another Bronze Age settlement, Syria's Hamoukar, was destroyed in 3500 BCE, in what appears to be a deliberate attack. Slings and thousands of clay bullets have been unearthed at the archaeological site.

Bronze-casting technology allowed armies to be supplied with sturdy swords, lances and shields. By the 4th millennium BCE, the horse-drawn chariot had been designed. With new weaponry at their disposal and large populations from which to recruit soldiers, empires grew and formed armies.

Over 11 seasons, marine archaeologists gathered over 15 metric tonnes (14.75 tons) of ancient trade goods from the wreck of the Bronze Age vessel, Uluburun.

SUNKEN TREASURE

Discovered off the coast of Turkey in 1982, the wreck of the ship *Uluburun* brought to light details of Bronze Age maritime trade. The ship, built using Lebanon cedar, carried a cargo sourced from, perhaps, ten different cultures. The cargo included copper, tin and glass ingots; ebony, ivory and tortoise shells from Africa; Egyptian gold and silver; and Greek weapons. The ship also contained collections of standard weights for use in trade exchanges. The ship is reckoned to have sunk during a voyage to mainland Greece around 1320 BCE.

A relief at the temple of Hatshepsut in Luxor, Egypt.

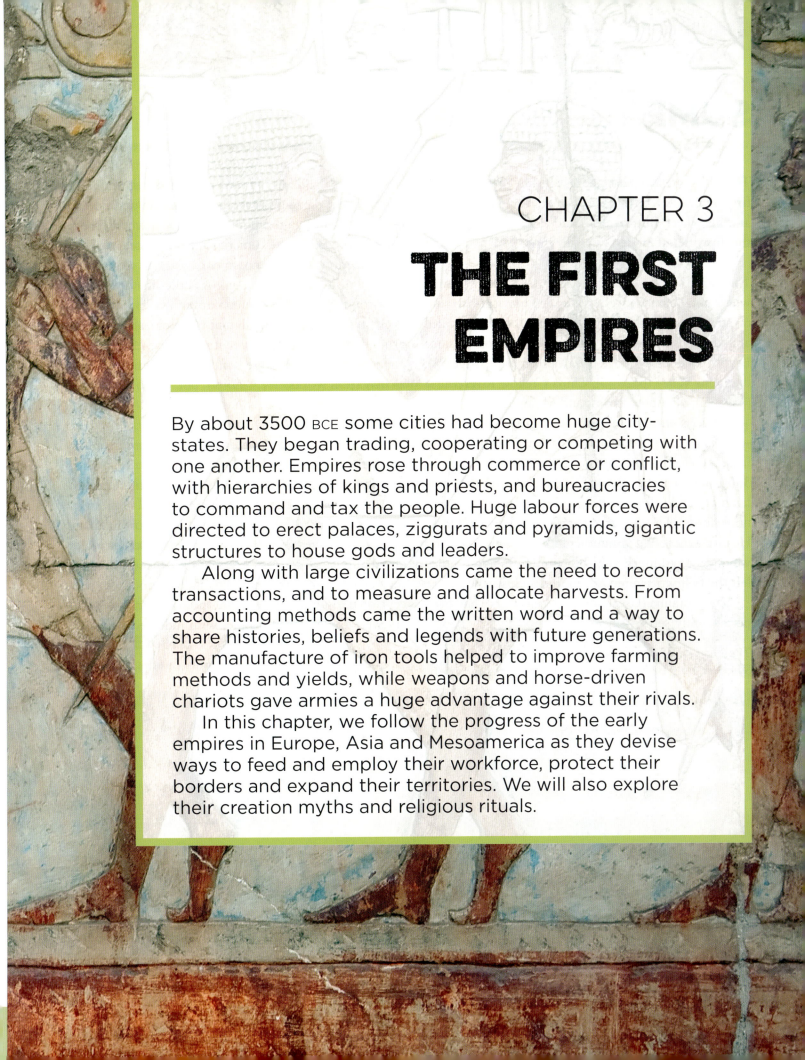

CHAPTER 3

THE FIRST EMPIRES

By about 3500 BCE some cities had become huge city-states. They began trading, cooperating or competing with one another. Empires rose through commerce or conflict, with hierarchies of kings and priests, and bureaucracies to command and tax the people. Huge labour forces were directed to erect palaces, ziggurats and pyramids, gigantic structures to house gods and leaders.

Along with large civilizations came the need to record transactions, and to measure and allocate harvests. From accounting methods came the written word and a way to share histories, beliefs and legends with future generations. The manufacture of iron tools helped to improve farming methods and yields, while weapons and horse-driven chariots gave armies a huge advantage against their rivals.

In this chapter, we follow the progress of the early empires in Europe, Asia and Mesoamerica as they devise ways to feed and employ their workforce, protect their borders and expand their territories. We will also explore their creation myths and religious rituals.

AKKADIAN RULE

The temple rulers of Sumer were gradually replaced with secular kings. They ordered great walls to be built to defend their cities and armies of infantry were recruited to take possession of surrounding villages and integrate them within the territories they controlled. Wars between neighbouring city-states were almost continuous, and Sumer was not invulnerable. Around 2234 BCE it was taken over by the Akkadian Empire, a rival civilization from the north.

The Akkadian leader Sargon the Great ruled Sumer and all of Mesopotamia for 56 years, from around 2350 BCE. His domain is considered the world's first empire. While the Akkadians spoke their own language, they adapted Sumerian cuneiform for writing.

The Akkadians were in time displaced by a rival dynasty known as the Gutians, but by the 22nd century BCE Sumer was once again under the control of Sumerians, who governed the land from the city of Ur. Here they built great monuments, including the Great Ziggurat (c.2100 BCE), but their new period of dominance would prove to be short-lived. Poorly irrigated soils and a dry climate led to local farmlands becoming saltier, and irrigation channels silted up. Wheat harvests became less abundant and the population shrank by about 60 per cent between 2100 and 1700 BCE. In the meantime, recurring raids by rival peoples further weakened the Sumerians, and the sack of the city of Ur by Elamites from Iran in 2004 BCE brought an end to the Sumerian civilization.

BABYLONIAN LAW

The fall of the city-states of Sumer led to a succession of brief takeovers. It was not until around 1792 BCE that Mesopotamia was united again, under the rule of Hammurabi, whose domain was the small (at that time) city-state of Babylon. Through a series of alliances and military advances, Hammurabi took control of the cities of southern Mesopotamia, including what was once Sumer. Hammurabi was much occupied with building and drafting legal codes. While his Babylonian empire did not last, he did leave one very important legacy – his laws.

A 2.4 m (8 ft) diorite stele discovered in 1901 is, perhaps, the greatest artefact from the period of Hammurabi's rule. Beneath an image of the king greeting the sun god Shamash, the carved stone bears lengthy cuneiform inscriptions listing the laws of the Babylonian Empire as decreed by Hammurabi. These include rules on criminal justice, marriage, adoption and inheritance. The laws did not consider all men equal (and women and the enslaved had no rights at all), but their strictures became a template for the legal codes of later civilizations.

This bust of an Akkadian ruler may represent Sargon of Akkad. Sargon retained control of Sumerian cities by placing his family in important positions. His daughters became high priestesses and his sons governors.

Dating from 1750 BCE, the Code of Hammurabi reveals much about Old Babylonian society with a lengthy proclamation of the laws of the empire.

THE STANDARD

The Standard of Ur is a great treasure unearthed at the site of the city's Royal Cemetery. This 4,600-year-old wooden casket is decorated with fine mosaics of lapis lazuli and shell. On one side it depicts peaceful activities and on the other the consequences of war, with prisoners being led away. It is notable for its portrayal of the tiers of Sumerian society from labourer and soldier, to councillor and king.

Among the many fine details on the Standard of Ur is one of the first images of a wheeled vehicle – a donkey-led war wagon.

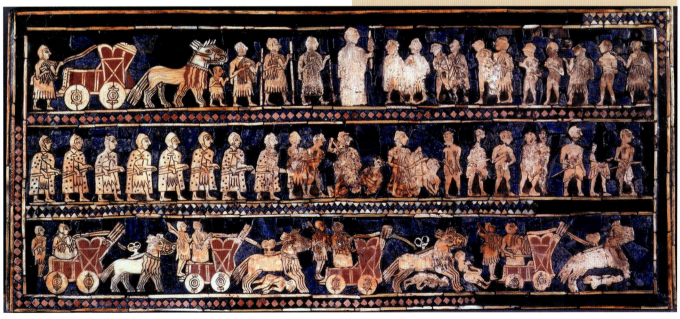

DYNASTIC EGYPT

Blessed by the fertile floodwaters of the Nile, Egypt rose to become the world's first nation state, ruled by kings who claimed descent from the gods.

As the city-states of Mesopotamia prospered between the Tigris and Euphrates (page 56), a rival civilization was growing along the banks of another major river further west. Led by rulers regarded as gods, the kingdom's success depended on a well-organized civil service of governors and tax collectors. Its impressive temples and tombs would surpass all that had gone before.

From antiquity, Africa's Nile, the world's longest river, could usually be trusted to burst its banks every year, delivering fertile silt to the surrounding lands and providing the nutrients needed for plentiful harvests. The Nile was the lifeblood of the towns that sprang up on its margins. Crops of emmer wheat, barley, lentils, chickpeas, sesame, flax, various vegetables and fruit (olives, figs, grapes) were cultivated along the river's plains. Local mines provided copper and gold. The bounty of this land delivered a profusion of food and materials that could support a non-farming hierarchy that included artisans, civil servants, priests and kings. The nation state that grew from the riverside towns survived periods of drought and division to become the longest-lasting civilization in early human history. It left behind some of the most remarkable buildings and relics ever created by humankind. This was Dynastic Egypt.

The beginnings of the Egyptian state are recorded on a 5,000-year-old ceremonial slate called the Narmer Palette. The slate depicts the towering image of King Narmer smiting a foreign captive with a mace. Narmer, also possibly known as Menes, was the first king of all Egypt, conqueror of Lower Egypt from the south and self-declared personification of the god Horus. His dynasty and the many that followed ruled for three millennia. Egypt became a powerful kingdom led by a monarch considered as a channel to the gods, with

The Narmer Palette commemorates the rise of the first unifying king of Egypt around 3100 BCE. Narmer wears the tall crown of Upper Egypt. The wearing of crowns may have been an ancient Egyptian invention.

a government led initially by the king's family. The kings would become known as pharaohs.

At its height, Egypt controlled most of the land surrounding the lower extent of the Nile to its delta in the Mediterranean. Under 31 identified dynasties, the nation state endured attacks from bordering powers, such as the Nubians, Assyrians, Hyksos and Libyans.

Running a nation state required a wealth of civil servants, local governors, a treasury and a taxation system to fund it. Just below the king, and advising and working directly with him, was the vizier, who oversaw local governors, called nomarchs. Temples acted as both places of worship and administrative centres for the collection of taxes. Without coinage, taxes were gathered in the form of agricultural produce. Some of this was redistributed to state employees, some was traded for profit, and some was set aside in granaries as insurance against times of poor harvest.

PATH TO THE GODS

The concept of death and renewal was at the heart of Egyptian religious beliefs, with the life-giving Nile pushing back against the encroaching desert, and pharaohs expected to join a pantheon of gods following their earthly demise.

During the reign of the first dynasties, several kings ordered gigantic memorial tombs for themselves directed towards their journey into the afterlife. Djoser, the first of the Third Dynasty kings, commanded that his tomb be built within a pyramid in Saqqara. Erected around 2667–2648 BCE, it took the form of a step pyramid and was possibly designed by Djoser's vizier, Imhotep. Djoser's pyramid inspired his successors to raise even more imposing testimonials to themselves. In some early tombs, the pharaoh's retinue were buried alongside him, willingly or not, to continue their service in the next world. Sometimes, the pharaoh's advisers and assistants were afforded their own splendid tombs. Examples include a mausoleum in Saqqara for Fifth Dynasty pharaoh Nyuserre Ini's manicurist overseers.

The peak of pyramid building came around 2570 BCE with the completion of the Great Pyramid in Giza for the pharaoh Khufu. With sides measuring 230 m (755 ft) and a height of 146.6 m (481 ft), the Great Pyramid was originally encased in polished limestone and was the tallest building in the world for almost 4,000 years until the completion of the central spire of Lincoln Cathedral in England in 1311. The pyramid was accurately aligned to true north to provide a direct ascension route for the deceased pharaoh into the realm of the gods.

Creating such monuments required an enormous workforce. While enslaved labour would have supplied some of the muscle, peasants were also enlisted for months of duty. Whether or not this labour was demanded or volunteered due to a genuine belief in the godlike power of the pharaoh is debatable.

The Great Pyramid was built from 2.3 million blocks of stone, each weighing one metric tonne on average. According to the ancient Greek historian Herodotus, constructing the pyramid required the services of 100,000 workers over several decades.

THE BOY KING

Diminishing power and poor harvests led to a decline in pyramid building for the pharaohs. From the beginning of the New Kingdom (c.1570–1069 BCE), royal tombs were being dug into the cliffs on the west bank of the Nile, now called the Valley of the Kings. It was here, in 1922, that the archaeologist Howard Carter uncovered the burial chambers of the boy pharaoh Tutankhamen (r. c.1332–1323 BCE), filled with gilded treasures, including a magnificent solid gold face mask inlaid with glass, obsidian and lapis lazuli. The discovery led to a huge renewed interest in Egyptology.

Tutankhamen took the throne of Egypt at the age of eight or nine. His death just nine years later may have left advisers ill-prepared and led to Tutankhamen being buried in a relatively small tomb rather than a site more worthy of his status.

ANCIENT INNOVATORS

As well as advanced techniques in stonemasonry and construction, the Egyptians are responsible for numerous innovations. These include the first hulls for ships and the plumb bob (a suspended weight for accurately measuring the vertical). Like Mesopotamia, Egypt had its own form of writing – hieroglyphics – to record trade and its history. Papyrus, a new medium for writing, was developed. This early form of paper was made from the reeds of an aquatic plant, by pressing out sheets from its pith that could be rolled into scrolls. The Middle Kingdom (2140–1782 BCE) saw a flourishing of the arts and literature, with sophisticated sculpture and epic tales, such as *The Story of Sinuhe*, written for the royal court, much of which, naturally, praised the kings.

THE ARD

Before the use of draught animals, people had to dig the earth to prepare it for sowing. Digging sticks, hoes and mattocks (axe-like tools) were used to turn the ground. The ard was a more sophisticated farming tool and was in use by the 4th millennium BCE in Mesopotamia and Egypt. The ard works like a plough, pulling a flint blade, or ploughshare, through the soil. Domesticated oxen were used to pull the ard, with a farmer guiding the stone (and later iron) ploughshare. This revolutionary implement allowed farmers to dig into harder land and to a greater depth, maintain larger crop fields and produce greater yields.

The defence of the realm required a strong army. Soldiers were recruited from Nubia in the south, and horse-drawn chariots, introduced by Hyksos invaders, helped bring rival states to heel. Peace also prospered through diplomacy. Letters survive of negotiations between the king Rameses II (*c.*1302–*c.*1213 BCE) and Hatusili III, ruler of the Hittites. These provide an early example of an international peace treaty. Rameses II was also responsible for ordering the construction of some of Egypt's most enduring temples and statues, such as those at Abu Simbel.

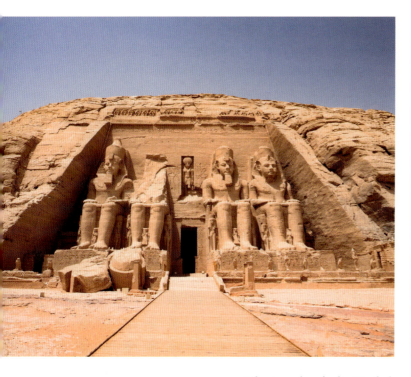

The temple of Abu Simbel.

As well as preserving human bodies, the ancient Egyptians embalmed many animals, particularly cats, which were held in high regard as representatives of the war goddess Bastet. More than a million animal mummies have been found in Egypt.

MUMMIFICATION

The deliberate preservation of the dead in Egypt began at least 5,500 years ago but, under the first dynasties, only kings were honoured with this service, as a way of ensuring their intact passage into the afterlife. Following the collapse of the Old Kingdom (*c.*2613–2181 BCE) anyone who could afford it could undergo this elaborate burial rite. The process, which could take 70 days, included the removal of organs, which were stored in limestone or pottery vessels known as canopic jars. The brain was scooped out via the nostrils. The heart, considered the source of thought and emotion, was left in place. The body was then stuffed with linen to retain its shape and soaked in preservatives before being wrapped in bandages and placed in a coffin with items meant to offer protection.

Egypt claimed superiority over its neighbours but did not decline the opportunity to trade, reaching out to lands as far away as Palestine, Turkey and Crete for goods such as incense, pottery, metals, quality timber, olive oil and slaves.

The power of the pharaoh waned over the centuries. Royal family members in government were replaced by able citizens. Mummification became available to the wealthy elite as well as the ruler (see panel). Even the pharaoh's advisers and assistants were afforded splendid tombs.

The nation of Egypt eventually succumbed to foreign takeover by the Assyrians (in 653 BCE, page 68), the Persians (in 525 BCE, page 82), and the Macedonian army of Alexander the Great (in 332 BCE), before becoming a province of Rome (page 88) in 30 BCE. Many of these new masters adopted the Egyptian style of governance and depicted themselves as pharaohs. While the dominance of the Egyptian dynasties faded, the legacy of this ancient kingdom has continued to fascinate and inspire archaeologists, writers and visitors.

THE WRITTEN WORD

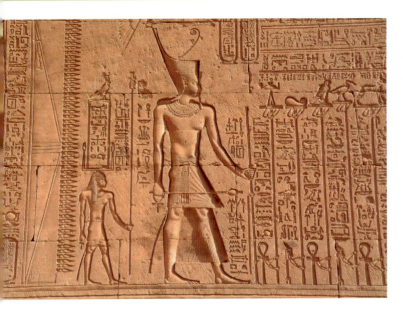

Egyptian hieroglyphs represented objects, words and sounds. Around 700 different symbols were used in the language.

The written word was one of the fundamental inventions of humanity, providing a record of trade, treaties and beliefs. Without it, much history would be lost to us.

One of the most significant advances for humankind, writing systems provided the means to keep an accurate record of transactions, to share laws, to pronounce the glory of leaders and gods, and to share stories that could survive the ages and become a record of history.

Anatomical studies show Neanderthals and *Homo heidelbergensis* had the neural and physical mechanisms to vocalize, but we have no way of knowing if they managed to build a language. *Homo sapiens* was certainly able to convey complex instructions to others and direct hunting parties. Language helped humankind collaborate on community projects, such as irrigation systems, to trade with other tribes and invent gods and myths. All of this knowledge was passed down the generations through word of mouth. Once forgotten, a story was lost.

The earliest-known examples of writing date from Mesopotamia and Egypt in the 4th millennium BCE, including numerous cuneiform administrative texts cut into clay tablets from Sumer and Assyria, and the hieroglyphics that adorn the tombs and temples built for Egyptian pharaohs. While these texts provide a picture of life for royalty and merchants in the Bronze Age, less is revealed about the daily life of those on the lower rungs of society.

Text may have originated through records of trade transactions, with small clay tokens that were placed in a sealed and labelled container. The picture label for the tokens replaced the need for the actual tokens. These pictures, recorded as marks on wet clay, led to more complex pictograms recording items and accounts. These pictures became increasingly simplified into more basic symbols.

CLAY, PAPER AND BONES

The Sumerian writing system, cuneiform, was transcribed using a cut reed as a stylus to make elongated triangular shapes in soft clay, hence its name, from the Latin word *cuneus*, meaning 'wedge'. The wet clay tablets could be recycled, or baked to retain a permanent record. The marks and symbols represented both objects and syllables from the spoken language.

Cuneiform was adopted and adapted by scribes from the city-states of the Assyrians, Hittites, Elamites, Hattians, Hurrians and, later, transcribed the Aramaic language. It survived as a writing system until the 1st century CE. A version of cuneiform, developed in Ugarit, Syria, around the 14th century BCE, was written from left to right and was composed of 30 consonant symbols. This script made its way to Phoenicia (page 76), then Greece, where it became the foundation of a 24-letter alphabet.

Egyptian hieroglyphics ('sacred carvings') are known to exist from about 3200 BCE and may have been inspired by Sumerian cuneiform, though they appear very different. Also representing both objects

Cuneiform script on a clay tablet, dating from the 1st millennium BCE.

and sounds, hieroglyphics were used for declarations on obelisks, temples and tomb walls, and for religious tracts. In late Egyptian dynasties, for more administrative texts a simpler writing style was used, known as demotic script (somewhat resembling the symbols used in modern shorthand). This was read from right to left, as Arabic script is today.

The need to record history and trade in ancient Egypt created a need for scribes. These men were the official state recorders, exempt from more back-breaking duties such as farming and construction.

They were trained to make their own ink, prepare brushes and accurately reproduce about 700 or so hieroglyphic symbols. Reading and writing were the preserve of scribes; rulers rarely shared this ability.

Evidence of writing in China dates back to around 6500 BCE, in the Henan Province, where turtle shells inscribed with symbols have been discovered. Oracle bones with markings used for divination have been found in Shandong Province that are more than 4,500 years old. During the Shang Dynasty (page 72), a full system of pictograms had been invented to describe objects and ideas. Early texts have survived, painted on bamboo slips and silk. The original pictograms have been adapted over centuries to become the script used in modern-day China, shared, in part, by Japan and Korea. With knowledge of how the symbols changed, scholars are able to translate the earliest documents from Chinese history.

An early written script also existed in the Indus Valley (modern-day Pakistan and northwest India) from after 3500 BCE. Only short rows of characters have been found, inscribed on seals, pots and tablets. Thus far, linguists have not been able to decipher it.

ROSETTA STONE

It took the discovery of the Rosetta Stone and several brilliant minds to decipher Egyptian hieroglyphics in the modern era. This fragment of a large stele included three versions of the same text, in Greek, Egyptian Demotic script and hieroglyphics. The text extols the virtues of the king, Ptolemy V. After many attempts to decode it, the French philologist Jean-François Champollion succeeded in unlocking the secrets of the ancient Egyptian language in 1822.

The Rosetta Stone was discovered in 1799 by a French officer arriving in Egypt as part of Napoleon's invasion force. It was being used as building material for a fort in Rashid (Rosetta).

THE IRON AGE

The technology to produce iron gave an advantage to the armies of the Near East and provided tools for poor farmers to cultivate new land.

For centuries, city-states and empires combined copper and tin to forge bronze for tools, jewellery and weapons of war, but there was another metal that was more widely available: iron. It was impossible to extract, however, as the pottery kilns of the time were not capable of reaching or sustaining the temperatures of 1,538°C (2,800°F) or higher needed to reach the melting point necessary for extracting iron ore deposits from the sedimentary rocks that contain it. The production of iron required the development of more powerful furnaces and the ability to remove impurities from the melted ore.

The Iron Age, the third designated age of humankind following the Stone Age and the Bronze Age, occurred at different times in different parts of the world. Iron production began in China from the 5th century BCE. The Chinese were the first people able to build blast furnaces capable of generating temperatures high enough not just to melt iron but to cast it, too. China's ability to produce cast iron gave it an advantage over other civilizations, which could only develop furnaces capable of heating iron ore enough to remove its impurities. This purified iron could then be manipulated, or wrought, by repeatedly heating and hammering it to give it shape.

This iron-bladed sword, with a bronze handle, was forged in Spain in the 6th century BCE.

A dagger with a smelted iron blade has been found in a tomb in Anatolia dating back to 2500 BCE. Signs of iron production have been found in Kaman-Kalehöyük, in Turkey, dating from 2200–2000 BCE. Iron may also have been used in India's Ganges Valley from about 1800 BCE. Iron production in the Near East is considered to have launched around 1200 BCE. Some experts believe its production was pursued due to a shortage in supplies of copper and tin during the trade disruption caused by the Bronze Age Collapse (see panel).

BRONZE AGE COLLAPSE

Until 1200 BCE, the kingdoms of the Near East and Greece, including Babylonia, Egypt, Mycenae and the Hittite Empire, had survived many major skirmishes and never tried to conquer each other. This was possibly due to their need to maintain trade relationships. Then, the kingdoms fell like a pack of cards. There are few records of the period, but it appears to have begun with mass migration and attacks on Canaan, Egypt and the Hittite Empire by naval raiders known as the 'Sea Peoples' (a coalition of tribes including the Sherden, Sheklesh, Lukka and Tursha). Other possible reasons for the sudden decline in regional powers include volcanic eruptions, earthquakes, drought and plague. A combination of some or all of these factors resulted in the end of the Hittite Empire and Mycenaean civilization (page 76) and a decline in the power of Egypt, while the less-powerful Assyria (page 68) shrank in size and was then revived as a mighty empire.

Assyrian soldiers carrying iron spears, from the North Palace in Nineveh, Iraq, c.645–635 BCE.

ARMIES IN IRON

Iron smelting was first practised in Anatolia or the Causasus. The technique spread to Europe, with iron slowly replacing bronze in tools and weapons. Iron was not as strong as bronze but it was easier to source and, by heating it in a charcoal fire, it was possible to convert it into steel, a much stronger carbon-iron alloy. The Hittites, in Turkey, may have been the first to manage this. With knowledge of the process, blacksmiths (named for the black oxides that appear on the metal when heated) would travel the land forging sickles and ploughshares for farmers, or swords and spears for soldiers.

Iron ploughshares allowed farmers to prepare land for agriculture that was otherwise too hard to dig. While bronze was generally restricted for use by the elite, the cheap availability of iron put tools and weapons into the hands of those who would previously have had to do without. Whole armies could now be equipped with armour, swords, spears and shields. One of the first civilizations to benefit from the production of steel was the Persian Empire (550–330 BCE, page 82). Persian warriors may have fought on horseback with both horse and rider protected with steel armour. Greeks (page 84) living on islands in the Aegean also took advantage of the technology and used it to conquer the Greek mainland.

ASSYRIA

Use of Iron Age weapons helped Assyria rise from a base in Upper Mesopotamia to become the strongest military power in the world, with an empire stretching from Iran to Egypt.

The city-state of Assur first came to prominence as a pioneer in free trade and was a wealthy part of a large network of cooperating cities. As neighbouring states declined or fell, Asur expanded to become the Assyrian Empire, with warrior-kings leading successful and, reputedly, bloody campaigns that gained territory including Babylonia and, for a time, Egypt. Assyrian kings were considered conduits for the god Ashur, acting out his will. This will was later interpreted as an instruction to bring order to chaotic neighbouring kingdoms.

Like many southwest Asian city-states around 1200 BCE, Assyria declined during the so-called Late Bronze Age Collapse (page 66). However, Assyria secured its heartland and stormed back under the command of

Ashurnasirpal II to reclaim lost territory and dominate the Near East. The ancient city of Nimrud was revived as the religious centre of the empire, with large palaces, temples, a zoo and botanical gardens, all surrounded by a perimeter wall 8 km (5 mi) long. By 800 BCE, it was the largest city in the world, with about 75,000 residents.

The new Assyrian Empire reached its height under Sargon II (r. 722–705 BCE) and his son Sennacherib (r. 705–681 BCE), who relocated the capital to Ninevah. The kings ordered glorious new building works. Palaces and temples were erected, with detailed, carved stone reliefs depicting their successes in war. The library in Ashurnasirpal II's Ninevah contained a vast collection of cuneiform clay tablets, recording observations on animals and the heavens, plus dictionaries, religious texts and myths, such as the *Epic of Gilgamesh* (page 56).

IRON EMPIRE

One reason for the success of the Assyrian army was its adoption of iron for tools and weaponry. By 845 BCE Assyria could boast the largest fighting force in the world, with warriors on horseback, 100,000 infantry and thousands of horse-driven chariots carrying both a driver and archer. The army employed engineers who could build bridges, dig tunnels, erect fortifications and set up siege engines. They struck terror into the hearts of their enemies by declaring their ferocity in battle with vivid imagery and texts, and by promising merciless retribution.

Assyrian kings protected their royal bloodline by naming their successors on taking the throne. Princes would gain experience by aiding the king, and potential wars of succession were avoided. The king also employed eunuchs as governors of the provinces, assured that they would not become a threat by launching a new royal bloodline.

Among the many innovations used by the Assyrians was a way of sharing news across the empire. With

The Assyrians left behind some of the most impressive art from the period in the form of lengthy wall reliefs and colossal statues. A popular subject was Lamassu, a god portrayed as a creature with the body of a bull or lion, a bird's wings and the head of a king.

relays of envoys travelling on mules between a series of rest stations, a message from the western border could be communicated with the capital 700 km (430 mi) away within five days. The speed of this national service would not be beaten until the introduction of the telegraph in the 19th century.

Assyria collapsed as an empire in 609 BCE after a series of invasions and rebellions, and a joint attack by the Medes and Babylonians. And yet, Assyrian identity survived the rule of its conquerors. An ethnic group claiming descent from this ancient civilization still exists today.

An Assyrian horse-drawn chariot and warriors as depicted on a mural at the Assurbanipal Palace, Ninevah, around 645 BCE.

SLAVE NATION

A consequence of the Assyrian wars was the recruitment of enslaved people from the defeated populace. Slaves were an intrinsic part of almost all the city-states during this period in the Near East, drawn from both the losers in battle and indebted peasants. The Assyrians also used mass resettlement to expand their empire, removing the population from defeated cities. An estimated 4.5 million people were relocated by the Assyrian Empire over three centuries. This suppressed revolt and resulted in a more diverse populace.

Stone panel from palace at Nineveh, c.640–620 BCE, showing Assyrians putting slaves to work.

THE INDUS VALLEY

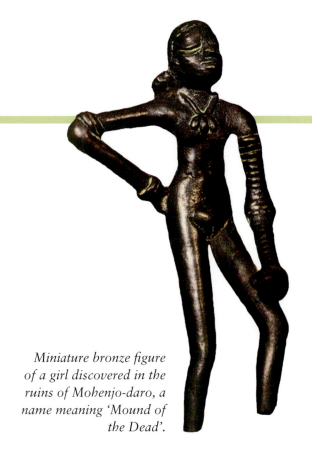

Miniature bronze figure of a girl discovered in the ruins of Mohenjo-daro, a name meaning 'Mound of the Dead'.

Undiscovered until the 20th century, the civilization that spread along the Indus Valley was as advanced and vast as that of Egypt and Mesopotamia, with urban planning, wheeled transport and sanitation.

The city-states of Mesopotamia (page 56) and Egypt (page 60) had grown under a hierarchical structure, with kings ruling powerful armies and priests guarding temples that dominated the cities. The culture that grew in South Asia's Indus Valley was strikingly different. While similarly sophisticated with disciplined building methods and sanitation, its cities lacked grand palaces or religious buildings. Nor did they appear to maintain an army.

The Indus river, which gave its name to India, flows from Tibet through Pakistan to the Arabian Sea. As with the Nile, Tigris and Euphrates, which fed the Egyptian and Mesopotamian civilizations, the Indus floods every year and replenishes the soils in the surrounding plains. Small agricultural communities emerged along the river and the plains surrounding it from about 6500 BCE. They farmed wheat, barley, rice, peas and cotton, and domesticated water buffalo for milk, to work in the fields and to pull wheeled carts.

By 2600 BCE, cities such as Mohenjo-daro and Harappa had been built, with over 40,000 people likely to be living there. Streets were laid out in a well thought out grid system, with standardized brick-built warehouses and wide boundary walls. Houses in the cities contained flush toilets linked to a complex sewer and drainage system, the earliest known sanitation system in the world. 'Wind catchers' were placed on roofs to feed cool air indoors as a form of air-conditioning. Mohenjo-daro also contained a large interior public bath the size of a swimming pool.

Unlike the contemporary city-states in the Near East, the Indus cities did not grow around a temple or palace complex, nor is there any evidence of a standing army. How they were run and what life was like there is a mystery, as the minimal writing found on seals and pots has proved indecipherable to modern scholars. Proof of trade has been found, however, between the Harappans and cities in Mesopotamia, such as the Sumerian city of Ur, where the Harappans were known as Meluhha.

Incredibly, this advanced culture was unknown until archaeologists properly investigated the sites in the 1920s. The name Harappa has been given to the civilization that sprang from the region and included 1,000 settlements stretching from Afghanistan to Delhi and the foothills of the Himalayas.

The Harappan civilization lasted for more than 1,000 years until 1700 BCE, when most of the cities were abandoned. The culture probably declined through a combination of circumstances, including weakened monsoons, drought and a reduction in trade.

THE ARYANS

The Aryans, as they have been called, were a race of Indo-Europeans probably from Central Asia who moved into the Indian subcontinent from about 1800 BCE as the Harappan civilization was beginning its decline. The Aryans do not appear to have employed

The ruins of the city of Mohenjo-daro in modern-day Pakistan. The city was built around 2600 BCE and contains a large public bath.

Of the many representations of animals made by the Harappans on sculptures and seals, one of the most curious is the 'unicorn'. The animal has the body of a bull, the head of a zebra and a single horn. Rather than describing an extinct creature, it is assumed to be the symbol of a region or trading order.

the written word or farming tools. What they did have was a mastery of the horse, chariots and dairy farming. Whether or not their arrival influenced the fall of the Harappans is unknown, but they did become a dominant culture, their language and religious beliefs spreading across the region. The Aryans spoke Sanskrit, the root of most dialects spoken today in Pakistan, northern India and Bangladesh.

THE CASTE SYSTEM

Soon after the arrival of the Aryans into the Indus Valley, the scriptures that formed the basis of the Hindu religion (page 100) were transcribed. The oldest of these, the *Rig Veda*, refers to the time of creation and a primeval man split into four. From his mouth came the priest, his arms became soldiers, his thighs traders, and his feet servants. This formed the basis of a division of society called the caste system.

This system arranged people into four main tiers: Brahmins, the spiritual leaders, at the top, followed by Kshatriyas, the public servants, Vaisyas, the artisans, and Shudras, the unskilled workers. There were many subcategories, including one below all of the others, the 'Untouchables', who were shunned. This system, which kept social groups apart and hindered opportunities for improvement, was banned when India became an independent nation in 1947, though elements of it still exist.

SHANG CHINA

The Shang was the first recorded dynasty to rule in China. Under the Shang, the country made huge advances in art, astronomy and technology.

China's Yellow River Valley is considered one of the cradles of civilization, where sophisticated culture developed into major city-states. Archaeological evidence reveals the foundations of villages from before 5000 BCE. As in the Near East, farming settlements grew into larger communities with ruling nobles.

The Shang, also known as the Yin, ruled the middle and lower Yellow River Valley from around 1600–1046 BCE. While there was an earlier dynasty, the Xia, the Shang was the first to be known through archaeological and written proof. The evidence reveals details of the dynasty's religious ideas, political structure, and advances in mathematics and military technology.

The capital of the Shang dynasty moved five times over the course of its reign, with the city of Zhengzhou possibly the first. Occupied from the mid-period of the dynasty, at its height Zhengzhou was a city covering 3.4 square km (1.3 square mi) protected by a wall 10 m (33 ft) high and 36 m (118 ft) wide at the base. Excavations suggest this was home to royalty, with numerous workshops for artisans using bronze, bone and clay. Skulls unearthed in the city's foundations hint that both human and dog sacrifices took place.

Tombs in the later Shang capital of Anyang include complete chariots, as well as the skeletons of their drivers and horses. The chariots are thought to be based on designs from Armenia. Some unearthed weapons may have origins in the Middle East, suggesting contact between the Shang and Bronze Age civilizations in the west took place. Among the tombs at Anyang is that of King Wu Ding's consort, Fu Hao. Finds here confirm stories of her acting as a military general for the king.

The value and usefulness of items buried with royalty suggest a strong belief in the afterlife similar to that of the ancient Egyptians (page 60). Kings were also buried with a retinue of servants. One grave dating to 1200 BCE contained the remains of 74 people beside the king, along with the bones of horses and dogs, all likely to have been sacrificed.

War chariots were buried in tombs to aid Shang-era kings in battles in the afterlife.

This bone was used for divination. During a ritual, which the king would sometimes lead, a question would be asked of ancestors and bones subjected to fire. How the bones cracked would be interpreted and the symbols on the bone are a record of the ancestors' replies.

MARKING TIME

The staple food for people living under the Shang was millet. Farmers also raised cattle, sheep and pigs. Shang rulers had access to plentiful copper and tin for making bronze and many fine ritual vessels were cast during the period (see panel). Jade was coveted by the elite. Cowrie shells from the coast far to the south were used for currency.

One Shang innovation was the use of calendars to mark dates for planting crops, based on 12 months of 30 days. The calendar considered both lunar and solar cycles. The Shang employed astronomers who were able to track the path of the planet Mars and various comets.

The last Shang Dynasty ruler was Di Xin, who was regarded as a cruel king. During an attack by the Zhou army in 1046 BCE, Di Xin recruited 200,000 slaves into his defence forces, but many defected to the Zhou. Facing defeat, Di Xin committed suicide by setting fire to his palace.

MASTERPIECES IN BRONZE

Bronze workers at the time of the Shang Dynasty were particularly advanced, using the piece-mould casting method which involved making a model, then covering it in clay to make a mould that would be cut into sections and re-fired as a whole. Production of bronze wares and weapons operated as a large industry, with a massive labour force involved in mining, refining and transporting ores to the workshops. The capital of Anyang contained a foundry covering 40,000 square m (430,556 square ft). Examples of fine Shang bronze artistry include wine vessels and ornate three-legged cauldrons known as ding vessels, used in sacrificial rituals.

This intricately decorated set of ritual bronzes, including wine vessels and an altar table, dates to the 11th century BCE.

CREATION MYTHS

Ancient civilizations developed their own stories to explain how humankind came to be, brought into being by gods to act in their service.

The craving for answers to life's mysteries defines humankind. In ancient times the ultimate question of where we came from was explained by creation myths, where gods brought earth and all of its creatures into being. The myths of different cultures have a lot in common. They imagined the gods bringing order from cosmic chaos, often a primordial ocean. The power of the gods was such that they could summon the earth from a void, with just a breath or a word.

Humanity is described as being moulded from the earth or from body parts of gods, which suggested we were more important than other animals on the planet. There is a recurring theme of chaos against order, light against darkness, good against evil, a battle humankind was expected to continue.

The ancient Egyptians had several creation myths associated with the gods of different major cities, but all followed the same theme, of order springing from chaos. The myth from the city of Heliopolis describes a mound of silt rising from a dark, lifeless water called Nu, with the sun god Atum appearing upon it. This parallels the annual rising of the Nile and its delivery of fertile silt to the surrounding land. Atum conceived the gods Shu (air) and Tefnut (moisture), and from them sprang divine personifications of the earth and sky. Other Egyptian creation myths describe the sun born from a cosmic egg and all creatures and plants being spoken into life or modelled from clay.

The Enūma Eliš, a Babylonian myth recorded on clay tablets, also imagines a watery chaos before the act of creation, with two initial gods giving birth to many more. Battle raged between the gods following the birth of the world until one named Marduk came to power and defeated the female god of sea and chaos, Tiamet, cutting her in two to form the earth and sky. Marduk then created humans from his blood.

Marduk would become the most revered of all the gods of ancient Sumeria and Babylon. His essence was believed to inhabit a statue in the Ésagila temple at Babylon. When the city was overtaken by invaders, as it was on many occasions, the golden statue of Marduk, protector of the city, was carried away in triumph by the winning army, to be reclaimed at a later date.

Myths of ancient Mesopotamia claim the gods created humanity to do the menial jobs they didn't want to do, such as planting crops, making buildings and herding animals. Humanity was brought into being to take on these roles and to provide for the deities who gave them water, grain and animals in return.

FROM THE EARTH

The formation of the earth and sky from nothing, followed by the creation of humans from an element of God mixed with earth, was repeated in the Jewish creation myth, which may have been inspired by earlier Babylonian texts. In the story that became the first two chapters of the Bible's Old Testament, the

Horemheb, the last pharaoh of ancient Egypt's 18th Dynasty, kneels before the god of creation, Atum.

Marduk slays Tiamet.

first humans are given a paradise to live in but they disobey the instructions of God in seeking knowledge. They are punished for their choices and cast out of the paradise known as Eden.

The ancient Greeks developed a vast pantheon of gods and monsters responsible for all manner of events. The creation, as related by the poet Hesiod, begins with another chaos. From this sprang the goddess Gaia, or Mother Earth. She birthed Uranus, the sky, to shroud her, along with the mountains and the sea.

The *Rig Veda*, an early Vedic text from India, describes Purusha, a giant being with a thousand heads, eyes and feet who envelops the earth. When the gods sacrifice him his body parts form the elements, humanity and all animals.

Ancient China described the initial chaos of the universe in the form of an egg with the opposing forces of Yin and Yang within. One day the first being, Pangu, broke free of the egg and separated earth and sky with a swing of his mighty axe. Over 18,000 years, Pangu held the earth (yin) and sky (yang) apart. On his death, his breath became the wind, his voice thunder, his eyes the sun and the moon, his head the mountains and his blood the rivers.

Humankind and all animals were born from Pangu's fleas. In another version, people were made from the mud of the Yellow river.

Pangu, the first being in Chinese mythology, holds the cosmic egg containing the Yin and Yang.

FINDING EDEN

The earth where humanity was placed by the gods is often described as a paradise in creation myths, with humans and animals living together as equals. In Judaic, Christian and Islamic religions, the Garden of Eden is considered the birthplace of the first humans, Adam and Eve, or a heavenly destination. In the Old Testament's Book of Genesis, the location of the garden is described as at the source of four tributaries. This has led some scholars to locate it on the banks of the Tigris, in Mesopotamia, where the first civilizations arose. The name Eden also comes from the Sumerian word *edin*, which means 'plain'.

THE MEDITERRANEAN WORLD

The world's largest inland sea, the Mediterranean became central to trade from the 3rd millennium BCE. With commerce came a new written language that provided the basis for the European alphabet.

Greek mythology recounts the story of Minos, king of the island of Crete in the Mediterranean. Every seven years he demanded a tribute of 14 Athenian youths to be sent to his labyrinth, where they became victims of the half-bull-half-man creature, the Minotaur. In the early 20th century, when the archaeologist Arthur Evans uncovered Bronze Age ruins on Crete, he chose to label the period it belonged to as Minoan, after the legendary ruler. What Evans found was evidence of the first civilization of note in Western Europe, the first in a long line of Mediterranean cultures and major players in the story of humankind.

Minoan society was at its height between 3000 and 1400 bce, with established sea-trading links with Egypt, Cyprus and settlements in the Aegean and Anatolia. The Minoans built impressive palaces, some four storeys high, decorated with fine frescoes. Their gods were all female and women may have played a major role in the priesthood. Minoan ceramics show a great deal of sophistication for the age. The remains of Minoan pots that once contained oil and ointments have been discovered in Egypt and Syria, evidence of their trade.

Minoan rule came to a sudden end around 1450 bce, possibly due to the fallback from a local volcano eruption and a takeover by Mycenaeans from the Greek mainland. The Mycenaeans are also connected to Greek myth through a supposed founder, the hero Perseus, and Agamemnon (page 84), a king who was said to have led the Greek army in the Trojan War. The Mycenaeans were also great palace builders and traders. On Crete, they adopted much of the Minoan culture.

THE PHOENICIANS

Around the same time as the Mycenaeans were trading across the Mediterranean, a network of city-states sited along the coast of modern-day Syria and Lebanon were finding their own markets. These people shared the same Semitic language and called themselves Canaanites. They gained the name Phoenicians from the Greek word for purple, *phoinix*, because of the purple-dye fabrics that they traded.

The Phoenicians were hugely influential in Classical antiquity, trading and sharing ideas between Mesopotamia, Egypt and Greece from around 1500 BCE. They did not seek to conquer and never established an empire, but their ability as intermediaries and their written language connected much of Europe.

Phoenician cities, such as Tyre, Sidon, Berets (Beirut), Ugarit and Byblos, became major hubs in the market for pine and cedar wood, dyed cloth, ivory and wine, and were home to artisans crafting fine glassware and metalwork. The Phoenicians acted as brokers between different cultures, not only exchanging goods but ideas and customs.

While the Late Bronze Age collapse (page 66) affected neighbouring states, the Phoenicians survived its effects and became the dominant traders for the region. They were advanced in building large merchant ships, developing the keel, and coating the hull in waterproof bitumen. They were the first sailors to navigate using the Pole Star, indicating north, enabling them to sail on clear nights. They crisscrossed the Mediterranean, establishing trading ports on the islands of Cyprus, Sardinia, Sicily and Malta, and along the coasts of North Africa and Iberia, where they founded Gadir (modern Cádiz). Carthage was established by the Phoenicians around 814 BCE, in what is now Tunisia. It would expand to become one of the richest cities in the ancient world.

The Phoenicians built up a maritime trade network across the whole of the southern Mediterranean.

THE ALPHABET

Perhaps the greatest legacy of the Phoenicians is their alphabet. Developed from about 1400 to 1000 BCE, the Phoenician alphabet was made up of 22 consonants read from left to right. It would be adapted by the Greeks around 800 BCE, who added five vowels. This formed the basis of the alphabet used by all European languages. The alphabet proved an easier model for language learning than cuneiform or hieroglyphics with their hundreds of signs. This allowed a wider population, not just trained scribes, to read and write.

While dominant in trade, the Phoenicians had no large standing army and were at the mercy of expansionist empires such as Assyria (page 68), which took control of Phoenician lands after 858 BCE and demanded tribute. Phoenicia then fell under the rule of the Babylonians, the Persians and the Macedonian king Alexander the Great. The Phoenicians retained some autonomy through their years under foreign rule but were finally absorbed into the Roman Empire in 62 BCE.

The revolutionary Phoenician alphabet comprised 22 letters representing consonants.

CURSED WRITING

The earliest surviving example of the Phoenician alphabet can be found on the sarcophagus of Ahiram, an ancient king of Byblos. The sarcophagus, dating from around 1000 BCE, bears an inscription translated as a curse to warn away those that may threaten Ahiram's city: 'Beware! Behold [there is] disaster for you down here.'

The sarcophagus of Ahiram bears the earliest-surviving Phoenician inscription, a warning carved around its rim.

aleph {A}   beth {B}   gimmel {G}   daleth {D}   he {H}   waw {W}

zayin {Z}   heth {H}   teth {T}   yodh {Y}   kaph {K}   lamedh {L}   mem {M}   nun {N}   samekh {S}   ayin {O}   pe {P}   tsadi {Ts}   qoph {Q}   res {R}   sin {S}   taw {T}

THE OLMECS

The Olmecs were the first known civilization to appear in Mesoamerica, influencing the empires that followed their demise. Independent of ancient Egypt, the Olmecs left a language of glyphs and giant pyramids.

The first great civilization that we know of to appear in Mesoamerica arose in the tropical lowlands of modern-day Mexico around 1200 BCE. Known as the Olmecs, these people left behind a large number of monuments, sculptures and artefacts, including numerous colossal stone heads. Independent of the cultures of Eurasia, the Olmecs designed cities orientated north–south, developed a sophisticated calendar, invented ball games and introduced the delights of drinking chocolate to the region.

We do not know what the Olmecs called themselves. The name Olmec was chosen by scholars from the Aztec word *Olmecatl*, which means 'rubber people'. Rubber was sourced from the trees in the area where the Olmecs lived. While their origin is a mystery, we do know something of Olmec beliefs through the glyphs they left carved into their monuments.

The people felt a connection with their environment, with mountains being the path to the sky and caves a route to the underworld. Olmec gods represented the life-sustaining aspects of earth, rain and maize. Their sky-dragon and feathered serpent gods would be adopted by later Mesoamerican civilizations, the Maya and the Aztecs.

The Olmecs are likely to have had kings and an order of priests presiding over events and rituals. These include ritual blood-letting, pilgrimages, offerings and sacrifices. They may also have believed that their gods could change their form and appear as eagles and jaguars. The jaguar was a significant creature for the Olmecs, representing both the ruler and fertility.

Olmec art includes many realistic ceramic sculptures, such as this figure of a crying baby.

To guard their monuments, the Olmecs placed 17 gigantic heads around their religious buildings.

CAPITAL AND CULTURE

There were no large animals available to domesticate along the coast where the Olmecs lived. Instead, they hunted and fished, subsisting on a diet of dogs, turtles and shellfish. The Olmecs grew maize, sweet potatoes, cassava and beans on their fertile land, and probably foraged for palm nuts. They also harvested and spun cotton for textiles.

At their height, a population of up to 350,000 lived in several Olmec towns – San Lorenzo, La Venta, Laguna de los Cerros, Tres Zapotes and Las Limas. The townsfolk traded far beyond their borders

An Olmec jade mask.

with pottery, rubber, obsidian, jade, feathers and polished mirrors made of ilmenite and magnetite.

San Lorenzo, potentially the first Olmec capital, featured what was probably a palace, along with ceremonial ponds and drains. This major centre was demolished, perhaps due to an invasion, and replaced by a larger settlement in La Venta. Here, a pyramid around 33 m (108 ft) tall was built, part of a deliberately planned religious layout for ritual events, with buildings positioned symmetrically, aligned north to south. Mosaic pavements were set on platforms, then covered up, while huge, carved stone heads were placed at strategic points, looking outwards. The heads were carved from basalt boulders, some of which are 3 m (10 ft) tall, that had to be transported from many kilometres away. The heads all differ, suggesting they were portraits of rulers.

While the remains of Olmec towns show remarkable skills in construction, most people lived outside these impressive complexes, in simple village homes nearby.

The Olmec calendar was based on cycles of 52 years. The 52nd year was feared as a time of great danger, and was observed with great religious ceremony. As well as a complex calendar, the Olmecs introduced the use of the number zero in their counting system.

Possibly due to a series of violent volcanic eruptions in the area or the silting of rivers, the Olmecs disappeared from history about 400 BCE. But their culture continued through later civilizations in the region – the Maya, Zapotec, Totonac and Teotihuacán people, who adopted some of the Olmecs' gods, games and culture.

THE FIRST BALL GAME

The Olmecs may have been the inventors of a ball game, *tlachli,* which was played by later Mesoamerican civilizations, and still is today by some indigenous populations in Mexico. The game involved a rubber ball being bounced between teams in a court, probably using their hips and knees, towards a goal hoop positioned on a high wall.

Circular goal used by ancient Mesoamericans in the rubber ball game tlachli.

A mosaic from Herculaneum depicting the deities Neptune and Amphitrite.

CHAPTER 4
CLASSICAL DOMINANCE

Some of the largest and longest-lasting empires known to history prevailed through the 1st millennium BCE. Along with vast bureaucracies that brought order, and disciplined armies that extended their territories, these empires gave birth to artistic, literary, dramatic, philosophical and scientific ideas that have lasted the ages.

These empires had the building and engineering skills to construct roads and canals that crossed continents, valley-spanning bridges, aqueducts and amphitheatres. Along with new material advances came new spiritual convictions, faiths that crossed borders, too, and converted emperors.

The Persian Achaemenid Empire was the largest empire in antiquity by population. The ideas of ancient Greece were disseminated throughout Persia, North Africa and India. At its height, the Roman Empire ruled 50 million people. The Han, one of the first dynasties to unify China, governed a population of many millions more. India saw its own Classical period of integration and artistic advancement under the Mauryan and the Gupta dynasties. At the fringes of these great civilizations, nomadic tribes left much less of a record but changed history nevertheless, threatening to bring several empires to their knees.

In this chapter, we chart the paths of the empires of antiquity, and see how they ruled huge populations through democracy or tyranny, invented new means of trade, and spread religious ideas.

THE PERSIAN EMPIRE

At its height, the Persian Achaemenid Empire ruled a greater percentage of population than any empire that followed. Conflicts between the Persians and Greek city-states determined the future for all of Europe.

The Persian Achaemenid Empire was the largest empire in antiquity, at its peak even greater in scale than the Roman Empire, with an estimated 44 per cent of the world's population under its rule. The name Achaemenid comes from Achaemenes, the supposed founder of the imperial dynasty, though there is no historical record of such a person existing. There are scant written records of the Achaemenids from the Persian side, while histories of the Achaemenid Empire from the Greeks and in the Bible portray the civilization as an aggressive Eastern tyranny threatening the liberty of the West. Archaeological records provide a more balanced perspective of a tolerant power that, while ruthless in crushing revolts, allowed freedom of language, administration and religion for its subjects.

What would become the greatest empire of the East originated in a small province of Persia, in modern-day Iran. From here the future Cyrus the Great led a successful coalition of peoples in revolt against the ruling king of Media, Astyages. Cyrus' armies continued their advances, conquering Lydia (Turkey) and other cities along the Ionian coast. In 540 BCE, Cyrus turned his attention to Babylon and took control, apparently without resistance. He put his son, Cambyses, in charge but allowed Babylonian administrators to continue governing the region. This pragmatic solution to keeping new provinces in order was one that Cyrus and his successors would continue.

Cyrus did not force his language or religion on the cities that he conquered, either. New Achaemenid subjects were allowed to continue in their beliefs, and the sanctity of their temples was respected. Indeed, Cyrus permitted Jews, who had earlier been deported to Babylonia, to return to Jerusalem and rebuild their temple. Such munificence was not the case for those who rebelled against the Persians. The people of defeated Lydia were relocated, while the inhabitants of the Babylonian city of Opis were massacred.

Persian archers painted on glazed brick panels from the Palace of Darius, Susa.

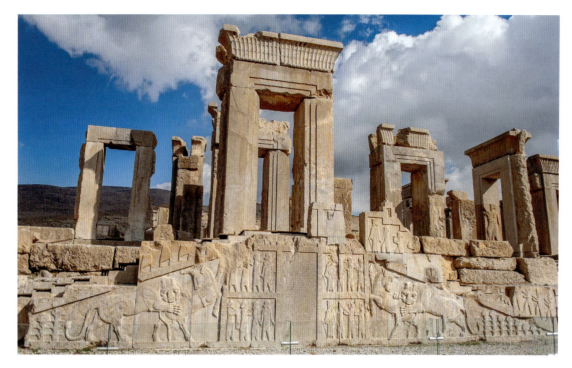

The remains of the Tachara Palace built for Darius at Persepolis, Iran. Wall carvings show servants bearing gifts for the king.

GREATEST OF ALL

On the death of his father in 530 BCE, Cambyses took charge and achieved one of Cyrus' unrealized goals, to take control of Egypt. Cambyses was given the pharaonic name of Mesuti-Re. Under his successor, Darius, the Achaemenid Empire reached its greatest extent, with borders in Libya, India and southern Russia. The kingdom was divided into 20 provinces, called satrapies, each with its own governor. Darius introduced coinage for trade, began a huge building programme in Persepolis, rebuilt the city of Susa to be his capital and instigated the digging of a canal to link the Nile to the Red Sea. This was a forerunner of the Suez Canal.

The Achaemenids believed in a creator-god, Ahura-Mazda, represented as a winged disc on reliefs. This faith developed into Zoroastrianism, the worship of Zoroaster (or Zarathustra). Unlike Greek and Roman religions, this was a monotheistic faith. It still has followers in Iran and India.

EAST VS WEST

During Darius' reign, the Persians came into conflict with the Greek city-states (page 84). Athens had supported Ionian cities in a revolt against the Persians, drawing the wrath of the empire. Xerxes (r. 485–465 BCE), the son of Darius, attacked and successfully captured and set aflame an evacuated Athens, but his navy was destroyed soon after. Had the Persians defeated the Greek city-states the complexion of Europe thereafter would have been very different, with eastern domination and Persian culture spreading across the continent.

The 4th century BCE saw the Persians occupied with fighting rebellions within the empire, including Egypt, which gained independence from the Persians for 60 years from 399 BCE. In 330 BCE, the Persians faced their most significant foe, the Macedonian Alexander the Great. Alexander's armies swept through Persian territory, adding its empire to their own.

MARATHON

In 490 BCE, when the Achaemenid navy landed at the Greek harbour of Marathon and was pushed back, legend has it that a runner, Philippides, was sent to share the news in Athens but collapsed and died from the effort. Another version has it that the victorious Greek army hurried to defend the city against the same retreating Achaemenid navy. The story and the distance covered, between 35–40 km (22–25 mi), inspired the competitive marathon race, named after the messenger's starting point.

ANCIENT GREECE

Emerging from a Mediterranean 'Dark Age', seafaring city-states began to share their learned culture far and wide. The ancient Greeks introduced new ideas in the arts, philosophy and science, and developed a new system of governance: democracy.

Almost three millennia ago, a group of city-states dotted around the Aegean Sea began to expand their reach through trade and war with their neighbours. The cities shared a common language, pantheon of gods and culture. Soon they would share a name – Greece – and launch what is considered a Classical age upon Europe.

Following a 300-year-long 'Dark Age' and a huge population drop across the eastern Mediterranean and Near East, small city-states around the Aegean began to thrive and spread their influence. These cities, called poleis, were ruled by citizens rather than kings. Some were small, with a population of just 1,000 individuals. Others, such as Athens, Sparta, Corinth and Argos, contained 10,000 individuals and held much greater sway.

A typical large polis would include an acropolis (high city) with a temple and an agora (an open meeting space for markets). While the people of these poleis considered themselves citizens of their individual city, as a whole they were known as Hellenes (Greeks). They spoke Greek, believed in the same gods, including Zeus, god of the sky, and Ares, the god of war, and treasured major literary works, such as the *Iliad* and the *Odyssey* (see panel). The culture and power of the Greeks spread across the Mediterranean, with colonies being established as far as Syracuse in Sicily, and Massalia (modern Marseilles) in France.

THE HOMERIC LEGENDS

The *Iliad* and the *Odyssey* are two lengthy heroic poems describing war and mythological adventures in ancient Greek history. Attributed to Homer, they were probably transcribed by more than one individual. The tales had been shared orally for centuries before versions were written down in Greek around 750 BCE. The *Iliad* describes two weeks of the Trojan War, a conflict that may have taken place between Troy and Greece in the 12th or 11th century BCE. The *Odyssey* recounts King Odysseus' perilous ten-year journey home from the Trojan War. His tale features shipwrecks, a death-defying sailing between rocks and a whirlpool, and encounters with a sorceress and the mighty Cyclops. The stories have continued to fascinate readers since they were first shared 29 centuries ago.

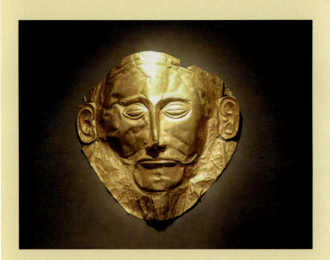

It has been claimed that this golden burial mask shows the face of the Trojan War's king, Agamemnon. While dating from around 1600 BCE, it is unlikely to be a depiction of the Greek leader from the Iliad.

The Temple of Concordia, Agrigento. The temple was built by Greek colonists on the island of Sicily in the 5th century BCE.

There were rivalries between the poleis, with wars common, but there were alliances, too, with coalitions based around Athens, Thebes, Argos and Sparta. Despite internal grievances, many of the poleis united when Greece as a whole was threatened by invasion from Persia in 490 and 480 BCE (page 82). The Greek armies developed an effective strategy in warfare called the phalanx. This involved soldiers forming tight units and overlapping their shields to form impenetrable defences. Successes against the Persian armies helped foster a pride in Greek identity.

DEMOCRACY AND SERFDOM

The ruling system of the Greek poleis went through many incarnations, including oligarchy (rule by a wealthy family or nobles) and tyranny (control under a single strong leader). In 594 BCE, Solon, the chief magistrate of Athens, ended debt slavery, reduced the power of the aristocracy and introduced a ruling council that allowed both rich and poor citizens to take part. Further revisions by Cleisthenes in 507 BCE divided Athens into 139 voting districts, called demes, and established a council of 500, with membership chosen by lot. Democracy was born, though this fairer voting system did not include women, foreigners or slaves.

The Greek economy was greatly bolstered through the labour of enslaved people, mostly taken from Anatolia and Thrace. An estimated 35,000 were forced to work in the dangerous and cramped silver mines in Attica. The militaristic state of Sparta enslaved the equivalent of seven individuals per citizen, subjugating most of the population of the territories of Laconia and Messenia. Called helots, this population supported the Spartan military machine by working in the fields, building and cooking. Once a year, young Spartan military graduates were encouraged to hunt and kill helots as part of their training. This annual 'cull' also helped to head off any possibility of rebellion by the subjugated people.

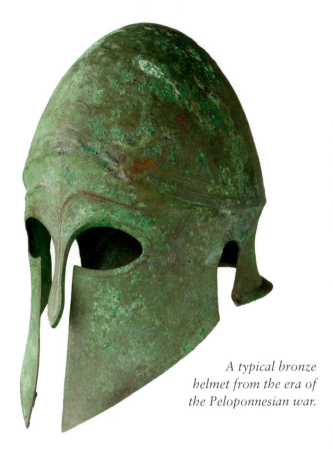

A typical bronze helmet from the era of the Peloponnesian war.

While the words science and scientists did not yet exist, 'natural philosophers' began questioning the workings of the world. Among the many theories put forward was that of Democritus (*c.*460–361 BCE), who suggested that matter was made up of tiny particles separated by empty space. He called these colliding particles *atoma* (atoms). Pythagoras (*c.*571–*c.*497 BCE) described mathematical laws involving right-angled triangles, while Archimedes (*c.*287–*c.* 212 BCE) engineered a screw device for raising water, designed large-scale catapults and formulated the value pi. Aristotle (*c.*384–322 BCE), known for his philosophical works, provided proof that Earth was round rather than flat. Soon after, Eratosthenes of Cyrene (276–194 BCE) succeeded in estimating the diameter of the planet with just one per cent inaccuracy.

From the 5th century BCE, Athens became a dominant power around the Aegean, forming the Delian League with other poleis, who all paid tribute to Athens to support its fleet. Athenian authority was challenged by Sparta, leading to a 30-year struggle called the Peloponnesian War (431–404 BCE). During this period, Athens completed the building of the Parthenon, a temple dedicated to the goddess Athena atop the city's Acropolis. Athens' Delian League eventually fell to Sparta, with the financial backing of Persia, but Spartan rule was brief and Athens regained its independence in 403 BCE.

ART AND PHILOSOPHY

The Classical Greek period saw the arts, philosophy and science flourish. Greek artists produced anatomically accurate sculptures of gods and heroes, depicting an ideal of human beauty. Theatre and public speaking were held in high regard. The playwrights Aeschylus, Sophocles and Euripides brought mythological and psychological drama to the stage. Thirty-two of their plays survive, including Sophocles' tragedies *Oedipus the King* and *Antigone*, which are still performed today.

A 4th-century sculpture of Hermes and the infant Dionysus, discovered in the ruins of the Temple of Hera in Olympia.

A mosaic showing Alexander the Great at the Battle of Issus, from the 2nd century BCE.

OLYMPIADS

The Greeks were captivated by sporting achievements. From 776 BCE until the late 4th century CE, major competitions took place in Olympia every four years. This was the origin of the modern Olympic Games. Truces were held between warring Greek states so that they could attend. Among the competitive events were horse-and-chariot racing, athletics races (some in heavy body armour), wrestling and boxing. Victors were given an olive-branch crown, heralded at home, and were sometimes commemorated with statues.

THE GREAT

In 338 BCE, Athens was conquered by King Philip of Macedonia, a country to the north. Following Philip's assassination, his son, Alexander III, took the throne at the age of 20. Taught by Aristotle, Alexander, known as 'the Great', created one of the most expansive empires the world has ever known. Alexander claimed to be the descendant of the Greek heroes Heracles and Achilles, and inspired his men by leading his cavalry from the front.

In just 15 years, Alexander took control of Persia, Egypt, North Africa and northern India. With the march of his men came Hellenic ideas. Alexander founded Greek-style cities in his army's wake, including Alexandria in Egypt. On reaching the Indian river Ganges, Alexander's men demanded they return home, which Alexander reluctantly agreed to. The conqueror made it back as far as Babylon, where he died from fever in 323 BCE. Greek ideas would hold sway over his empire for almost 300 years under his generals, the Diadochi, in an era called the Hellenistic period (see panel).

THE DIADOCHI

Following the death of Alexander, his generals fought for 47 years over who should be his successor. The lands that Alexander conquered were divided among these men, called the Diadochi. Three kingdoms of note were established: the Seleucid dynasty in Asia; the Ptolemaic kingdom in Egypt and Palestine; and the Antigonid kingdom of Macedonia and Greece. Hellenic ideas continued to be disseminated among the conquered people, through Greek political systems, city planning and architecture. The philosophies, literature, music and scientific ideas of this Hellenistic period spread from Central Asia to North Africa and northern India where they fused with local culture.

THE ROMAN EMPIRE

The Roman Empire was the longest lasting empire to rule the Western world. The laws and political institutions of this military superpower provided the template for modern republics.

According to legend, Rome was founded in 753 BCE by the twins Romulus and Remus. Abandoned as infants, they were said to have been suckled by a she-wolf then raised by a shepherd on the Palatine Hill. The truth is far less fanciful. What would become one of the greatest and most enduring empires in history had its origin in a string of villages on the hills above the Tiber river in the 8th century BCE. By 600 BCE, this collection of villages had transformed into a city-state ruled by a king and a council of clan elders, or Senate.

The siting of Rome, on a major trading crossroads between Europe and North Africa, brought wealth and ideas into the city. Under the influence of the neighbouring Etruscans, Rome implemented improvements in sanitation and officials began wearing the toga. Greek developments in art, architecture and philosophy were taken on board, too, as was the alphabet, which was adapted to become the written form of the Roman language Latin (the root of Spanish, Italian, French, Portuguese and Romanian). While absorbing ideas from abroad, the Romans were pioneers in their own right, particularly in building, with concrete production supporting the construction of many large-scale projects by skilled engineers.

KINGDOM TO REPUBLIC

The rule of Rome's kings came to an end in 509 BCE, when the city's final monarch, Tarquinius Superbus (Tarquin the Proud), was overthrown by an alliance of Roman aristocrats. In his place they established a republic led by a law-making Senate and two consuls elected by the citizens. Roman society was divided into patricians (wealthy citizens), plebeians (other citizens) and enslaved persons who, along with women, had no vote. Even at home, women had little say. Every Roman household was under the control of a

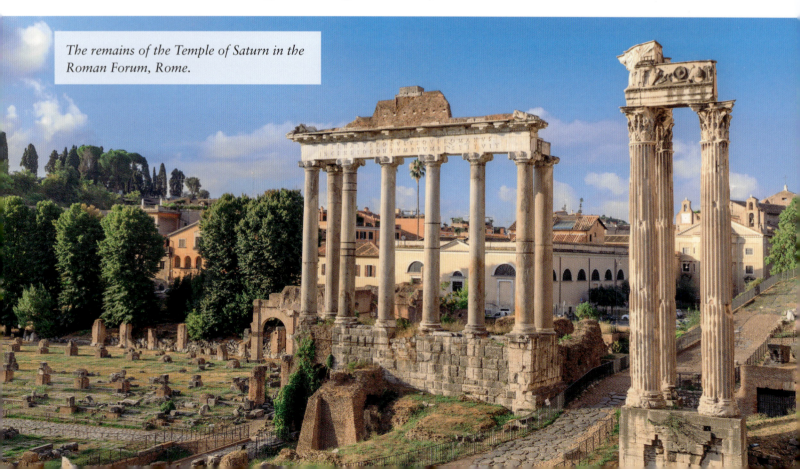

The remains of the Temple of Saturn in the Roman Forum, Rome.

paterfamilias, the oldest male member, who among other things had the power of life and death over his family members and slaves. While attempts were in time made to put curbs on individual rule and involve the working classes in decision making, the highest positions in state and society were generally taken by Rome's wealthiest male citizens.

Rome's ambitions to increase its territory were not without setbacks. An attack by Celtic Gauls in 390 BCE saw a 15,000-strong Roman army wiped out and the capital burnt to the ground. The Gauls were persuaded to leave the city in exchange for gold and Rome was rebuilt with stronger defences that would protect it for another eight centuries.

When Rome did begin to extend its borders its successes came primarily via the efforts of its disciplined land army. By 264 BCE most of Italy was ruled from Rome. Success in the Punic Wars against the maritime trading power of Carthage in North Africa saw Roman rule extend over the whole of the western Mediterranean, including Spain and the islands of Sicily, Corsica and Sardinia. Defeat for the Phoenician city of Carthage, in modern-day Tunisia, resulted in the city's total destruction in 146 BCE. The city was razed and the population enslaved.

The taking of North Africa was vital for the expansion and success of the Roman Empire. While Carthage was destroyed, its wheat fields were claimed and exploited as the breadbasket of Rome, producing on average one million tonnes of cereals every year, as well as olives and olive oil. Roman agriculture benefitted from an unusually warm period in European history, the so-called Roman Climatic Optimum, which saw regular rains over North Africa and 650 years of temperatures close to modern-day figures.

For many defeated powers Roman authority meant the paying of taxes and the supply of soldiers in tribute, but it often came with something close to Roman citizenship. Roman culture was adopted by the new colonies. Cities were built and rebuilt following a Roman plan, including public squares (forums), bathhouses, temples and amphitheatres.

THE RISE OF CAESAR

Roman armies would return from their campaigns with huge amounts of booty, including slaves. Great battles were commemorated in Rome on triumphal arches and columns. While the ruling Senate gained wealth from these military operations, soldiers, often recruited from farms, lost out. A people's movement gained traction, demanding fairer wealth distribution and a say in governance. In the turmoil that followed, the politician-generals Pompey, Caesar and Crassus rose to positions of power and formed an uneasy alliance,

Bronze statue of Julius Caesar in Rimini, Italy.

the so-called First Triumvirate. On the death of Crassus in 53 BCE, the Senate supported the more traditionalist Pompey over the more populist Caesar, leading to civil war.

Following campaigns in what is now Britain, France and Germany, Caesar returned to Italy and refused orders to disband his army. In 49 BCE, as Pompey and his enemies in the Senate fled, Caesar seized Rome itself and took dictatorial power. He instituted land reforms, pensions for war veterans, and introduced a new calendar (see panel on page 90). This assumption of total control of the state by a single man was unacceptable to republicans, and in 44 BCE Julius Caesar was assassinated by a group of senators led by Gaius Cassius Longinus and Marcus Junius Brutus (a descendant of Lucius Junius Brutus, the man who led the conspiracy against Rome's last king, Tarquinius Superbus, 450 years earlier). Fourteen years of civil war followed until order was finally restored under Octavian, Caesar's adopted son.

THE FIRST EMPEROR

Octavian took the name Augustus and effectively became Rome's first emperor. For the next 200 years there was relative peace in the empire, the *Pax Romana*. Great works of Latin literature were written during Augustus' reign, with the emperor himself becoming a patron of some of the era's greatest writers. This was the golden age of the poets Horace and Ovid, and the historian Livy. The origin of Rome was mythologized in Virgil's epic poem the *Aeneid*, written between 29 and 19 BCE, which followed the fortunes of Aeneas, a character from Homer's *Iliad* (page 84) and his involvement in the foundation of the city. It swiftly became part of the Latin school curriculum.

By the 1st century CE Rome was the most populous city in the world, with half a million inhabitants. The Roman Empire included a population of 50 million people and could call upon an army of 300,000 soldiers. A network of roads stretched from Rome in many directions across a network 80,000 km (50,000 mi) long, with impressive bridges, viaducts, aqueducts and harbours. Many Roman roads (or the routes they once followed) are still in use today.

ROME OF THE EAST

When new provinces were brought under Roman rule their local gods were absorbed into the Roman pantheon, helping to tie the conquered peoples to their conquerors. However, two monotheistic faiths – Judaism and Christianity (page 102) – rejected the idea of a multitude of gods and were considered a threat to the status quo. Christians were falsely blamed by the emperor Nero for the Great Fire of Rome in 64 CE, and were rounded up and put to death. A revolt against Roman rule in Jerusalem in 66 CE led to the destruction of the city and the dispersal and killing of most of the population, possibly as many as one million people.

Then, in 306 CE, the emperor Constantine converted to Christianity, supposedly after a vision on the eve of a major battle. He made Christianity the religion of the empire and built a new capital on the border of Europe and Asia where the Black Sea meets the Mediterranean. He named the city Nova Roma (New Rome) but it became known as Constantinople (now Istanbul in Turkey).

As the imperial focus shifted towards the east, Rome saw its fortunes decline. The Antonine Plague of 165–180 CE, which may have been smallpox, had destabilized the empire before the rise of Christianity, wiping out an estimated five million people and reducing the number of recruits for the army. Later, migrations of warrior peoples, including Goths and Vandals, crossed the borders of the empire to escape the Huns, nomads from the steppes of Asia (page 104). Some of these peoples allied with Rome and helped defend the empire but, in 410 CE, Rome was sacked by the Visigoths led by Alaric, then by the Vandals, in 455 CE. When the military leader Odoacer took Rome in 476 CE and deposed the last emperor, Romulus Augustulus, the city's time of imperial rule was ended

The Roman Empire
in 117 AD, at its greatest extent

The Roman Empire at its greatest extent in 117 CE under the reign of Trajan, whose campaigns claimed modern-day Romania, Moldova, Armenia and parts of Syria and Iraq (Mesopotamia).

once and for all. The eastern Roman Empire, known later as the Byzantine Empire, survived for many centuries from its base in Constantinople until the city was finally taken by Mehmed II and his Ottoman army in 1453 (page 138).

BURIED IN ASH

Much detail about the Roman way of life has been revealed through the excavation of Pompeii. The city, along with other settlements such as Herculaneum, was buried under ash and rock following the eruption of the nearby volcano Vesuvius in August 79 CE. Among the remains revealed by archaeologists are fine mosaics and wall paintings in villas belonging to the wealthy, 31 bakeries, public baths, a meat market, amphitheatre, remains of meals and lewd graffiti.

BREAD AND CIRCUSES

Keeping the urban population fed and entertained was essential for the Roman leadership, to pacify the public and to gain their votes. Little expense and few lives were spared. In Rome, grain was subsidized and loaves were handed out to the people. Much entertainment was also provided for free, sponsored by the ruling class and, later, by the emperors. City dwellers had a choice of theatrical shows, chariot races and bloodthirsty sports to enjoy.

Roman plays were often supplemented with music and dancing. Actors would sometimes wear grotesque masks and padded costumes to play comical characters. Amphitheatres in the Roman cities were host to brutal and often deadly battles between gladiators and wild animals. Chariot races took place in the cities' hippodromes. Emperors also arranged wild animal spectacles which might involve imported herds of elephants, lions, leopards, bears, rhinoceroses and hippopotamuses.

UNIFIED CHINA

The Qin and Han Dynasties unified China for the first time and introduced a powerful bureaucracy to control the country's vast population. Major infrastructure projects were initiated, along with world-changing inventions.

China gets its Western name from the dynasty that unified the country. The Qin (pronounced 'Chin') brought stability to the area after 250 years of inter-regional war. From 316 BCE, the Qin people, from the western end of the Yellow River Valley, had competed with rival warlords for supremacy until, in 221 BCE, the Qin king, Qin Shi Huang, was able to declare himself the first emperor of the unified lands.

The emperor set to work bringing the country together. The Qin standardized the scripts used in the regions to produce a national written language, and established official weights and measures, currency and new laws.

With the western borders troubled by the Xiongnu, raiders from the steppes (page 104), the emperor ordered the building of a Great Wall in the north to monitor and deter outside attacks. Exceeding the Romans' road-building efforts across their empire, the Qin built a network of long, straight roads from the capital Xianyang. One road stretched 800 km (500 mi) to the Ordos region. These enormous infrastructure projects, including a vast canal system, were facilitated through central government taking control of the peasant classes away from aristocrats and landowners. The Qin put 300,000 peasants and convicts to work.

Later dynasties recorded that Qin Shi Huang also set about controlling history, burning books and killing scholars to ensure only his version of events survived. Whether or not this took place, the plan did not succeed.

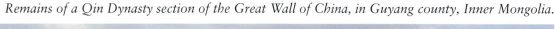

Remains of a Qin Dynasty section of the Great Wall of China, in Guyang county, Inner Mongolia.

On his death in 210 BCE, the first Qin emperor was buried within a huge pyramidal mound in Xi'an, with an army of terracotta statues nearby, along with the emperor's wives, concubines and the tomb's designers, said to have been sacrificed on the orders of his successor.

The first emperor died in 210 BCE. Obsessed with immortality, he had ordered work to begin on his own massive mausoleum two years earlier. Set in a large pyramidal mound, it incorporated a model of his empire, primed crossbow traps set to fire on potential tomb robbers and, nearby, an army of 13,000 terracotta warriors and horses to protect the emperor in the afterlife. The dynasty did not survive long after Qin Shi Huang's death, however. His son was forced to commit suicide by his chief minister and there was a period of unrest until a new dynasty arose, called the Han.

THE HAN

Liu Bang, who established the Han Dynasty in 202 BCE after four years of instability, benefitted from the bureaucracy and legal structures put in place by the tyrannical first Qin emperor, but he proved a more liberal and pragmatic ruler. Ideals put forth by the philosopher Confucius (see panel on page 94), that had been repudiated under Qin rule, became official state ideology, with Confucian academies founded to train students for imperial administration work.

The Han instituted military conscription for all adult males. From the age of 23 (or 20, for a brief period), conscripts spent a year in training, followed by a year on the frontier. From the 1st century BCE, a professional army was employed, paid for in land, as it was in the Roman Empire. Battles to secure borders and subdue rebels were waged with large forces on horseback, armed with crossbows.

The seventh and longest-serving Han emperor, Wu (141–87 BCE), failed in his attempts to quell attacks from invading nomads from the steppes. He sent an ambassador, Zhang Qian, to form alliances against the Xiongnu, but Zhang was captured by the enemy. Zhang's escape and exploration of the territory west of China laid the foundations of the major trading route later known as the Silk Roads (page 108). While nomads remained a threat, Wu was able to extend Chinese territory in the south to include Korea and north Vietnam. Military campaigns were part funded through the nationalization of the country's salt and iron industries.

Wu, as emperor, made himself the master of all military and civil affairs, with limitless decision-making powers. He claimed that his authority was divinely ordained, calling it the Mandate of Heaven. Placing such unchallenged control in the hands of an individual left the empire vulnerable to rule by unstable or unsatisfactory characters, as was manifested by the many examples of unbalanced Roman emperors.

EAST AND WEST

By the turn of the millennium, almost half of the population of the world was ruled by the Han and Roman empires. Both were led by emperors who claimed divine right, with a centralized government, regulated currency and powerful military forces spread across vast territories. Both were intimidated by nomadic tribes at their borders.

By 2 CE, according to the country's first census the Chinese empire comprised more than 57 million people. But there was not complete harmony among its citizens. The Han Dynasty was overthrown in 9 CE by Wang Mang, who established the short-lived Xin Dynasty. Wang Mang's efforts to redistribute land and change the currency led to rising costs and workers' rebellions. This was at a time when major floods had caused the Yellow river to change course, forcing a destabilizing mass migration of peasant farmers. By 25 CE, Han rule had been re-established and the emperor Guang Wu established a new capital city at Luoyang.

The later Han Dynasty witnessed the arrival of merchants from the Roman Empire, the dissemination of Buddhist literature translated into Chinese, the invention of paper (see panel on page 95) and advances in agriculture, including the invention of the seed drill and the production of iron tools. Creatively,

Statue of the philosopher Confucius at Shanghai Confucian Temple, China.

CONFUCIANISM

Confucius (Kǒng Fūzǐ) was a philosopher and teacher who lived between 551 and 479 BCE. His moral teaching recommended a respectful way of living, behaving in a way in which you would want others to behave towards you. He believed in worshipping ancestors and the importance of family, obeying one's parents and those of higher status. Many Confucian schools were established under the Han Dynasty, particularly for the education of civil servants.

PAPER PRODUCTION

The invention of paper is credited to Can Lun (c.50–121 CE), the Han Dynasty court eunuch and director of the Imperial Workshops at Luoyang. Prior to this, wooden and bamboo strips had been used as writing material. Can Lun is said to have soaked and pressed a mix of plant fibres and then dried them on wooden frames. The resulting 'paper' was easy to produce and was quickly adopted across China, with quick-growing bamboo used as the main source material from the 8th century. The secret of paper-making is said to have been extracted from Chinese prisoners of war by the Arab Muslim empire around this time and a paper mill established in Baghdad, before the knowledge spread to Medieval Europe.

the period produced the finest of lacquer work and new genres of poetry. Silk became one of the country's most prized products. While the secret of its production remained within China, its worth as a means of payment or a peace offering was enormous. Such was its value and cachet that peasants were forbidden from wearing it.

Allowing for the brief interruption of Xin rule, the Han proved to be the longest surviving Chinese imperial dynasty, lasting for more than 400 years. It finally collapsed in 220 CE, after further incursions by nomadic raiders, rebellions within the empire and court eunuchs asserting their power over the emperors. Its name has continued, however, with the ethnic majority of modern-day China identifying as 'Han people'.

Emperor Guang Wu, who restored the rule of the Han Dynasty in 25 CE and established the capital at Luoyang.

CLASSICAL INDIA

Beyond the reach of Alexander the Great, India began its own period of Classical history with empires that promised religious tolerance and delivered a flourishing of the arts and literature.

When Alexander the Great's army ended its empire building at the banks of the Indus river (page 87), the Macedonians had little or no knowledge of the breadth and variety of the landscape that lay on the other side, or of the cultures that stretched out of their reach. The India that they turned away from was already a mighty empire by the time they arrived in the 4th century BCE.

The Mauryan Empire was established by Chandragupta, with the help of allies, around 321 BCE. Chandragupta took over the dominant state of Magadha and led his armies to expand their dominion north and south. At its height the empire would encompass all but the southern tip of the Indian subcontinent.

Where Alexander had turned back, his successors, the Seleucids, marched forth. In 305 BCE they faced the Mauryan armies head on. They were defeated and were forced to cede their territory in Afghanistan.

Much of what we know of the early Mauryan Empire is derived from the reports of the Seleucid ambassador, once peaceful relations between the two powers had been re-established.

After 25 years of expanding his empire's borders, Chandragupta gave up the throne and became a Jain monk. In his stead, his son continued to expand the empire. Chandragupta's grandson, Ashoka (*c.*304–232 BCE), inherited a kingdom with borders in Iran, the Himalayan mountains and India's Deccan Plateau. His attempt to claim the Kalinga region on the northeast coast led to a bloody conflict resulting in an estimated 100,000 deaths and even more deportations. Ashoka is said to have felt repentance for the bloodshed. He ended his campaigning for new territory and turned to Buddhism, a new religion that had emerged in the Himalayas (page 101). He reduced the size of his army and invested instead in public education and health. Ashoka sponsored missions to spread Buddhist teachings beyond his empire's borders, to Greece, Egypt, Libya and Sri Lanka. His own son and daughter were employed as missionaries. Ashoka shared his new principles on a series of inscribed stone

Ruins of the Gupta Empire Buddhist monastery Mahavihara.

pillars positioned throughout the empire. He extolled the virtues of religious tolerance and non-violence.

Ashoka's successors failed to keep the empire intact. After almost 150 years of rule the Mauryan Empire ended with the assassination of the last emperor, Brihadratha, in 185 BCE. The empire split into smaller kingdoms that squabbled for 500 years until a new dynasty was able to reunite most of northern India in the 6th century.

GUPTA EMPIRE

The disintegration of the Mauryan Empire led to several invasions from the north, including the nomadic Kushans from Central Asia. Their cultural influence included Hellenistic sculptural styles, particularly in their depiction of Buddha (page 101). After 500 years of fragmentation and power divided among the regions, a new dynasty arose that brought stability and a golden age to India.

The Gupta Empire begins in 320 CE with Chandragupta I (sharing his name with the founder of the Mauryan Empire), heir to the throne of Magadha on the Ganges Plain. Through marriage and a strong cavalry-led army, Chandragupta expanded his lands in the north and adopted the title Maharajadhiraja, 'Great King of Kings'. His son, Samudragupta (c.335–375 CE) led his army to claim even greater territory. Not quite on the scale of the Mauryan Empire, Gupta dominion would stretch from its centre in Patna, northeast India, to the Himalayas and Afghanistan north and west, and to the Godavari river in the south, and the Arabian Sea, where a lucrative maritime trade developed, exporting silk, cotton, spices, gems and iron, and importing horses, ivory and other goods from Africa, China and the Middle East.

Samudragupta and his successors invested in education and the arts. Sanskrit became the most widely used written language. Poetry, epic dramas and literature flourished, in particular with the work of the poet and playwright Kālidāsa. The *Kama Sutra* was written during this period. A guide to living well, it revealed something of the preoccupations of the court elite. Gupta law appears to have been lenient; capital

punishment and torture are not reported during the reign; offences were punished with fines.

Despite having seen off border attacks from the Huns (see page 104), the Gupta dynasty crumbled from within due to clan rivalries and poor administration. The empire collapsed around 550.

GOLDEN AGE

The Gupta period is considered a golden age for North Indian art. Surviving works are mostly religious sculpture. The sandstone figures of Buddha are of particular note. At this point, Buddha (see page 101) was revered as a god rather than a spiritual teacher. His depictions were influenced by Hellenistic art, with fine, unfolded cloth draped over his body. Exquisite painting from the period is preserved in the Ajanta Caves, a series of Buddhist monuments in western India that date from the 2nd century BCE to the final years of the Gupta Empire.

Gupta period cave ceiling painting in Ajanta, India, depicting the Buddha.

NEW FAITHS

The Classical period of Eurasian history saw the spread of major religions that still count hundreds of millions among their devotees today – Hinduism, Buddhism, Judaism and Christianity.

The Roman, Han, Mauryan and Gupta empires witnessed the birth and spread of major religions that would survive the centuries and retain many millions of followers in the modern era. These faiths were shared and spread by traders and missionaries, and also by conquerors, some of whom were converted to a new belief during their reign.

Considered the oldest surviving religion in the world, Hinduism can be traced back over 4,000 years to sometime between 2300 and 1500 BCE. It originated in the Indus Valley and was an amalgamation of various regional beliefs that coalesced into a whole. Unusually, it does not have a named founder.

Sculpture of Brahma, Vishnu and female servants, Shree Ganga Godavari temple, Nashik, India.

The roots of Hinduism possibly developed from the beliefs of the first Indus Valley civilization (page 70) or may have arrived with a group of tribes called the Aryans, from Central Asia around 1500 BCE. It is believed that the earliest Hindu scriptures, the Vedas (see panel) were written around this time, which is known as the Vedic Period. Considered to have always existed prior to being transcribed into Sanskrit, the Vedas contained details of rituals to be performed, including sacrifices (animals, milk, butter) to the devas, the gods of the sky, fire and weather. Very few

of these early gods became major figures in Hinduism as it developed over the centuries.

During the 4th and 5th centuries under the Gupta kings (page 99), the worship of deities in temples would become common practice, particularly towards the gods Vishnu the protector, Shiva the destroyer and Devi the restorer of *dharma* (law, truth). New inspirational texts would be written, including two epic dramas of gods and princes, the *Mahabharata* (the world's longest epic poem) and the *Ramayana*.

With its roots in many early beliefs, Hinduism is more a way of life than an organized doctrine, involving the desire to know one's self, to pursue good and, through this path, to find god. While there is one creator god, Brahma, recognized above all others, lesser gods and goddesses are accepted and paid tribute to.

The cycle of birth, life, death and reincarnation (*samsara*) is part of Hindu belief. The law of karma determines the quality of the next life depending on how considerate one has been in their current existence. This belief of reincarnation and karma is shared by Buddhism, which emerged from Hinduism hundreds of years later.

THE VEDAS

The Vedas are the oldest Hindu religious scriptures, with one, the *Rig Veda*, dating from about 1500 BCE. Along with poetic descriptions of conflict and rule by the Aryans, the Vedas include hymns and descriptions of rituals, sacrifices and philosophies. They are still spoken in the ancient Sanskrit language they were composed in, a language which is otherwise no longer in use. Verses from the *Rig Veda* are included in Hindu marriage ceremonies. The Vedas are also the source of the traditional system of Indian medicine, Ayurveda, still practised today.

The gigantic statue of Buddha in Leshan, China, was carved into the mountain from 723 CE under the guidance of a monk named Hai Tong.

BUDDHISM

According to tradition, Buddhism began with Siddhārtha Gautama, a prince born in the shadow of the Himalayan mountains sometime between 550 and 420 BCE. He left his wife, young son and a life of plenty for a seven-year wandering to experience a simpler way of living, to study and to contemplate the sorrows of the world. Through meditation, including 49 days sat beneath a pipal tree, Gautama came to the realization that humanity could escape from the endless cycle of birth and rebirth by shedding the desires and cravings that can lead to disappointment. Living a good and unselfish life would improve one's karma and lead to happier rebirths before finally reaching a peaceful state called nirvana. Gautama was now the Buddha, meaning 'enlightened one'.

The first Buddhist texts include no mention of Gautama. His story was pieced together and elaborated on by followers in later centuries. The teachings of the Buddha spread slowly via devotees from the Ganges valley throughout India. The religion gained a hugely influential advocate in the 3rd century BCE when the Mauryan emperor Ashoka (page 98) renounced his warring ways and accepted Buddhist teachings.

Variations on the initial Buddhist teachings were pursued by different schools. One feature that was not endorsed by the Buddha but became accepted by his followers was the veneration of his image. Where once there were images of the pipal tree, a wheel or footprints to signify the presence of the Buddha, painted and sculpted images of Gautama were adopted from the 1st century CE in Gandhara, modern Pakistan, and Mathura in northern India. The Buddha appeared serene, sat in a lotus position for meditation, sometimes with one hand raised to indicate reassurance. Figures of the Buddha were usually placed around sacred mounds called stupas. So it was that Buddhism gained some of the trappings of other religions – icons, written guidance, even accompanying music. Semi-enlightened figures called Bodhisattvas were anointed to guide others on their journey towards nirvana.

While Buddhism did not become a major religion within India, where Hinduism remained the predominant belief, it thrived in China. During the Han dynasty (202 BCE–220 CE, page 93) the religion spread through merchants crossing into the country. By the 6th century Buddhism had around 30 million adherents in China.

JUDAISM

Judaism, the monotheist religion of the Jews, emerged from the southern Levant about 4,000 years ago. The Jewish people describe themselves as the descendants of Abraham, a patriarchal figure whose faith in God, the creator of the world, earned him the promise of a land for his descendants. Abraham's people, the Hebrews, suffered enslavement in Egypt before an exodus led by the prophet Moses. Moses delivered the Hebrews to Mount Sinai, where they received the Torah, their book of laws. From there, they were guided to the land of Israel, where they built a temple in the capital, Jerusalem.

In 587 BCE, the site was destroyed by Babylonians and the Jews were deported and held in captivity in the Babylonian Empire before being allowed to return home by the Persian ruler Cyrus the Great 50 years later (page 82). For much of their history, the Jewish people were settled away from their ancestral lands as part of a diaspora across the world. From this great religion came another monotheist faith which shared many of its scriptures.

Dating from 408 BCE, and discovered in caves in the Judean Desert in 1946, the Dead Sea Scrolls are the earliest-known fragments of Hebrew scripture used in the Old Testament and later included in the Christian Bible.

CHRISTIANITY

With Roman and Jewish records reporting Jesus' trial and death, few historians doubt that the figure who would inspire Christianity actually lived. What is generally understood is that a man named Jesus emerged from Galilee in modern Israel towards the dawn of the 1st century CE. He was baptized and became a healer and teacher from about the age of 30. But, his rejection of wealth and power and claims to speak the word of God brought him into conflict with both Jewish religious leaders and Roman authorities. This led to his being put on trial as a revolutionary and his crucifixion around 30–33 CE. Jesus was then reported to have been raised from the dead as the Son of God. The concept of death, resurrection and received divinity was not such an outrageous concept for the time; the Roman rulers Julius Caesar and Augustus were awarded divine status on their deaths.

Missionaries, including Paul from Tarsus, in Anatolia, began to spread the news of Jesus through the Near East and into Greece. They gave Jesus the name Christ, after the Greek word *christos*, 'anointed one'. Initially, the ideas of Christ were spread by Jewish Christians. Jewish texts had foretold that a messiah would appear and bring about a revived Kingdom of God, freeing the Jewish people from foreign captivity. Strict Judaism did not accept that Jesus Christ was a messiah, however.

Paul's interpretation of Christianity welcomed all to the fold, without the need to subscribe to Jewish laws. Faith in Christ was enough to lead one to forgiveness of their sins and a path to heaven, the home of God. Christianity separated from Judaism while adopting the Hebrew scriptures as the Old Testament, alongside a New Testament that told the story of Jesus and his disciples. The New Testament was compiled around the mid-2nd century and consisted of letters written by Paul, a series of gospels ('good news'), plus other histories and prophecies.

Following a period of persecution of Christians, and the destruction of their churches under the Roman emperor Diocletian from 303 to 305 CE, the fortunes

This mosaic roundel from a Roman villa in Dorset, England, is a 4th-century CE representation of Christ.

of the faithful changed dramatically. After success in a battle against his rival Maxentius, Constantine, ruler of the Western Roman Empire, claimed that beforehand he had received a vision of a cross that suggested the Christian God had helped him triumph. Constantine converted to Christianity and declared it the official religion of the empire. The Christian faith took hold across the empire from Asia to Ethiopia, Gaul (France), Iberia (Spain) and Britannia (Britain).

CONTINUED FAITH

Buddhist teachings have found devotees across the globe. It is estimated Buddhism now has around 500 million practitioners worldwide.

Hinduism in India survived Muslim domination, religious suppression, the destruction of many of its temples from the 13th century, and 200 years of British rule from 1757. Today, an estimated 95 per cent of Hinduism's 900 million followers live in India.

There are estimated to be more than 14 million Jews today, of which almost half live in Israel.

Christianity, in its various forms, became the world's most widespread faith, especially in the west. More than two billion people identify as Christians today.

DIVISIONS

As with many religions, there were divisions between Christianity's followers, particularly regarding whether or not Jesus was a man or god, and whether Mary, as a human woman, was able to give birth to a divinity. The Roman emperor Constantine attempted to force a consensus without much success. The Eastern and Western Churches took different paths, leading to the 'Great Schism' of the 11th century and later breaks between Catholicism and Protestantism.

NOMADS OF CENTRAL ASIA

For thousands of years, away from the city-states, nomadic groups rode across the Central Asian steppes and terrorized the empires of the East and West with their raiding parties.

The steppes are vast, windswept grass and shrublands that stretch across 8,000 km (5,000 mi) of Central Asia, from the fringes of Europe to the borders of China. For thousands of years they were home to nomadic peoples such as the Scythians, Parthians, Cimmerians, Huns and Xiongnu. These people are often neglected by history, as they left scant written records and few, if any, buildings. They roamed the land, setting up camps and leading herds of sheep and cattle to fresh pasture.

Scythian golden plaque of a hunting scene dating from the 5th or 4th century BCE.

Wild horses were domesticated around 4000 BCE. They provided transport, meat and milk for the nomadic groups. The people trained to fight and plan raids on horseback. Their invention of the stirrup in the 2nd century BCE allowed them to ride in armour and freed their hands so that they could use a short bow to fire arrows or wield axes. As raiders they were much feared. There were rumours that they drank the blood of their enemies and fashioned coats from their scalps. Yet archaeological finds at grave mounds, called kurgans, reveal a more sophisticated culture than reports of the raids suggest.

The Scythians, as named by the Greeks, were a group of Iranian origin that pillaged northern India and Bactria, and controlled a vast area of Central Eurasia from Siberia to the eastern European border, in the 7th century BCE. While they robbed and demanded money from settled communities in their range, they had no ambition to conquer. As they left behind no cities, we know them by the fine golden decorations they crafted, featuring birds of prey, cattle and griffins, and from the buried remains of their ancestors, interred with stallions, chariots, fine textiles and carpets.

Unlike the Scythians, the Parthians were semi-nomads, living on the edge of the central Asian steppe, farming the land as well as extorting money from peasants. Their prowess at fighting on horseback helped them to defeat the army of the Roman general Crassus in 53 BCE. They established a considerable empire that reached from the Mediterranean to India and lasted from 247 BCE to 224 CE.

THE HUNS

In the mid-4th century the westward movement of the Huns, the period's most notorious nomad army, created a domino effect that brought the Roman Empire to a new low, as people fled the approach of this aggressive group.

Fear of the Huns pushed the Goths towards the Roman Empire, where they demanded sanctuary. After themselves threatening Rome in the past, the Goths had settled as farmers in what we now call Romania. They were allowed into imperial lands by the eastern emperor, Valens, in 376 CE. Further Hun attacks in 405 CE drove more Germanic peoples across the Roman borders. Events worsened for Rome as a

19th-century illustration of Attila the Hun leading his army.

new king named Attila led the Huns to conquer cities across the Balkans, and then to invade Gaul (France) and Italy. Rome tried to keep his forces at bay by offering huge tributes of gold before teaming up with the Goths to give Attila a rare bloody nose at the Battle of Maurica (also known as the Battle of the Catalaunian Plains) in 451 CE. Attila was unable to reap revenge. He died two years later of a haemorrhage during a drunken wedding celebration. Without his command, the Hun Empire disintegrated.

EASTERN NOMADS

China's Qin Dynasty (page 92) faced similar threats from nomads facing east. Based on the fringes of the steppes, the Xiongnu were a loose group of different peoples that regularly attacked Chinese territory in the 3rd century BCE. Led by the warlord Maodun, the Xiongnu looted Qin Dynasty lands with an army of mounted warriors, possibly 300,000 strong, outmanoeuvring Chinese chariots. The building of China's Great Wall only slowed the Xiongnu raids. The early Han Dynasty emperors tried appeasing the Xiongnu, offering various princesses as brides to Xiongnu leaders, along with annual gifts of silk, wine and rice. This failed to stop the attacks.

Finally, the young emperor Wudi weakened the Xiongnu with a decade of army assaults from 129–119 BCE, at great cost to his own forces. By 51 BCE, what was left of the Xiongnu had accepted Chinese rule. Some were assimilated into the Han Empire, given land and conscripted into the army to fight other nomads.

UNSEEN THREATS

Confrontations with nomads resulted in more than theft and arrow wounds. Records suggest that the peoples of Central Asia carried pathogens that infected those they came into contact with during their conquests. In 161–162 CE, one third of the Chinese army sent to combat nomadic tribes was brought down by an unknown infection. A few years later, Roman soldiers were similarly affected while fighting the Parthians in Syria. Repeated outbreaks of plague were recorded over the next decades, then again a century later with even greater casualties, with up to 5,000 people dying each day in Rome.

The Baptism of Clovis from a 14th-century French manuscript.

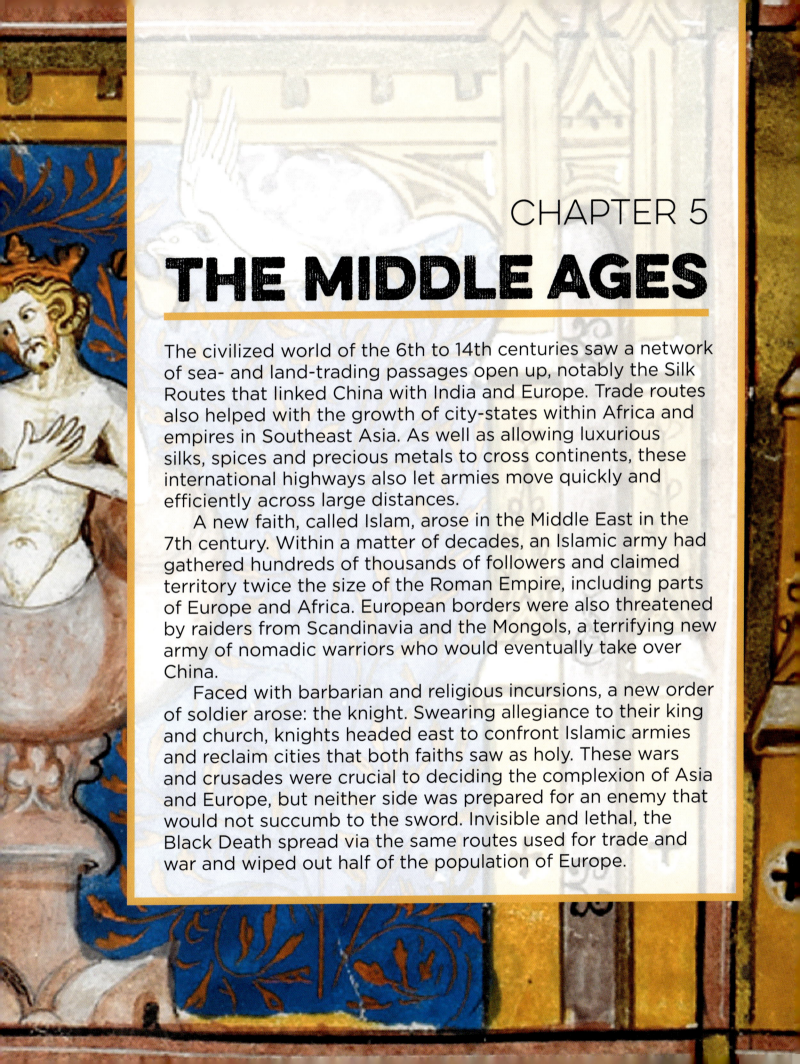

CHAPTER 5

THE MIDDLE AGES

The civilized world of the 6th to 14th centuries saw a network of sea- and land-trading passages open up, notably the Silk Routes that linked China with India and Europe. Trade routes also helped with the growth of city-states within Africa and empires in Southeast Asia. As well as allowing luxurious silks, spices and precious metals to cross continents, these international highways also let armies move quickly and efficiently across large distances.

A new faith, called Islam, arose in the Middle East in the 7th century. Within a matter of decades, an Islamic army had gathered hundreds of thousands of followers and claimed territory twice the size of the Roman Empire, including parts of Europe and Africa. European borders were also threatened by raiders from Scandinavia and the Mongols, a terrifying new army of nomadic warriors who would eventually take over China.

Faced with barbarian and religious incursions, a new order of soldier arose: the knight. Swearing allegiance to their king and church, knights headed east to confront Islamic armies and reclaim cities that both faiths saw as holy. These wars and crusades were crucial to deciding the complexion of Asia and Europe, but neither side was prepared for an enemy that would not succumb to the sword. Invisible and lethal, the Black Death spread via the same routes used for trade and war and wiped out half of the population of Europe.

THE SILK ROUTES

The Silk Routes, or Silk Roads, were a series of trade highways that connected China with the Mediterranean. For thousands of years exotic goods and ideas were shared via this caravan route.

The Silk Routes (or the Silk Roads) were used by traders to cross between China, India, Greece and Europe between the 2nd century BCE and the mid-15th century. They acquired their name in the 19th century for the much-prized silk that was exported from China and were first used during the Chinese Han Dynasty (page 93).

The Silk Routes were not the first major land roads between countries. The Persian king Darius I (page 83) had overseen a 2,600 km (1,600 mi) Royal Road between his capital Susa (modern Iran) and Sardis (modern Turkey) in the 5th century BCE. China was aware of Western powers before the Silk Routes, too. The generals who ruled the remains of Alexander the Great's empire may have made contact with China as early as 200 BCE. (The ancient Greeks and Romans called the land to the east Serica, meaning 'the place that silk came from'.) The possibility of profitable trade with the West was made clear from reports brought to the Chinese Han emperor by his envoy Zhang Qian (see panel) around 125 BCE.

The 6,400 km (4,000 mi) Silk Route that opened soon after started at the Han Dynasty capital of Chang'an (Xi-an) and followed the way of the Great Wall before passing around the Taklamakan Desert, and arriving at the oasis town of Kashgar. From here, traders pushed on over the Pamir Mountains (in modern Tajikistan) through Bukhara to reach the Near East and sea crossings to Alexandria in Egypt or Constantinople (modern-day Istanbul, Turkey) with links to Venice, Italy. Branches of the Silk Routes also led to India and Tibet.

LUXURY GOODS

Merchants followed the routes in caravans made up of camels, horses or bullocks. Few merchants traversed the entire route. Instead, trades were arranged at stop-off points, some of which grew into substantial cities. Smaller inns, or caravanserai, were built en route too. These gave travellers an opportunity to rest and to feed pack animals.

Of the goods that changed hands, the fine silk produced in China was the most prestigious. It also had the benefit of being lightweight, and therefore easy to carry. While the method of silk production was kept secret in China until the 6th century CE, it remained in high demand in Rome, Greece and Egypt as a luxury good. The wearing of silk in the Roman Empire demonstrated wealth but, for some, its semi-transparency was an outrage against public decency. Silk was also used in religious ceremonies; Christian priests added purple-dyed silk to their vestments, while Buddhists donated the material to monasteries, where silk banners were raised.

Along with Chinese silk came tea, dyes, perfumes and porcelain. Paper and gunpowder would follow later on. These were exchanged for horses, gold, silver, woollen textiles, honey and glassware. The Silk Routes also conveyed ideas, with Buddhism and Christianity (pages 101–2) expanding their reach via merchants and missionaries.

MONGOL CONTROL

The rise of Arabic armies in the Levant in the 7th century (page 110) made crossing the Silk Routes perilous and deterred much traffic, but the way was revived under the Mongol Empire of Kublai Khan from the mid-1200s (page 118). While Kublai Khan's grandfather Genghis Khan had terrorized the empires bordering Central Asia, the Mongol control established by his descendant over an area that reached from China to the Black Sea provided a guarantee of safe passage for merchants. The route was famously travelled and described by Marco Polo in the 13th century.

Along with trade, unseen viruses such as smallpox, measles and whooping cough spread along the route.

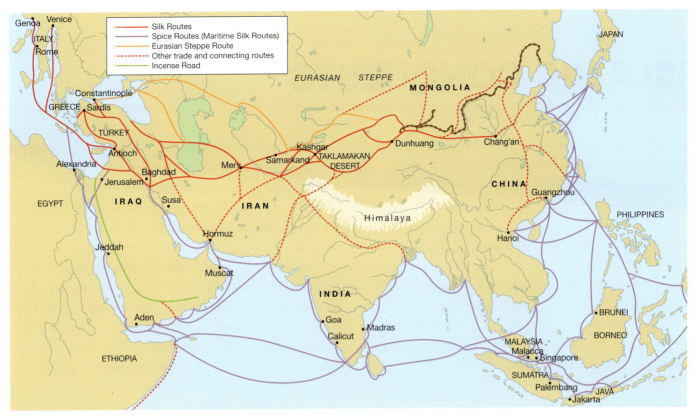

Map showing the different routes taken on the Silk Roads.

Bubonic plague crossed the sea to Genoa in Italy, where its consequences were given the foreboding name 'the Black Death' (page 124).

Trade in both goods and unwanted diseases was halted in the 15th century. The route was unceremoni-ously blocked under the Ottoman Empire (page 138) whose sultans cut ties with the West in 1453. This forced European countries to seek other ways to reach the Chinese market, leading to the great voyages of discovery (page 144).

ZHANG'S MISSION

Around 138 BCE, the Han emperor Wudi instructed his envoy Zhang Qian (c.195–114 BCE) to make contact with the nomadic Yuezhi tribe, seeking an alliance with them against the Xiongnu who had been troubling Chinese borders. Instead, Zhang was captured and imprisoned by the Xiongnu for ten years. Zhang married and fathered a child during his decade of imprisonment, before escaping and resuming his mission. While Zhang failed to forge an alliance with the nomads, the reports he submitted after this 13-year sojourn, of the demand for Chinese goods in the West, led to further missions abroad to foster trade relations. Neighbouring states began to send envoys to the Han court and trading routes were opened, leading to the creation of what we now know as the Silk Routes.

Zhang Qian and his entourage leave emperor Wudi, from an 8th-century Tang Dynasty mural.

ISLAMIC CONQUESTS

Inspired by the prophecies of Muhammad, Arab armies established a vast Islamic empire from the 7th century, exploiting weaknesses in the Byzantine and Persian empires.

According to historians, Muhammad bin Abdullah, the figure who would inspire Islam, one of the world's leading faiths, came from the oasis town of Mecca in Arabia (now Saudi Arabia), where he worked as a merchant. Around 610 CE, Muhammad is said to have received a vision of the angel Gabriel while meditating in a cave. The angel told Muhammad to recite verses and that he was to be a prophet of Allah (God), the last prophet, in fact, in a lineage that included Abraham and Jesus.

Muhammad began sharing the messages he had received but faced opposition from the religious establishment in Mecca. With his safety and that of his followers threatened, Muhammad took flight to the city of Yathrib (now Medina) in 622. Here, Muhammad founded a religion, known as Islam, that's name means 'submission to God's will'. This date would become the first year in the new Islamic calendar. The prophet was able to raise enough acolytes, called Muslims, to form a 10,000-strong army that could take Mecca.

The Islamic shrine the Dome of the Rock was built on one of the most sacred spots in Jerusalem under the caliph Abd-al-Malik, from 691–692 CE.

Prior to Islam, the Arabian Peninsula was populated by disparate nomadic groups who spoke different tongues and followed various polytheistic religions. Muhammad's teachings, in Arabic, managed to unify the people under Islam and the one language within a decade.

The first converts turned towards Jerusalem to pray, but the focus was soon changed to Mecca, which had been a place of pilgrimage for decades. Here, kept within a large block called the Ka'ba, was a black meteoric stone said to have been delivered by an angel. Muslims were urged to make a pilgrimage to the site. This pilgrimage, the hajj, remains an important part of Islam today, with millions visiting the site each year.

SCHISM

Muhammad died in 632 without naming his successor. There was much dispute over who should continue his mission to spread the word of Islam. Three of the first four caliphs (spiritual and political leaders) who took power after Muhammad were assassinated. Divisions led to two distinct groups forming: the Sunni, who backed Muhammad's advisor and father-in-law Abu Bakr as the first caliph, and the Shia, who backed Ali, the husband of Muhammad's daughter, Fatima. This split endures today.

Despite disagreement over interpretations of the prophet's teachings, 20 years after Muhammad's death his teachings, said to be the direct word of Allah, were transcribed into the holy book, the Qur'an, a word meaning 'recitation', whose verses are meant to be read aloud.

DIVISION AND DOMINATION

Both the Byzantine Empire and the Sasanian Empire of Persia were depleted by repeated wars and the spread of plague. They proved unable to withstand the Islamic armies that swept north and west through the 7th century. The Islamic armies believed in jihad, that their campaign had a holy purpose. They ben-

The Islamic Empire in 750 encompassed much of Spain, North Africa, Arabia, the former Persian Empire and Central Asia, an area twice the size of the Roman Empire at its height.

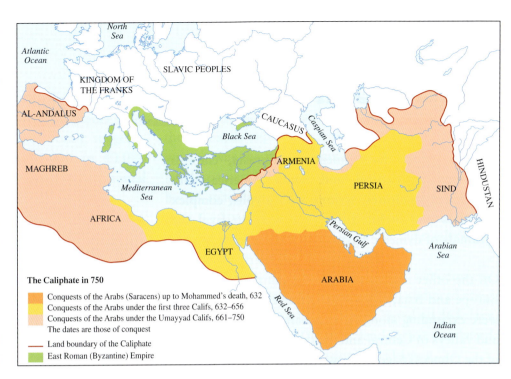

North Sea

Atlantic Ocean

SLAVIC PEOPLES

KINGDOM OF THE FRANKS

AL-ANDALUS

CAUCASUS

Black Sea

Caspian Sea

ARMENIA

HINDUSTAN

MAGHREB

Mediterranean Sea

PERSIA

SIND

AFRICA

Persian Gulf

Arabian Sea

EGYPT

ARABIA

Red Sea

Indian Ocean

The Caliphate in 750

- Conquests of the Arabs (Saracens) up to Mohammed's death, 632
- Conquests of the Arabs under the first three Califs, 632–656
- Conquests of the Arabs under the Umayyad Califs, 661–750
  The dates are those of conquest
- Land boundary of the Caliphate
- East Roman (Byzantine) Empire

efitted from the use of two key animals – the camel, a beast of burden able to carry goods and weapons across deserts, and the horse, for whirlwind raids.

By 651, Arab armies had forced the Byzantines out of Syria, conquered the Sasanian Empire and claimed the holy city of Jerusalem. On taking control, the new Muslim rulers did not insist on conversion to Islam; they allowed local Christians to continue in their faith. Indeed, some Jews and Christians welcomed the arrival of the devout forces of Islam as fellow worshippers that shared their early prophets and a belief in one God. While Jews and Christians avoided conversion and military conscription (though not taxes), pagans faced enslavement or even death if they did not accept the new religion.

The march of Islam continued, with both Egypt and Afghanistan conquered, but when the armies reached France in 732 they met with fierce resistance. The Islamic Empire was pushed back to Spain, and proved unable to capture the Byzantine capital of Constantinople, despite many attempts. This pushback preserved most of Western Europe as predominantly Christian lands. In the East, Islamic armies reached the borders of China by the mid-8th century, where they halted their advance.

The Islamic Empire thrived for centuries. After four caliphs, the Umayyad Dynasty took power from 661 to 750, followed by the Abbasid from 750 to 1258. Profits from trade along the Silk Routes (page 108) helped finance the building of magnificent cities such as Córdoba in Spain and a new capital in Baghdad, Iraq, a cradle for a flowering of art, poetry and science (see panel).

A GOLDEN AGE

The 9th and 10th centuries under the Abbasid Dynasty are considered a golden age for the Islamic Empire, when interest in astronomy, mathematics, poetry and literature blossomed, and some of the most impressive architectural masterpieces were erected, particularly mosques.

In mathematics, Arabic numerals, based on an Indian system, replaced the Roman use of letters and introduced the concept of zero. The Greek astrolabe was improved upon, primarily to locate Mecca. This astronomical device proved a useful tool for measuring latitude. Classic literary, philosophical and scientific writings were translated into Arabic from Greek and Persian. Obtaining paper production methods from the Chinese (page 95) supported this endeavour. These texts, ignored in Europe following the fall of the Western Roman Empire, were later translated into Latin and prompted European artistic and scientific revolutions in the 16th century (page 156).

An Arabic astrolabe from 1291.

Dating from about 725, this Mayan limestone lintel from Yaxchilan, Mexico, depicts a blood-letting ritual involving the threading of the tongue.

In terms of personal beauty, the Maya had an unusual taste for elongated heads. They would compress the heads of newly born babies between boards to give them oval-shaped skulls, and hung wooden balls between their eyes so that they developed squints.

The Mayan population shrank by a half around 900 CE. There is no agreed explanation for the decline of the civilization; it was likely due to several causes, including drought and agricultural practices that degraded the soil, making it impossible to use the land to feed increasing numbers of people. War broke out and the power structure crumbled. People abandoned the cities which were then taken over by another tribe, the Toltecs. The Mayan culture and language survived beyond European conquest, with 6 million people continuing their traditions and speaking Mayan today.

THE AZTECS

Around 1325, a tribal group known as the Mexicas (the source of the name Mexico), later known as the Aztecs, settled on an island in the middle of a shallow lake called Texococo, 2,100 m (7,000 ft) above sea level. They built up areas, called *chinampas*, for agriculture within the lake, bailing water on to their crops from canoes. In the valleys surrounding the lake, the Aztecs dug terraces for the planting of maize, squash, beans, tomatoes and chilli peppers. They also harvested cacti to ferment beer.

The success of their culture led to the population of the island city of Tenochtitlan and its surrounding settlements to rise to 2–3 million people. Tenochtitlan (now buried beneath modern Mexico City) covered an area of 8–9 square km (3–3.5 square mi).

Expansion came as a result of a formidable army recruited from all adult males. These warriors, including elites named after the eagle and the jaguar, wore padded cotton armour and wielded extremely sharp obsidian sword-clubs, called *macuahuitl*. The warriors gained battle experience through organized 'flower wars'. These were planned conflicts between the Aztecs and neighbouring rivals, involving equal numbers of participants waging war on a mutually agreed date.

This Aztec vessel, carved into the shape of a jaguar, was used to hold human hearts removed during ritual sacrifices.

Both flower wars and larger-scale offensives also supplied the Aztecs with prisoners of war who could be dragged back to the capital. Prisoners were offered as ritual sacrifices to appease the gods in an effort to postpone the end of the world. Living participants were held down and their still-beating hearts cut out to be offered to the Aztec deities. Of the pre-Columbian cultures that ruled Mesoamerica, the Aztecs spilled the most blood in rituals. The Aztecs believed in the necessity of sacrifice for life to continue, and that the sun would fail to rise without regular 'feeding' of the gods. They did not see death as an ending but as a bridge to another existence, including rebirth as a hummingbird for those most worthy.

Inca interlocking carved stone walls at the ruins of the Sacsayhuaman fort in Cuzco, Peru.

THE INCA

Along the west coast of South America, from the early 13th century, people settled in the shadows of the Andes mountains, growing potatoes and quinoa. They domesticated llamas and alpacas for meat, wool and carrying loads. The Inca were the dominant tribe, controlling an estimated population of 7–12 million people and an empire that grew to become the largest in American history, covering modern-day Peru and parts of Chile, Ecuador, Bolivia and Argentina.

The Inca built their sacred capital, Cuzco, in a mountain valley, erecting a complex of temples including one lined with gold and another with silver. Inca architecture did not use mortar to fix together bricks; instead, stonemasons cut interlocking blocks that fitted neatly together and could withstand earth-quakes. They also laid the stones for around 25,000 km (15,000 miles) of roads, easing the movement of llama trains and armies.

The Inca lacked writing but kept records on painted sticks, woven into textiles, or with an unusual system of knotted strings called the *quipu*. According to their belief that the human spirit survived the death of the body, Inca rulers were mummified, their bodies housed and brought out for meetings and feasts.

Though suppressed by the Spanish conquest, the Inca did manage to retain some of their culture. The native Quechua languages are still spoken by millions of indigenous people in the Andes.

MACHU PICCHU

The 15th-century Inca complex of Machu Picchu was lost from history for hundreds of years following the Spanish conquest in the 16th century. Sited on a hard-to-reach mountain ridge, the citadel had returned to the jungle and been largely forgotten. The site was rediscovered in the 19th century and excavated by the American explorer Hiram Bingham from 1912. Machu Picchu is believed to have been originally used as a retreat for the Inca emperor Pachacuti (1438–1472) and was probably called Huayna Picchu.

The ruins of Machu Picchu are sited on a Peruvian ridge 2,430 m (7,970 ft) high.

THE VIKING AGE

Norsemen sailed from their homes in Scandinavia to trade, raid or claim lands across the sea. They brought fear to the coastal towns of northwest Europe and discovered new lands far across the ocean.

In the 8th century, Norway, Sweden and Denmark were home to pagan farming cultures that fished, bred sheep, cattle and goats, and grew oats and barley, though quality agricultural land was limited. Collectively known as Scandinavia, these countries made friendly contact with England and the Netherlands through the Danish fur trade. To the rest of Europe their inhabitants were known as the Norsemen (Northmen). They would soon gain a new, notorious title.

Whether to support a growing population, satisfy a craving for loot, or simply to sate a warrior lust for adventure, the Norsemen sailed forth in the 790s and began a series of violent raids on coastal targets in Scotland, England, Ireland and France. They were now identified as Vikings, a word that can loosely be translated as 'seafaring raiders'. While the Vikings have a reputation for pillaging, they also traded with and settled in other countries. Their legacy is not just one of blood spilled but of bloodlines established.

The Vikings improved their boatbuilding skills to fashion fast and lightweight craft, perfect for lightning coastal raids. The longship was constructed from oak and measured up to 28 m (92 ft) in length. Its single square sail was made of wool, and could be lowered on sight of land. With a shallow keel, the ship could then be rowed right up to the shore. The longship could carry more than 100 men armed with swords, spears or axes, along with their booty. Viking ships were light enough to be lifted out of the water and dragged overland to rivers. Examples of longships still exist today

thanks to the Vikings' tradition of burying their great men in ships for their journey to the next world.

For the Norsemen, European crossings were relatively simple, with coastal landmarks remembered through chants and rhymes. Over greater distances, across the Atlantic Ocean, sailors had to gauge their direction by the Pole Star on clear nights and by the position of the rising and setting sun.

RAIDING AND TRADING

The first-recorded Viking raid took place in 793, at Lindisfarne monastery just off the Northumberland coast of northeast England. Monasteries were prime targets for raids from the sea. They were often remote, unguarded and contained religious treasures made of precious metals. The Vikings were not Christians like most of Europe; they believed in a pantheon of warrior gods, such as Odin and Thor, and had no respect for Christian artefacts. Further Viking forays took place against island monasteries off the coast of Scotland, Ireland and the Netherlands, along with the Islamic kingdom on the Iberian Peninsula.

A preserved Viking ship discovered at Oseberg, now on display at the Viking ship museum, Norway.

As well as treasures, the Vikings took away people to sell as slaves. (A thousand people were enslaved following a Viking raid on Armagh, Northern Ireland, in 869.) Slaves, or *thralls*, were important to Viking society, as servants, construction workers and for trade. Their position in society was below the *Karls*, free peasants who could own farmland, and a ruling class called the *Jarls*.

Viking tactics became bolder as they took advantage of divisions within Europe, sending larger fleets out on raids and demanding protection money from potential targets. The Vikings also began to build settlements in the lands that they attacked, taking control of northern Scotland, Shetland, the Hebrides and the Orkneys. They established bases in Ireland, including Dublin and Limerick, from where they could trade or launch attacks on England. The French ports of Rouen and Nantes were also captured.

By 851, Vikings, mostly from Denmark, had claimed much of England. A diagonal line across the country separated the Danish half, the Danelaw, comprising north and eastern England, from the half ruled by Alfred, the king of Wessex. The settled Scandinavians farmed the land and established Jorvik (York) as a major trading city.

VIKING COLONIZATION

A mostly Norwegian company sailed west in the 9th century, to colonize Iceland. The Icelandic settlers wrote great histories and legends of the Scandinavian medieval period, called the Sagas. By the 10th century, Vikings had also settled on the southwest coast of Greenland, during a warm period when some livestock and crop farming was possible. From here, there is evidence that some made it as far as North America. Scandinavian explorers, possibly led by Leif Ericsson, called the land that they discovered Vinland (Wineland) and built a temporary settlement at L'Anse aux Meadows in modern-day Newfoundland, Canada.

In 1013, further raids on England led to the whole country coming under Scandinavian rule. After a period of Danish kings, in 1066 England was conquered by invaders from Normandy in France. The Normans were themselves of Scandinavian stock, descendants of Viking settlers in the area who had claimed the territory under their leader Rollo in the early 10th century.

1066 is considered the end of the Viking Age, as the invaders had now become settled in the countries they had previously attacked and replaced their belief in Norse gods with the prevailing Christian faith.

THE RUS

By 862, Swedish Vikings had crossed the Baltic Sea and sailed along the Dniepr and Volga rivers to trade and settle in Novgorod in present-day Russia. They formed a state called Kievan Rus', the source of the names for both Russia and Kyiv. Rus merchants also travelled as far as Baghdad to trade with the capital of the Islamic Caliphate. The Rus failed in their attempts to take the Byzantine capital of Constantinople in the 9th and 10th centuries but, decades later, supplied mercenaries to the Byzantine emperor for an elite group of bodyguards known as the Varangian Guard.

Ninth century Viking graffiti left in Hagia Sophia, Istanbul (former Constantinople).

MONGOL ARMIES

The medieval empires of the East and West were unable to hold back fast and ferocious assaults from a nomadic army trained from childhood to live and fight on horseback.

Empires had expanded from towns and city-states, where buildings, fortifications and roads had proclaimed their might and reach. None of them could have predicted their fall would come not from a rival empire but from a coalition of nomads without cities. Led by shrewd leaders who knew how to spread terror ahead of their army's advance, the Mongols destroyed the status quo in Eurasia and built their own empire, from Eastern Europe to Korea, and established a new dynastic rule over China. Theirs would become the largest land empire known to history, but it was one that left little trace behind it in architecture or art.

The Mongols were nomadic herders that led their sheep, goats, camels, yaks and horses to graze across the plains and steppes of Central Asia in what is now known as Mongolia. For centuries the steppe nomads had existed as separate groups of people, on the fringes of so-called civilization. Limited by the natural resources they could access, they struggled against harsh weather and sometimes frozen ground. The nomads subsisted on the meat and milk of their herd, fashioning clothes from wool, leather and fur. They lived in felt-covered, circular-framed tents called *gers*, which could be quickly erected and taken down as they moved with the seasons.

Portrait of Genghis Khan, who unified the Mongol tribes and helped build the world's largest land empire.

What they lacked – iron for horse bridles, stirrups and weapons, wood for wagons, or vegetables and grains – they could barter for from farms, or simply steal in raids. And, as raiders, the Mongols were a force to be feared. They bred and trained their stocky, pony-sized horses to respond to whistles. Mongol children were put on horseback from the age of three so that riding became as natural to them as walking. Warriors were trained to fire arrows at a target while their horses raced at a gallop.

UNIVERSAL LEADER

Years of infighting between tribal confederations had prevented the Mongols from being more than a nuisance to the empires surrounding the steppes. This all changed under the leadership of Genghis Khan. Born around 1162, he was originally named Temüjin

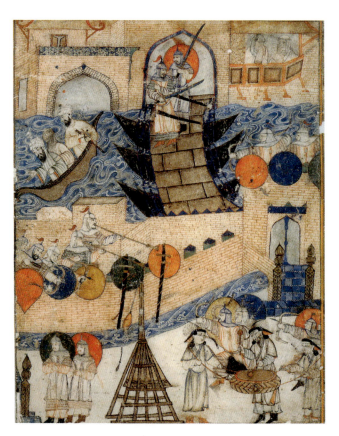

A 14th-century illustration of the fall of Baghdad to the Mongols in 1258.

and was the son of a chieftain. Like all Mongol boys, he was trained to ride and hunt, but while still a child he was deserted by his father and endured a spell of poverty, living by his wits outside of his tribal group. In time, he began to gather allies and raised an army with the aim of ending the wars between the Turko-Mongol peoples. By promising and delivering booty to his fellow warriors, through repeated raiding parties, Temüjin gained their loyalty and, by the age of 44, he was the leader of all of the tribal peoples of the steppes. From a population of around 1 million people, he had an army of 129,000 men at his disposal. In honour of his pre-eminence, Temüjin was given the name Genghis Khan, meaning 'Universal Leader'.

Men gained rank in Genghis' army for their proven ability and loyalty, not for any tribal relationship. On horseback, the army could cover vast distances at speed, preventing any warning of attack. With a choice of horses, warriors could ride for ten days, without setting up camp, and survive on a diet of milk paste and raw meat tenderized under their saddles. Genghis employed engineers to build siege ladders and giant catapults to help his army take heavily fortified towns.

Genghis led his army eastward, conquering areas of China and taking control of the Silk Routes (page 108). Reports spread of atrocities committed by Genghis' army, of the total annihilation of towns that failed to surrender, with every man, woman, child and animal being slaughtered and settlements razed to the ground. With their reputation for merciless brutality preceding them, the Mongols merely had to approach a town in order for it to surrender without offering any resistance. In these cases, mercy was shown and people were allowed to continue with their trade and beliefs, so long as they paid tribute to their conquerors. Towns that fell to Genghis' army were sometimes rewarded with investment in new building. While these facts reveal a more magnanimous side to Genghis Khan, the reports of violence were also true; millions were put to death by his Mongol armies.

The Mongol Empire continued to expand after the death of Genghis Khan in 1227, with his third son, Ögödei, chosen as the new leader. The nomad army also gained a capital city, Karakorum in central Mongolia. Genghis' grandson, Batu, led forces into Europe, claiming the cities now known as Kyiv and Moscow by 1241.

On reaching Vienna, the Mongols returned to Karakorum to debate succession issues. In 1260, the empire spilt into four, with a separate khan ruling each quarter. Eleven years later, Kublai Khan, the grandson of Genghis, established himself as the Chinese emperor, the first in the Yuan Dynasty (1271–1368). He chose what would become Beijing as his capital. The other three khans converted to Islam.

Mongol rule was severely weakened, as was all of Eurasia, by the spread of the Black Death (page 124), a plague that had its origins in Central Asia. Mongol trade and conflict across the region helped spread the bacterium that caused the deaths of tens of millions. This plague would prove far more lethal than hordes of raiding nomads.

THE YUAN DYNASTY

The Chinese Yuan Dynasty, initiated by the grandson of Genghis Khan, was a period of relative peace in the country, not least because external Mongol invasions had become a thing of the past. Kublai Khan protected the eastern end of the Silk Routes. Trade flourished and foreign visitors were welcomed, including the Venetian merchant Marco Polo, who wrote an imaginative account of his travels and the time he spent in the khan's court. Kublai's palace at Shangdu would be immortalized in poetry as Xanadu. Chinese innovations were shared with Europeans. These include the magnetic compass in 1180, and the wheelbarrow and horse collars from 1250. Most influential of all was the formula for gunpowder, which would change the balance of world power dramatically.

ENVIRONMENTAL DECLINE

Population growth, and the overuse and degradation of fertile land, are not just 21st-century issues. Empires of past millennia declined and disappeared due to environmental changes.

Early civilizations, living in small towns, with minimal population growth, could barely have imagined that the targets of their hunts might become extinct or that harvests might regularly fail. But, over time, humanity's effect on the environment became hard to ignore.

To protect regular weather patterns and food supplies, the first cultures worshipped fertility gods and sacrifices were made in order to appeal to divinities. Drought and crop failures were assumed to be the result of the gods being angered. Only in recent centuries have we understood exactly how our impact on natural resources could cause famine and changes in weather patterns.

Early empires were typically sited on land regularly fed by flooding rivers. Egypt relied on the annual Nile floods. The great empires of Sumeria, Assyria and Babylon thrived on the floodplains of Mesopotamia, between the Tigris and Euphrates rivers. In Southeast Asia, the Mekong river burst its banks every year to wash nutrient-rich silt over surrounding fields. The Niger river supported emerging African civilizations in the 1st millennium BCE.

Hierarchical societies were able to command populations to build large irrigation systems to water crop fields, but, as a rising population made more demands on the land, soils lost their nutrients. Irrigation failures caused the earth to dehydrate in hot climates. Harvests shrank and populations with it. The Sumerian city-states (page 56) over-farmed their lands which as a result suffered salinization under the hot sun. By 1800 BCE, farming in Sumeria was all but impossible.

DEFORESTATION

Forests were cut down for wood and to clear land for farming. Without the trees' root systems holding the soil in place, rains washed away the top soil. Greek philosopher Plato noticed this environmental phenomenon 2,500 years ago, when he wrote of an area of land that he was observing: 'All the richer and softer parts have fallen away, and the mere skeleton of the land remains.'

Salinization and deforestation also meant that the Indus Valley communities (page 70) lasted just 500 years. To provide wood fuel for the kilns that fired clay bricks for building, the Indus Valley people cut down their hillside forests, resulting in serious erosion. Farmers in the northern plains of Song Dynasty China also caused erosion through deforestation and agriculture. Silt slid into the Yellow river between 1048 and 1128 CE, blocking it and causing floods and major loss of life.

Set on an African plateau a kilometre above sea level, Great Zimbabwe flourished as a trading centre between the 13th and 15th centuries. The city was abandoned around 1450 due to a decline in trade, the reduced availability of gold and environmental issues. To support a population of up to 18,000 people, the

A painting by the Song Dynasty artist Ma Yuan (1160–1225) shows the Yellow river flooding.

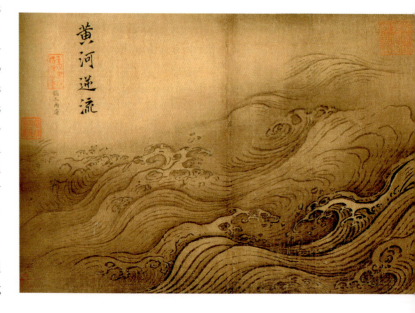

A row of moai facing inland on Easter Island.

surrounding lands had been overgrazed by cattle and over-cultivated for crops. It was unsustainable. Supplies of water ran out or became contaminated. Woods were cut down for fuel. The ecological effect of more than a century of exploitation of the land means that, even today, certain species of tree will not grow on the site.

The overexploitation of land forced people to leave their homes. Sometimes, their migrations caused conflict as cultures fought over plots of land and water sources. A balance was needed and still needs to be found, using the land in a sustainable way to support the population while protecting it for future generations.

NATURAL CAUSES

Not all environmental declines were caused by human intervention. Natural cycles of temperature change and reduced rainfall also beset civilizations.

Evidence in tree rings records a decade-long cool period from 2354–2345 BCE which may have precipitated the large-scale collapse in Near Eastern cultures. What is now referred to as the 4.2-kiloyear event (because it happened 4,200 years ago, around 2200 BCE) created a drought that affected much of the northern hemisphere over most of a year. Agricultural land in northern Mesopotamia was abandoned. Around 2150 BCE the annual Nile floods were severely reduced. Crops on the floodplains suffered and the resulting famine may have helped provoke the collapse of the Egyptian Old Kingdom that built the pyramids.

The Late Bronze Age Collapse of the 12th century BCE, that saw large cultures in the Eastern Mediterranean shrivel into villages and empires within the Levant collapse, has been blamed on many things, including volcanic eruptions and invasions. The volcano theory proposes that the eruption of Iceland's Hekla volcano left ash suspended in the atmosphere, reducing sunlight. A period of drought led to migrations.

KNIGHTS AND SERFS

11th-century Norman knights and archers from the Bayeux tapestry.

Armoured soldiers found greater employment in Europe from the 8th century. Loyal knights and nobles were rewarded with a parcel of land and a contract of service that became known as the feudal system.

Europe had faced attack by mounted armies, including the Arabs and Mongols, since the 7th century but, while sometimes arriving on horseback, European armies chose to dismount and fight as infantry. In the

The medieval fortified town of Carcassonne in France is one of the largest surviving medieval walled cities in Europe.

8th century, to expedite his campaigns, the Frankish king Charlemagne chose instead to employ proper mounted and armoured soldiers, fighting with swords, lances and spears. With these knights leading his army, Charlemagne succeeded in unifying Western Europe for the first time since the Roman Empire. He was crowned Holy Roman Emperor in 800.

Knights, like those of Charlemagne, were expected to follow a chivalrous code of honour, obeying their king, protecting the Church, fighting non-believers, respecting women and keeping their word. When not on campaigns, knights competed in tournaments, showing off their skills in jousting contests and battles that could deliver serious injuries or even death.

Just as ancient Roman emperors remunerated their soldiers with property (see page 88), Charlemagne rewarded his loyal captains with parcels of land, called benefices. These were then divided and let to soldiers of lower status. The use of knights and the division of land in lieu of service or funds became common practice across Europe. Plots of land, called fiefs, were given to nobles, or vassals, as they were called. This division of land, sublet for service or produce, was later called the feudal system.

VASSALS AND FIEFS

Becoming a vassal involved a formal ceremony, with a noble kneeling and swearing loyalty and service to the king. Vassals were expected to attend the royal court and recruit soldiers should they be needed for war. The vassals also helped fund royal undertakings, such as castle-building and weddings.

This contract between the king and his vassals was just the peak of a pyramidal set-up. The bottom of the heap were the serfs, or villeins, peasants who worked the land without pay for their landlords so that they could provide food and lodgings for their family. Virtual slaves, the serfs were not allowed to leave the area where they lived and worked. This was just another legalized form of the hierarchical structures that had existed since the first large settlements. Where the system did differ, however, was in providing a power shift from the Church to local nobles.

The 9th and 10th centuries were a time of much castle construction, as vassals and knights desired homes of prestige where they could provide entertainment and suitable lodgings for the king as he toured his realm. Castles were used for the administration of the noble's fiefdom, provided a site of defence against rivals and acted as a launchpad for raids.

The feudal system was seriously disrupted by the spread of the Black Death (page 124). With a huge percentage of the population wiped out by this plague, there was a shortage of tenants for land and workers for the fields. Peasants gained leverage over landlords and could more easily barter for greater pay, or else relocate for better working conditions or employment in towns and cities.

BARONS v KINGS

While appointed by the king, the nobles that managed lands across England began to challenge royal power in the 13th century. King John (r. 1199–1216) had led unsuccessful wars in France and triggered a rift with the Catholic Church of Rome. This, and the extra tax burdens he placed upon the nobles, or barons, led to a confrontation. In 1215, King John agreed to sign a charter, the Magna Carta, which relieved the barons of some of the demands placed on them by the Crown and gave them the power to seize the king's assets should he break the contract.

The agreement did not last and a year of civil war broke out as the rebel barons sought to place a French king on the English throne. Peace was restored soon after John's death and the terms of the Magna Carta were accepted by the new English king, Henry III. The rise of baronial power to balance that of the king led to the institution of the English Parliament.

THE BLACK DEATH

Warring armies had caused empires to crumble, but the deadliest foe of civilizations was invisible, spread by rodents and encouraged by close contact: plague.

The bubonic plague has its origins in Central Asia. Its intermittent spread across Asia and Europe led to the deaths of tens of millions and the decline of empires. In the mid-14th century it was called the Black Death. It remains the deadliest pandemic in human history.

The source of the plague has been traced back through DNA evidence from cemeteries, with the cause identified as the bacterium *Yersinia pestis*. This bacterium was borne by rodents but developed to transmit itself via rat fleas. These are what caused the plague to leap from rats to humans.

Four lead mortuary crosses from the period of the Black Death found at the old Grey Friars Monastery, London.

The virus thrived in crowded communities, as did rodents. The black rat, in particular, was a carrier of disease-infected fleas. It was drawn to places where food was stored, such as granaries and storehouses, where its fleas were able to hitch a ride on any passing humans who happened to be living, working or shopping nearby. Flea-infested rats also made their way into the holds of ships, and were thus transported across the globe, helping the plague to spread more quickly. Poor sanitary conditions and inefficient waste disposal in human households was another open invitation for rats to move in.

The plague spread from Central Asia along with human populations and armies. While the bacterium existed before the 6th century BCE, it was human migration, agriculture and empire building that prepared the ground for major outbreaks. Once it infected a human, the plague could be passed on through droplets breathed out by its victim, putting that person's family, fellow workers and carers at major risk. Plague symptoms included large swellings, called buboes, around the neck, armpit or groin. These were followed by a fever and, for two-thirds of the infected, death within days.

Yersinia pestis had caused devastation in Europe before. The Roman Empire, under the emperor Justinian, was battered by the plague spreading from northern Egypt from 541 CE. It could have arrived there by sea or land trade routes and reached Constantinople with rats stowing aboard Alexandrian grain ships bound for the capital. The plague would haunt both the Byzantine and Persian empires. It weakened their ability to hold back the Islamic armies inspired by Muhammad (page 110).

MEDIEVAL MENACE

The second major wave (1346–53) lasted three centuries and wiped out about half of Europe's population. It was a period of great connectivity, with trade links from China to Persia, from Africa to India, and from Constantinople to Italy. Populations were at a high. Countries were ripe for attack from *Yersinia pestis*.

This new wave of plague has been traced back to Kyrgyzstan, possibly encouraged by the movement of the Mongol hordes (page 118). Mongol tribes caught wild marmots for their meat and fur. These rodents could have been carrying the bacterium.

Records show the plague reached the Egyptian port of Alexandria, spreading south and taking up to 20,000 lives in one day as it turned major cities such as Cairo into ghost towns. By 1348, it had raced across Italy to France. It is estimated that 40 million people perished in Europe due to the Black Death. China is said to have lost at least a third of its population, an estimated 50 million souls.

The plague returned with more local outbreaks in the centuries that followed, emerging more widely across Continental Europe in the 17th century, assisted by troop movements during war. The cause of the plague was unknown at the time. The plague of the Middle Ages was seen as the wrath of God visited on humanity for its sins.

Plague victim burials in Tournai, France, 1349.

CRUSADES

The Seljuks were a mercenary army whose territorial gains led to conflict with the Byzantine Empire and a series of bloody religious wars, the repercussions of which persist today.

The Seljuk Dynasty, which would dominate Eastern Asia and eventually threaten the Byzantine capital, had its origins within a group of mercenary soldiers that offered their services across Central Asia. Descended from Turkic nomadic groups based around the Aral Sea, the Seljuks converted to Islam in 985. After helping a number of local rulers in their wars, the Seljuks began to claim an empire of their own, including Khurusan in the Iranian Plateau in 1046, followed by the former Abbasid capital of Baghdad in 1055.

The Seljuk army, expert soldiers on horseback, also crossed into Byzantine territory and clashed with that empire's forces in the area now known as Georgia. The ensuing battles left the Byzantines in no doubt that the Seljuks were a serious threat to their borders. Led by the Sultan Alp Arslan, the Seljuks claimed both Armenia and Georgia and began more serious incursions into Byzantine land from 1068, claiming most of Anatolia (modern-day Turkey).

Seljuk tile design from c.1160s–70s, Konya Köşk Palace.

In 1071, the Byzantine emperor Romanos IV Diogenes took the decision to push back. He led a large army from Constantinople to strike against the Seljuks and neuter their threat against his empire. But, rather than face the Byzantines on a battlefield of their choice, the Seljuks led the Byzantines away, before turning back and vanquishing the Byzantines at the Battle of Manzikert. Emperor Romanos was captured and forced to the ground, under the foot of the Seljuk leader Alp Arslan. Rather than kill the Byzantine emperor, Arslan chose to free him on the promise of an annual tribute. Humiliated, Romanos returned to Constantinople where he was blinded by a rival and soon died. This Seljuk victory is still celebrated today as the birth of the Turkish state.

A year after Manzikert, the Seljuks occupied Jerusalem and closed it off to Christian pilgrims. Arslan's successors expanded the Seljuk Empire across Central Asia from China in the east to Byzantine territories in the west. A capital city was established at Isfahan, in modern Iran. The spread of the empire led to the building of many madrasas (Islamic schools) and mosques across Central Asia, including the addition of domes to the Great Mosque of Isfahan.

For two decades following the Battle of Manzikert, the Seljuks cooperated with the weakened Byzantine Empire. This détente ended in the 1090s, as the Seljuk Empire splintered due to a series of wars of succession between tribal groups and heirs. The Seljuks found themselves occupied with their own internal battles when they needed to be united. While these internal troubles continued, in 1096 a 'holy war' was launched from the west, encouraged by the pope. This was the first of the so-called Crusades.

HOLY MISSION

In 1081 a new emperor, Alexios I Komnenos, took the throne of Constantinople. A veteran of the Battle of Manzikert, he knew very well the danger that the Seljuks posed to the Byzantine Empire. With his armies depleted, he called for help from the western half of the former Roman Empire and the Christian pope based in Rome. Relationships between Rome and Constantinople had been fractious, but the plea was well received by Pope Urban II. He dutifully rallied to the cause, whipping up a fighting force to march eastwards to repel the 'pagan' forces threatening Christendom and to retake Jerusalem for the Catholic Church. As the Islamic armies believed their jihad was a divine instruction to spread Islam, European men took arms on their own holy mission to defend their faith. The opportunity to ransack palaces and temples and to claim booty along the way provided an extra incentive.

The first Crusaders were a ragtag collection of French and German peasants and zealots happy to follow the call to kill without conscience while looting Eastern lands. These would-be fighters made up what was known as the 'People's Crusade'. Ill-disciplined and inexperienced in warfare, they were slaughtered by the Seljuks.

The Great Mosque of Isfahan, Iran, was modified and repaired during Seljuk rule between the 11th and 12th centuries.

Peter the Hermit leading the 'People's Crusade'.

A larger group led by Christian knights, including 4,000 armed soldiers on horseback and 25,000 infantry, made far more formidable opponents. They defeated a large Seljuk army in Dorylaeum, in modern Turkey, then proceeded to Antioch, where, after a six-month siege, they breached the city gates in 1098 and massacred thousands of soldiers and citizens.

A depleted group of Crusaders made it to Jerusalem. Once again, they lay siege, broke through defences and committed slaughter, not just of Muslims but Jews, too. This holy war had achieved its aim of returning Jerusalem to Christian control but in a bloody fashion. Jerusalem was just one city taken by the Crusaders. Much of the coastline of the Levant was claimed, cutting off the Seljuk Empire from the Mediterranean Sea.

THE FIGHTBACK

When the vulnerable Crusader state of Edessa (in modern southeastern Turkey) was taken by Turks in 1144, the pope at the time used the opportunity to call for a new Crusade. This one attracted European royalty to the cause, with the kings of France and Germany leading the charge. It was a disaster; the Turks sent them packing. Further Crusades were launched, this time towards Spain and Portugal to remove the Iberian Peninsula's Muslim rulers.

The sporadic attacks of the Crusaders helped unify Muslims in the Middle East. Under the sultan Saladin, they pushed back against the Christian armies, taking Jerusalem, where they spared Christian lives. By 1291, Saladin's successors managed to conquer the Crusader states, removing the Christian knights from the Holy Land.

The Crusades had turned the Middle East into a battleground between West and East, between Christian states and Islam. Both sides saw huge losses of life, and hostile feelings would linger.

KNIGHT MONKS

Following the successful taking of Jerusalem by the Crusaders, new brotherhoods of religious knights were formed, swearing off the trappings of wealth for a monastic way of life, of chastity and prayer. The Knights Templar swore to protect the pilgrimage routes to Jerusalem, while the Knights Hospitaller sought to provide medical help for ill or injured pilgrims. Both continued to wield swords and joined Jerusalem's army when needed, playing an active role in Crusades up to the 14th century. They attracted members and patronage by offering a curious mix of charity and violence. The Knights Templar were disbanded in 1312. The Knights Hospitaller continued as a chivalric rather than an armed order.

The castle of Krak des Chevaliers, Syria, built in the 12th century by the Knights Hospitaller.

EMPIRES OF SOUTHEAST ASIA

A bountiful landscape enriched by floods and maritime trading provided for the rise of major empires in Southeast Asia. They left behind some of the most spectacular temple architecture the world has ever known.

Every year, meltwater pours off the Himalayan glaciers and flows along the Mekong river in Southeast Asia, swelling the Tonle Sap lake in Cambodia to three times its size. The water and red silt it carries nourishes the surrounding land, providing for rich rice harvests and fishing. For the first centuries of the last millennium, empires fought for this abundant land and the maritime trade routes that delivered great wealth with spices, ivory and gold exchanged for silk and metals.

The Mekong river basins were coveted by several empires. From the 1st to the 6th centuries, the loosely connected states known as Funan ruled the area surrounding the delta, building large walled cities linked by canals that stretched for tens of kilometres. The Funanese were influenced by Indian culture, worshipping Hindu gods and following Buddhist teachings. The Champa, based in modern-day Vietnam, were also Indianized. They were a strong seafaring race who gained control of the commercial spice and silk route in the South China Sea between the 8th and 10th centuries. They also indulged in piracy. Both cultures traded with China and India but, when the sea-trading routes were redirected, Funan began to decline in power.

The maritime trading route through the Strait of Malacca was dominated by the Srivijaya Empire based on the island of Sumatra, in modern-day Indonesia. From the 7th to the 12th centuries, Srivijaya was a major hub for the spread of Buddhism.

In the 9th century, the Funan were superseded by the Khmer under Jayavarman II. His reign from 802 is accepted as the beginning of the Khmer Empire. Jayavarman's dynasty lasted for two centuries. He encouraged his subjects to see him as a god king, meaning that his orders went unquestioned.

THE KHMER

The Khmer were impressive builders, laying down a network of roads, canals and reservoirs, and erecting numerous temples, most notably the complex of Angkor Wat. Inaugurated under King Suryavarman II, around 1122, this vast temple complex took 30 years to construct. The sandstone walls featured carved reliefs depicting the king and his court, along with scenes from Hindu mythology. There are signs and reports that suggest the building was once layered with gold.

Angkor, which means 'Holy City', was established as the capital of the Khmer Empire. The city covered an area of 1,000 square km (386 sq mi), the largest urban centre of the era, comparable with modern-day Los Angeles in scale. The Khmer enjoyed a rich cultural life of music and dance. Women were given much responsibility for running trade.

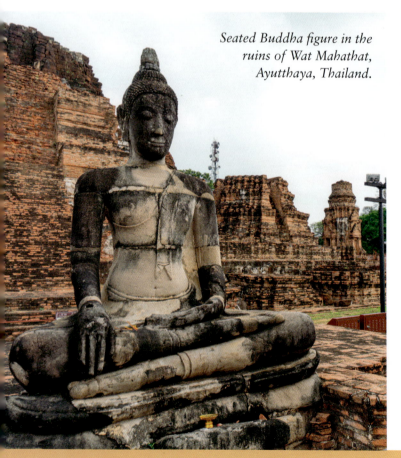

Seated Buddha figure in the ruins of Wat Mahathat, Ayutthaya, Thailand.

Cambodia's Angkor Wat is the largest religious complex in the world. Built in the 12th century, the site is dedicated to the Hindu god Vishnu and covers an area of 260 ha (642 acres).

The Khmer often came into conflict with the Champa, before conquering and absorbing them into the empire. The kingdom grew larger than the Byzantine Empire, covering most of modern Cambodia, Thailand, Laos and southern Vietnam.

From the 12th century, the Khmer empire saw its fortunes fade as the Thai began to migrate into Khmer lands from the north. Following Mongol attacks in China, the slow migration turned into a flood. Thai kingdoms claimed land along the western parts of the Khmer Empire. In 1431, the kingdom of Ayutthaya took Angkor, forcing the Khmer to retreat to what would become the future capital of Cambodia, Phnom Penh. The Ayutthaya kingdom would develop into the country of Thailand.

All of the cultures that developed in Southeast Asia were influenced to some extent by their contact with India, particularly in regard to architecture and religion. Buddhism remains the predominant religion in Cambodia, Laos, Thailand and Myanmar, while Malaysia and Indonesia turned to Islam from the 15th century. The temple complex of Angkor Wat was mostly abandoned by the mid-15th century and was hidden by the encroaching jungle, but its rescue and restoration in the 20th century turned it into a major visitor attraction.

BOROBUDUR

A century before the completion of Angkor Wat, Borobudur, the world's largest Buddhist temple, was built on the island of Java, Indonesia, under the rule of the Sailendra Dynasty. With nine ascending platforms, this 9th-century structure represented a path for pilgrims from a life of desire at the base to a formless world at the top. The temple included no fewer than 504 statues of Buddha, and thousands of relief panels depicting daily life in 8th-century Java. It may once have been brightly painted. The temple was abandoned, possibly around the 10th century, and buried under volcanic ash and overgrowth until its rediscovery in 1814.

The ruins of the 9th-century Borobudur temple, near Yogyakarta, Java, Indonesia.

AFRICAN STATES

Trade with Arabic nations and the desire for gold, ivory and slaves were among the factors motivating the activities of states in sub-Saharan Africa.

South of the empire of Egypt and the arid Sahara, smaller African states developed with their own fine arts and culture. Several became wealthy thanks to trading relations with Arabs. One of the earliest of note was the Kingdom of Aksum, which may have been founded in the 1st century CE. Based in Ethiopia, Aksum rule spread to modern-day Eritrea, Djibouti, Sudan and even southwestern Arabia for a while.

Aksum served as a major trading post for goods crossing the Red Sea between Rome and India. African exports included ivory, rhinoceros horn, gold and incense, as well as slaves. Aksum minted its own coins in gold, silver and bronze, and developed Africa's first indigenous written script.

Evidence of the Aksum Empire includes towering stele up to 33 m (108 ft) tall and over 500 tonnes (492 tons) in weight, that were erected to memorialize Aksum rulers. This practice was discontinued when the country adopted Christianity as the state religion in the 4th century. Ethiopia remains a predominantly Christian country.

By about 500 CE, Aksum, the city that shared its country's name, was large enough to house a population of 20,000. This was about the limit that could be fed by farming the surrounding land. Forests had been cut down to feed wood furnaces and to provide land for tilling, and soils had lost their nutrients due to over-farming and floods. Trade disruption in the late 6th and 7th centuries, followed by reduced rainfall, sounded the death knell for Aksum. The city was all but deserted by the end of the 7th century.

CENTRE OF TRADE

Djenné-Djenno in Mali was one of the earliest large urbanized centres south of the Sahara. The city occupied the inland Niger delta from 250 BCE to

A statuette of a woman from Djenné, Mali, 13th–15th century.

900 CE, when it was surrounded by a 2 km (1.2 mi) mud-brick wall. The city predated trading routes used by North African Arab traders across the Sahara. Estimates suggest Djenné-Djenno had a population around 27,000 people around 800, yet it was unusual in being a city without a main administrative focus or obvious hierarchy.

The increase in population for Djenné-Djenno was due to the successful mass production of rice. The city's position led to it becoming a natural waypoint for traders, and the city's rice may have been exchanged for salt, copper and dried fish. No major architecture was erected in Djenné-Djenno, but many fine terracotta pots and statuettes have been unearthed, depicting humans, snakes and horses.

The caravans of camels bringing traders across the Sahara also helped stimulate the growth of urban cen-

The ruins of Great Zimbabwe, outside Masvingo, Zimbabwe. The purpose of the conical tower is unknown.

tres such as Timbuktu and Gao in Mali, Aoudaghost in Mauritania, and Kano in Nigeria. Salt from the desert was a major cargo for the camel trains, a luxury ingredient warranting highly inflated prices by the time it reached the coast. Another export with a high value was the kola nut, which was popular as a stimulant. Grown in the equatorial rainforests of West Africa, it eventually became a key ingredient in cola drinks.

GOLDEN YEARS

Great Zimbabwe in southeast Africa became an important source of gold from the 11th century, connecting the western gold fields with the trading posts on the Swahili coast. In the language of the Shona *zimbabwe* means 'houses of stones', and Great Zimbabwe was just the largest of hundreds of stone-walled habitations in the area.

The settlement covered an area of 7 square km (2.7 square mi) of the Zimbabwean plateau. Some of the city's walls were 5 m (16 ft) thick and 10 m (33 ft) tall and were built without mortar to cement the bricks together. At 1,000 m (3,280 ft) above sea level, the city thrived thanks to tsetse-fly-free grazing for cattle and fertile land for crops of millet, sorghum and beans.

As for trading, evidence of long-distance dealing found at Great Zimbabwe includes fragments of Chinese dishes and Persian ceramics. Local artists worked in soapstone to carve subtle images of birds, including an eagle statue which has become the symbol of modern Zimbabwe.

Gold was not prized by Africans; as a soft metal, it was of little use for fashioning tools. It was, however, coveted by Egypt, Greece and Rome, then Arab traders. Once the use of camels made it possible to transport heavy goods across the Sahara, gold became a major export from West Africa. By the late Middle Ages, Great Zimbabwe and the Kingdom of Mali were the world's leading suppliers of gold. Lust for gold encouraged the Arab conquest of North Africa, which led to the spread of Islam in the north of the continent.

THE ARK

The legendary Ark of the Covenant is among the ancient treasures said to have made their way to Ethiopia. A gold-lined box constructed to house the tablets engraved with the biblical Ten Commandments, it was supposedly brought to Aksum from Jerusalem at some point in ancient history. Today, what is claimed to be the Ark resides in a small, lightly-guarded and modest chapel in the northern Ethiopian city. At least, that is what visitors are led to believe – the Ark is not kept in public view and belief in its existence is purely an act of faith. The Ark, however, remains a powerful symbol in Ethiopian Christianity and replicas of it are held in thousands of the country's churches.

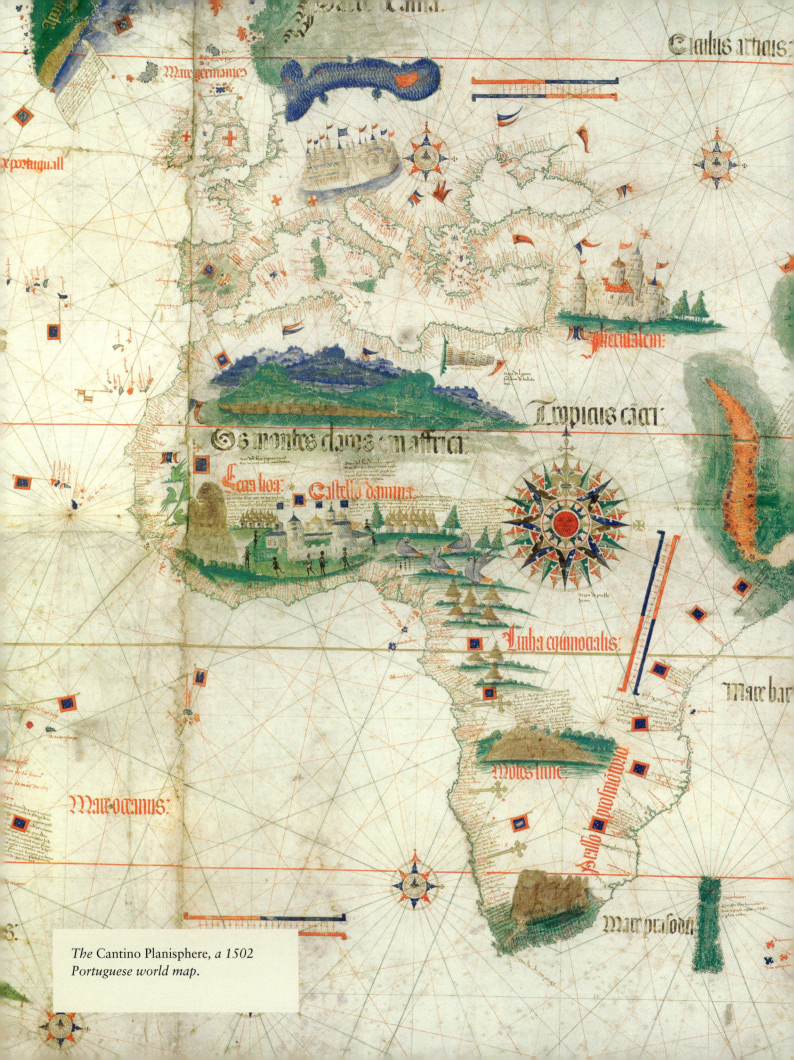

The Cantino Planisphere, *a 1502 Portuguese world map.*

CHAPTER 6

NEW HORIZONS

The 15th century saw huge fleets leave the ports of Ming Dynasty China for the shores of India, Africa and Indonesia, while a new Islamic power took hold of North Africa and claimed the capital of the Eastern Roman Empire in Europe. An ocean away, American cultures and empires remained in ignorance of the events in other continents. That was all about to end. When the Ottomans cut off overland trade to Asia, Europeans sought new maritime trading routes. They landed on the American east coast and began staking their claim to this New World.

Small armies of conquistadors defeated and enslaved the people of Central and South America, and brought with them the viruses of the Old World which had a far more devastating effect. Europeans claimed islands in the Caribbean, too, cutting down forests to plant sugar cane to satisfy Europe's sweet tooth. To work in the plantations, they turned the ancient trade in slaves into a major commercial enterprise, relocating millions of captured Africans to the Americas.

The international trade in American food and metals led to modern capitalism and the concentration of huge wealth in private hands. In turn, some of these funds were used to sponsor artists and scholars, leading to a boom in the arts and scientific progress.

THE OTTOMAN EMPIRE

Christian Constantinople finally fell with the arrival of the Turkish Ottomans. For 700 years, the Ottomans led an Islamic empire that, at its height, reached across Eastern Europe, the Middle East and North Africa.

After defeating the Byzantine army and humiliating its emperor, the Turkic Seljuks (page 126) gained control of Anatolia (modern-day Turkey) and an empire that covered most of Central Asia. But, by the early 12th century, the empire was divided after internal rows over succession. The splintered Seljuk realms not only had to deal with revolts from within but crusades from the west and attacks from nomad armies. The killer blow was dealt by the Mongols, who invaded Anatolia in the 1260s and divided it into small territories governed by beys, or chieftains. One bey, governing the area called Bithynia, was an ambitious man named Osman.

With the Mongols maintaining a weak grip on the region, Osman took advantage of Bithynia's position close to the Byzantine Empire and began laying siege over the border. Osman and his successors, named the Ottomans after their founder, took strategic control of the Balkans, including the Dardanelles, the strait that divided Asia and Europe at the mouth of the Black Sea.

While the Ottomans were generally tolerant of non-Muslims, in the 14th century they instituted the system of *devshirme*, 'levy of boys', which required Christian families to give up one in five of their male children to be converted to Islam. Many joined the military, with one powerful group of infantry, the Janissaries, made up of mostly Christian converts. This system provided a considerable standing army for the empire.

Interior of the Ottoman-era Blue Mosque, Istanbul.

Following a defeat to the central Asian conqueror Timur (page 137) in 1402, and a civil war, the Ottomans regrouped under a dynamic new sultan, Mehmed II (1432–81). In 1453, Mehmed led the Ottomans to attack Constantinople, the Byzantine capital that was considered impregnable. The Byzantines had blocked the nautical route to their city with a large chain across the main waterway in, but the Ottomans navigated this by dragging their ships overland and bombarding the city walls using gunpowder weapons, including the world's largest cannon with an 8 m (26 ft)-long gun barrel. Thanks also to an army of 160,000 men, Mehmed II claimed the capital as his own, and took tens of thousands of its population captive. The former capital of the Roman Empire was in Islamic hands. The city's ancient cathedral, Hagia Sophia, became a mosque.

After Constantinople, the Ottomans expanded their empire further, claiming Serbia, Bosnia and Greece in the west before taking Cairo by 1517. The Ottomans managed to secure control of the holy cities of Jerusalem, Mecca and Medina and assert themselves as the caliphs of the Islamic world. Under the reign of Suleiman the Magnificent from 1520–66, the Ottoman Empire reached its peak, its territory extended across three continents.

The Ottomans closed the important Silk Routes (page 108) to the west, forcing their foes to seek new maritime trading routes. The Portuguese successfully navigated around the southern tip of Africa to reach Iran and India. Voyages west in search of new trade routes led to the discovery of the Americas (page 144).

ARTISTIC LEGACY

While building an empire that would survive for centuries, the Ottomans also left a fine artistic legacy. Of note are the decorative tiles and pottery made in Iznik, in modern Turkey, with repeated floral patterns, often in blue on white, suggesting the early influence of Chinese Ming porcelain (page 136). The Ottomans' spectacular architectural heritage includes the Topkapi Palace, home of the sultan in Constantinople, and hundreds of sublime mosques (see panel).

The empire began a slow decline in the 17th century, suffering from poor leadership and corruption. Defeats in Vienna (1683) precipitated the empire having to give up territory in Austria, Venice, Poland and Russia. Despite its reduced scale, the Ottoman Empire survived into the 20th century.

DOMES AND MINARETS

During the Ottoman rule of Suleiman and his son, Selim II, their chief architect, Mimar Sinan, designed an incredible 80 mosques, 60 madrasas (religious schools), 32 palaces, 17 hospices, three hospitals and numerous bridges and bathhouses. Among the most impressive of his works is Selimiye Mosque in Edina, Turkey. Its dome is slightly greater in scale than Istanbul's Hagia Sophia and the four minarets on its corners, at 71 m (233 ft), are among the tallest erected under the Ottomans.

Built between 1568 and 1575, the Selimiye Mosque is considered to be architect Sinan's masterpiece.

THE PRINTED WORD

Gutenberg's printing press led to a book publishing industry in Europe that provided access to Classical knowledge as well as more controversial material.

Access to the written word was limited in the early Middle Ages. Most European books were laboriously copied by clerks or monks, dipping quills into ink pots and writing on stretched sheets of parchment. It could take months for one book to be completed. The results were expensive and, thus, only available to the wealthy, the clergy and royalty. This all changed with the advent of paper production and the printing press. Books were instantly cheaper to manufacture. Religious, philosophical and scientific ideas could be more widely shared with the reading public, including some that those in power would prefer not to be distributed.

Moveable type, shaped in clay, wood or metal, was invented in China in the 11th century and was used to print books in Korea from 1377. The availability of literature, particularly fictional epics, created an upturn in literacy levels, but preparing type for Chinese novels was a lengthy process, with hundreds of

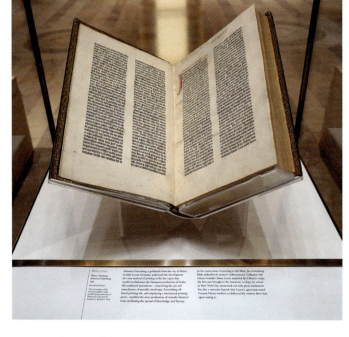

A Gutenberg Bible, printed around 1453.

characters required. The limited alphabet of the West was far easier to deal with.

The technology for printing arrived in Europe in the 1440s, when the German inventor Johannes Gensfleisch zur Laden zum Gutenberg (*c*.1398–1468) developed a wooden hand-press along with moveable metal type and an oil-based printer's ink. His innovations and publications quickly found a market, especially the so-called 'Gutenberg Bible', which was produced in Mainz from 1454–55. Within 50 years, more than a thousand printing shops had opened across Europe, putting out 10–20 million volumes each year in many languages. In England alone, 400 different books were published in the 1600s. By the 1640s, the number had leapt to 20,000. Literacy rates rose accordingly.

Relief showing the 15th-century printing process in Mainz, Germany.

As well as the Bible, philosophical works by Plato, Ptolemy, Aristotle, Cicero, Ovid and Horace were made commercially available. Classical theories on cosmology, medicine and mathematics by Archimedes, Euclid, Hippocrates and others were now more freely at the disposal of inquiring minds.

CENSORSHIP AND PROPAGANDA

The Church became concerned about the spread of texts, particularly religious tracts which might challenge its doctrine and it began to censor publications it considered dangerous. The first council of censorship opened in Mainz, the origin of the European press.

The ease and speed of running off hundreds of identical pamphlets led to a rise in propaganda. Governments could now spread notices of laws, opinions and dangers by posting and pinning broadsides in market places and on church doors within days. Equally, opposing opinions could be disseminated quickly. When the German monk Martin Luther (page 142) disagreed with aspects of the teaching and the administration of the Catholic Church in the early 16th century, he printed leaflets sharing his thoughts. These were widely circulated and caused a huge schism in European religious practices.

In 1538, the Senate of Milan issued the first list of banned publications. Over the years of its publication, banned titles in the Index of Forbidden Books included Luther's writings, works on biology and medicines, plus the astronomical texts of Nicolaus Copernicus that positioned Earth in orbit of the sun (page 158). The Index was regularly updated until 1948, then abolished in 1966.

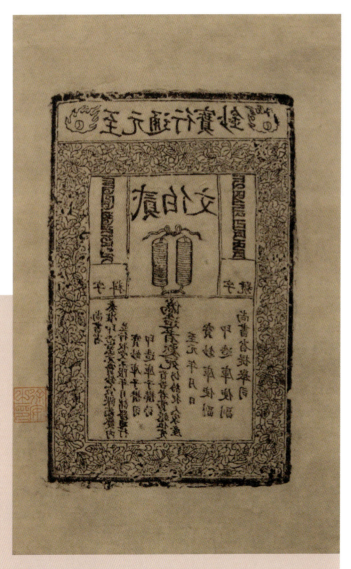

A Yuan Dynasty banknote.

BANKNOTES

Printing using woodblocks on paper existed in China in the 7th century and was copied across Asia. The earliest-dated publication is a woodblock-printed Buddhist Diamond Sutra dated from May 868. Moveable type was conceived by the Chinese engineer Bi Sheng in the 11th century, using porcelain characters. Moveable metal type, which produced a more consistent result, was introduced in the later Song and Yuan dynasties, and provided the first examples of printed paper money.

THE REFORMATION

Protests against corruption within the powerful Catholic Church led to a theological split across Europe, religious revolution, persecution and war.

The Catholic Church, the dominant religious power in 16th-century Europe, allowed believers to receive forgiveness for sins and a reduction in their period in purgatory after death through acts of repentance, prayer and pilgrimage. Payments to the Church were also gratefully received. These indulgences, as they were known, were lucrative for the Church but were perceived by many theologians as a profiteering exercise by the clergy.

One such critic was the university-educated German monk Martin Luther (1483–1546). In 1517, he became infuriated by clerical efforts to raise funds for the rebuilding of Rome's St Peter's Basilica through the selling of indulgences. Luther shared his criticisms in 95 statements, or theses, nailing them to the door of the Wittenberg castle church, according to legend. His theses were quickly disseminated through sermons and the recently developed printing press (page 140). Luther also questioned the Church's belief in transubstantiation (the idea that bread and wine shared during church communion become the body and blood of Christ), as well as celibacy for priests and papal rule.

Luther wished only for change within the Church but his opinions gained a following and brought him to the attention of religious leaders. Whereas previous critics of the Church had been labelled heretics and burnt at the stake, Luther avoided punishment thanks to the protection of his local elector, Frederick the Wise. Luther was able to continue sharing pamphlets attacking the pope and demanding reform. In a dramatic demonstration of his grievances with the Church, Luther set fire to a papal order of excommunication in 1520. Thrown out of his own church, Luther proceeded to set up his own and began a translation of the Bible from Latin into German, thereby providing access to the holy book for the ordinary lay person.

Lutheranism spread beyond Germany, into Scandinavia. Similar treatises on religious reform were distributed by Huldrych Zwingli and John Calvin in Switzerland. This new reformed version of Christian belief, rejecting the pope, was later named Protestantism. An unforeseen benefit of the Protestant movement was increased literacy levels in the peasant classes, as reading the newly translated Bible was encouraged.

COUNTER-REFORMATION AND CONFLICT

In the early 16th century, the English king Henry VIII, frustrated in his attempts to have his marriage annulled by the pope, took advantage of Reformation ideas and disconnected his states from papal power to found a Church of England with himself at its head. Several other European nobles supported his and similar movements, whereby not just religious affairs but matters such as land rights and succession issues were decided by local monarchs and rulers rather than the pope.

Despite the pope's protestations, a treaty was signed by the Holy Roman Emperor Charles V in Augsburg in 1555 which permitted European states to choose between Catholicism and Lutheranism as their official

95 Theses.

Martin Luther debates theology with the Swiss Reformer, Ulrich Zwingli, in 1529.

faith. Followers of the Puritanical form of Christianity, Calvinism, were excluded from the treaty. Power struggles between French Catholics and Calvinists erupted in nine wars of religion between 1562 and 1598. Later attempts to impose Catholicism on the Holy Roman Empire led to the bloody Thirty Years' War (see panel). Religious divisions would continue.

Partly in response to the Protestant Reformation, the Church of Rome launched a Counter-Reformation after a series of councils from 1545 to 1563. It agreed to deal with corruption and the sale of indulgences, reasserted its core beliefs and instituted the structured training of priests. The Church refused to come to any accommodation with the Protestant movement, however. At a time when the public were able to read the Bible for themselves, the Catholic Church insisted that only its interpretation was the spiritual truth. This truth was spread by a new religious order, missionaries known as the Jesuits. The Jesuits became the vanguard for the spread of Catholicism in the newly discovered Americas (page 144), Japan and China.

THIRTY YEARS' WAR

The ascension of the Catholic Ferdinand II to the throne of the Holy Roman Empire preceded one of the bloodiest conflicts in Europe. Ferdinand disregarded the 1555 Augsburg peace accord and tried to force all of the empire's citizens to follow Catholicism. This led to the Thirty Years' War (1618–48), a pan-European conflict that saw an estimated 8 million soldiers and civilians die in battle or as a result of famine and disease. The eventual peace deal created new borders on the continent. Spain lost control over Portugal and the Netherlands; the Catholic Church lost its grip on many European states. Many of the Continent's nation states began to take on the shapes that we recognize today.

Many soldiers involved in the Thirty Years' War were mercenaries who plundered towns and villages in lieu of pay. Painting: Sebastiaen Vrancx, 1620.

THE COLUMBIAN EXCHANGE

The arrival of Christopher Columbus in 1492 opened the floodgates for the movement of goods, people and ideas between the Old World and the New. But, while Europeans exported new crops and silver, the indigenous population was almost wiped out by imported diseases.

Christopher Columbus sailed back to Europe in 1493 after his voyage of discovery, convinced he had succeeded in finding a sea route to Asia. He had, in fact, arrived in the Caribbean, and set foot upon islands including Cuba and Hispaniola. The array of parrots and other exotic birds Columbus brought back with him, not to mention the captured natives and reports of abundant farmlands, spices and gold led to a wave of colonists, priests and conquistadors sailing west to seek wealth and to subjugate this 'New World'. The ensuing import and export of plants, animals, people and metals between Afro-Eurasia and the Americas has been dubbed 'the Columbian Exchange'.

Far from a fair trade-off, while Europeans profited greatly from commerce and theft from the New World, the indigenous population saw their livelihoods and lifestyle threatened, and faced diseases their immune systems were totally unprepared for. It is estimated that 80–90 per cent of the native population of the Americas were wiped out by viruses during the 16th century.

NEW HARVESTS

Crops that are now considered part of traditional menus in Europe originated on the American continent. Staples such as potatoes and maize (corn), along with tomatoes and capsicums were first cultivated by indigenous Americans. Tobacco, made from the dried, cured leaves of the nicotiana plant, was used in religious ceremonies in the New World. It was adopted as a medicine and would soon fill the pipes of gentlemen in Europe, then become a habit for millions worldwide. Cacao, delivered to Europe by the Spanish, was used to produce chocolate drinks before it became a sweet confectionery.

Portuguese settlers in the Americas took cassava and corn from the New World to Africa, where they would supplant popular crops such as sorghum and millet. Quinine, sourced from the bark of the Andean cinchona tree, proved an effective treatment for malaria in Africa after testing in the mid-19th century, and helped to facilitate the further European investigation and exploitation of Africa's interior (page 182).

Eurasians transported cattle, sheep, pigs and goats to the continent as well as horses. The arrival of horses would transform the culture of the indigenous people of North America; many would give up their farms for a nomadic lifestyle, following and hunting herds of native bison.

Spanish traders receiving goods from indigenous Americans.

CHANGING TASTES

Some of the crops that moved between the Americas and Afro-Eurasia

NEW WORLD	OLD WORLD (Source)
Maize/Corn	Apple (Central Asia)
Tomato	Banana (Africa)
Potato	Citrus fruits (Asia)
Sweet potato	Mango (Asia)
Cassava	Onion (Asia)
Chilli peppers	Rice (China)
Tobacco	Wheat (Middle East)
Cacao	Sugar cane (New Guinea)
Vanilla	Coffee (Africa)

DEADLY EXPORTS

Unseen perils also moved across the Atlantic. The sexually transmitted disease syphilis returned from the Caribbean with European crews. Reaching a dreadful height in the years 1494–95, this 'Great Pox' killed up to 5 million people.

Far more devastating was the effect of diseases brought westward. Swine influenza took a huge toll on the Caribbean island of Hispaniola (modern Dominican Republic and Haiti), where an estimated population of 500,000 was reduced to fewer than 500 individuals by 1526. The deadliest of all diseases delivered was smallpox. Originating in domestic farm animals and spreading in tight communities, it had laid waste to large numbers in the Old World but, over time, had triggered some local immunity against its worst effects. The native Americans had no such defences.

Very likely arriving aboard a Spanish ship, American cases of smallpox were first recorded in 1518. Forty per cent of the population of the Aztec capital Tenochtitlán (now Mexico City) died. The Incas of Peru (page 115) were next to fall. Smallpox and other imported diseases, such as measles, whooping cough, bubonic plague and typhus, would eventually wipe out an estimated 80–95 per cent of the indigenous people of the Americas within 150 years of Columbus setting foot on Caribbean soil.

SILVER AND RUBBER

While tales of golden cities would lead Spanish conquistadors into the South American interior, it was silver that dominated exports from the Americas in the 16th and 17th centuries, with 80 per cent of the world's total being extracted from mines in Bolivia and Mexico. The precious metal gained usage in trade, particularly with China, in exchange for silk and porcelain, and helped fund Spain's numerous wars at home.

Natural rubber is made from latex, that 'bleeds' from cuts made in hevea trees first found in Central and South America. The latex was worked and used by native Americans for boots, tents, balls, containers and glue. It wasn't until the 19th century that New Englanders took advantage of it and began commercial production for footwear. The process of vulcanization (making the product both stronger and more elastic) led to rubber production expanding into a vast, competitive industry across Asia and Central Africa.

Without doubt the exchange of food, materials and people following the 15th-century discovery of the Americas by Europeans transformed the health, wealth and way of life for people on both sides of the Atlantic. While Europeans tasted new foods, hoarded precious metals and planted their flags on foreign soil, millions in the Americas died from shared diseases and Africans were forced into slavery (page 152) to maintain farms on land claimed from natives. As horizons opened, the inequalities between peoples persisted.

CONQUISTADORS

In the wake of Christopher Columbus' discovery of the Americas, a new wave of Spanish sailors crossed the Atlantic with a thirst for gold and land.

Two years after Christopher Columbus located islands off the coast of the Americas, Spain and Portugal were drawing maps to divide the new continent between them. With Hispaniola and Cuba taken, the Spanish turned towards the mainland. The Europeans saw the indigenous American peoples as godless and sought to convert them to Christianity. While the local people fought with clubs, arrows and spears, the Spanish had armour, horses, swords, lances and a limited number of guns. America was ripe for exploitation.

In 1519, the nobleman Hernán Cortés left Cuba, commanding a fleet of 11 ships, to explore the Yucatan coast (in modern Mexico) for evidence of gold. Like many of the conquistadors (conquerors) that followed, Cortés was not a trained soldier but an opportunist, unsanctioned by the Spanish crown. His exploits in Mexico were a private enterprise, and a bloody one, leaving a trail of tens of thousands of Aztecs dead.

Having heard rumours of a great empire inland, Cortés recruited local guides and led a group of 15 horsemen and 400 soldiers into the interior. On the way he was joined by the indigenous army of the Tlaxacalan, a people who were enemies of the Aztec kingdom Cortés sought. Late in 1519, they arrived at the great Aztec capital of Tenochtitlán (page 114), one of the largest cities in the world at the time.

Concerned by the military strength of the Spanish, the Aztec emperor, Motecuhzoma II, attempted to appease the visitors with gifts and accommodation. Diplomacy failed. The Spanish took Motecuhzoma prisoner, killed several Aztecs and incited a revolt. Cortés escaped with just a quarter of his soldiers but returned with a greater force and conquered Tenochtitlán, which was now much weakened by an epidemic of smallpox (page 147) brought during the first invasion. The golden Aztec treasures that Cortés seized were melted down for transport to Europe and thousands of Aztecs were made to work the land, now called 'New Spain'. A new capital was built on the ruins of Tenochtitlán, using wood cut from the forests. Cattle, pigs and sheep were imported along with European agricultural methods. The Aztec irrigation canals were left to dry up.

SUBJUGATING THE SOUTH

Further south, in 1527, the Spaniard Francisco Pizarro and his ships pulled ashore at Tumbes (modern-day Peru) and made contact with the Inca Empire. The initial trade interactions between them revealed that the Inca had access to gold, silver and jewels. Within four years Pizarro was back with firepower, bent on claiming the Incas' riches for Spain.

As with the Aztecs, the Inca had been brought low by imported disease and had lost their ruler. Taking

An 18th–century portrait of Atahuallpa (c.1502–1533), the last Inca emperor.

advantage of an Incan civil war, Pizarro's men killed at least 7,000 unarmed Inca and kidnapped the new emperor, Atahuallpa, before demanding a huge ransom of 6,100 kg (13,420 lb) in gold, and 11,800 kg (26,000 lb) in silver. By 1533, Pizarro's army had taken the Incan capital of Cuzco and controlled the empire via a puppet regime.

Other conquistadors led armies to claim land in what is now known as Ecuador, Chile, Colombia, Bolivia (where great silver mines were discovered) and Argentina. The wealth in gold and silver taken from South America helped fund the expansion of Spanish territories in Europe and the building and decoration of palaces and churches.

FIREPOWER

The first conquistadors to arrive in Central and South America terrified the locals with their firepower, but their guns were just a fraction of the armoury they used. Cortés' initial force brought 10 cannons with them, but only 13 men carried handheld, long-range firearms. These were arquebuses, early muskets, which were heavy and took a minute to reload. These gunpowder weapons were lethal, but the noise they created probably had as much effect in terrifying the Aztecs, who thought the invaders capable of raising thunder.

A 16th-century Spanish arquebus.

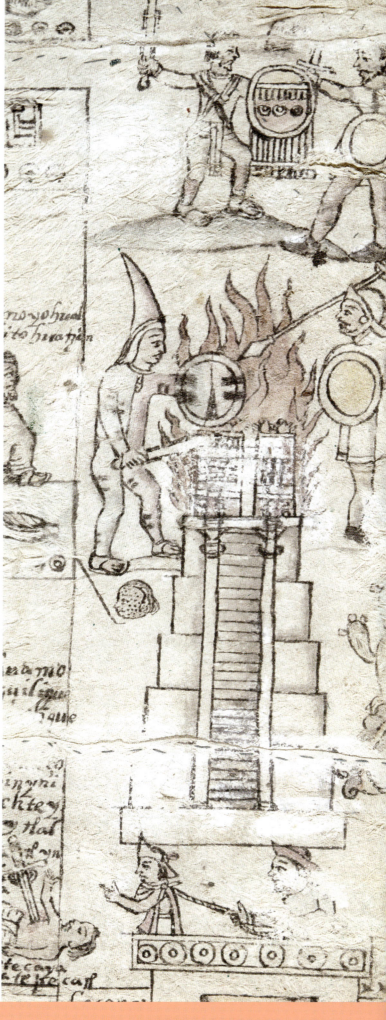

A fragment from a 16th-century codex showing a fight between an Aztec warrior and a Spanish conquistador.

AMERICAN COLONIES

The 16th century saw European settlers arrive in the Americas to take land for plantations or for a life of religious freedom. Indigenous people were brushed aside or forced into labour by new landlords.

Having found a lucrative route to the Americas, European countries established bases to protect and serve their trading fleets. Spain exported gold, silver and sugar from Central and South America, France set up camp in North America, collecting furs and fishing off the east coast, but it was the English, late to the game, who first started settling in the New World.

There had been peoples living in North America for millennia (see panel), but European settlers were unconcerned with natives and fenced off their communities, avoiding contact with indigenous people as much as possible. When contact was made, it was not always friendly. As far as the European arrivals were concerned, without contracts or fences, the natives had no claim on the land. The New World was up for grabs.

In 1585, the English explorer Walter Raleigh built a settlement on Roanoke Island, in modern North Carolina, but was unable to maintain it. A more successful attempt at occupation took place in 1607, when the Virginia Company of London set up a colony in Jamestown, Virginia. Their aim was to farm land and become wealthy, something they achieved as the first North American exporter of tobacco.

The so-called Pilgrim Fathers and Mothers that landed in New Plymouth in 1620 were seeking a new life rather than riches. They wanted to be free to follow their own religious beliefs. Half of the 102 settlers who made the crossing on their ship the *Mayflower* died from sickness in the first year. The rest would have starved had they not received help from native peoples. The pilgrims' relief in making it through a year was celebrated with a Thanksgiving, an annual tradition that continues in the United States.

Other religious groups followed the Plymouth pilgrims, including Puritans who settled in Massachusetts in 1630, Catholics in Maryland in 1634, and Quakers in Pennsylvania in 1682.

OPENING MARKETS

In the wake of Christopher Columbus (page 146), the Spanish began settling in the Caribbean and Central and South America. They compelled the indigenous people to pan for gold or work on their plantations as part of the *encomienda* system. This was an arrangement whereby the Spanish crown granted a local labour force to conquerors who could demand from it tribute in exchange for protection and religious education.

Spain had been the leader in transatlantic trade for decades, but after losing much of its armada in a decisive naval battle against England in 1588, maritime routes were opened up to other nations. France set up a trading network in the north of the continent. It established a colony called New France in modern-day Quebec in 1608, gaining a firm foothold in what would become Canada. From New France, French trappers headed up the St Lawrence river to trade with Native Americans for fox, ermine, squirrel and sable pelts. In exchange, the local peoples gained guns, metal tools and alcohol.

New Amsterdam (New York City) in 1656, from a 19th-century engraving.

The Netherlands and Sweden joined the rush for New World wealth by setting up companies to export goods. In 1626, the Dutch West India Company bought an island in the Hudson River from the Manhattan tribe for the giveaway price of 40 guilders (around $1,150 in modern money). They would name the island New Amsterdam; we now know it as New York City. Supported by a system of bank loans, the Dutch became Europe's most extensive international trading country for some time (page 154), but both Dutch and Swedish regional rule ended in 1664 as the English pushed them out to claim the North American eastern coast from New England to Georgia.

In the south, growing crops for export became big business. There was huge demand in Europe for American tobacco, cotton and, especially, the sugar derived from sugar cane. To work on the farms, the settlers began shipping over enslaved men and women from Africa (page 152). Europe had a sweet tooth and pioneers hurried to satisfy the market. The English and French cleared forests for plantations in the Caribbean in the 1650s. The deforestation undertaken to plant sugar cane led to erosion and changed the climate on the islands. Malaria, a virus harboured by enslaved workers from Africa, was then carried by mosquitoes that thrived in stagnant water. Both malaria and yellow fever spread throughout the Americas.

It took just decades for European traders and settlers to change the identity of a continent. Imported diseases wiped out many indigenous people. Those that survived would find themselves regarded as second-class citizens in a new European outpost.

NATIVE AMERICANS

European settlers showed little interest in the indigenous peoples they encountered when they began staking out territory from the 16th century, but these groups had been living, hunting and farming the land for thousands of years. While a hunter-gatherer lifestyle was predominant, especially in the forests and tundra of Canada, corn from Mesoamerica had become a staple crop in southern North America and supported large societies, such as the Cahokia in the Mississippi Valley, where large mounds attest to the longevity of their settlements. The diverse peoples of the Pacific northwest coast shared many traditions and beliefs. Finely carved totem poles, raised to celebrate special events, are a feature of their cultures. While not constructing cities on the scale of those found in Central and South America, the indigenous people of North America were self-sufficient and formed complex cultural groups. The arrival of Europeans led to a huge decline in their population, mostly as a result of diseases such as smallpox and measles brought over with the colonists.

Replica Pacific Northwest Coast totem pole on display in Vancouver, Canada.

THE SLAVE TRADE

The demand for workers on American plantations supported centuries of trade in slaves. Millions of Africans were captured, sold and transported in cruel conditions to North and South America and the Caribbean.

The 3.4 million Europeans that settled in the Americas between 1492 and 1840 were far outnumbered by the 11.7 million enslaved men, women and children they brought from (mostly) West Africa to work on their farms, growing both native and imported crops such as sugar cane, cotton and tobacco.

For almost 300 years, Portuguese and Dutch, then English and French slave traders transported Africans to sell to plantation owners. They replaced the local workforce which had been almost wiped out by small-pox and measles. These forced workers were more resistant to the Old World diseases. The descendants of the enslaved would eventually form the majority populations of Caribbean islands such as Haiti and Jamaica, as well as representing a sizable proportion of the mainland's ethnicity.

Slavery is as old as the written record. Slaves, usually a defeated population in wars or raids, or workers unable to pay their debts, were employed in ancient Sumeria, Egypt, Rome, China, Persia and Israel. They

Enslaved workers at the Cassina Point plantation, South Carolina, 1862.

were compelled to work in the fields, in mines, and ordered to build monumental temples and defences for their new overlords. Those taken as prisoners of war could be sent back into battle, fighting for their enemy. They often died in service, and their children were born into servitude. In some rare cases, enslaved men or (less commonly) women rose to positions of responsibility. The Mamluk Sultanate that ruled Egypt from the mid-13th century was formed from a caste of freed slave soldiers; the Ottoman Empire's janissary system (page 138) employed enslaved Christian boys as infantry, though they received a wage and were eventually allowed to retire. The trade in humans from the 15th century onwards was on a much greater scale, however, and offered no opportunity for emancipation and little chance of escape.

Slave capture, transport and trading became a major international industry, tearing millions of people from African towns and villages, shipping them in foul conditions to foreign lands to face back-breaking toil, with the constant threat of punishment.

ATLANTIC CROSSING

On the voyage that took Christopher Columbus to the Caribbean in 1492, he kidnapped several indigenous people and offered them as gifts to his royal patrons back in Spain. Despite orders to the contrary, Columbus later sent 500 more West Indians back as slaves. While slavery was outlawed in Spain, it was legal in the New World.

Portugal had been using African slave labour to work on its sugar-cane plantations on islands off the coast of Africa; they simply continued this operation in their new territories in Brazil in the 1580s. Here, enslaved persons were only expected to survive hard labour for about seven years, so there was always demand for new workers. The English colonists in Jamestown, Virginia, accepted African slaves in a trade with a Dutch ship in 1619 and treated them as

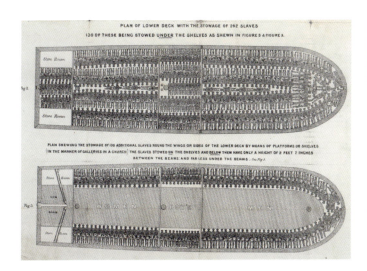

A poster showing how slaves were packed on board ships during the era of the slave trade, produced in 1788.

indentured servants for several years. Slavery became fully institutionalized in North America in the 1660s.

For an enslaved person, the journey from Africa to the Americas was appalling. Only about 80 per cent were expected to survive the voyage. Men, women and children were placed in cramped conditions below deck in almost complete darkness. The men were kept in manacles. They were provided with little food and water, and inadequate toilet provisions. Those that died en route were simply thrown overboard.

When the American War of Independence erupted in 1775, many in the enslaved population expected the call for liberty would extend to them – but it would be 75 more years before slavery was ended in the north. It took a civil war to see it abolished in the south. The Atlantic slave trade was ended by Britain and the US by 1808. While this meant Africans did not have to endure the inhumane crossing, over the next 50 years about a million Africans were forcefully relocated within North America to the west and south to work. By 1860 there were 380,000 slave-owners in the United States.

Slavery was finally outlawed in England in 1833, in France in 1848, the United States in 1865, Spain in 1886 and Brazil in 1888. The African slave trade officially ended in 1914.

SLAVE REVOLTS

Not all enslaved people suffered a fate of enforced servitude. Some fled their shackles or fought against their masters. Famously, the enslaved Roman gladiator Spartacus led a revolt in 73 BCE, leading an army possibly 90,000 strong before his death in battle two years later. His followers were crucified for their defiance. Many enslaved people died fighting slave traders before they were shipped away. The Stono Rebellion of 1739 saw a group of 20 enslaved men in South Carolina raid a warehouse for arms and head towards Florida and freedom. The uprising grew to more than 100 strong, but was put down in a week-long battle. Most survivors were executed. More successful were the Maroons in Jamaica, a group of unfree workers that escaped English sugar-cane plantations in 1728 to establish and defend their own community in the mountains. Maroon communities also succeeded in Brazil, Suriname, Puerto Rico and Cuba.

A 19th-century illustration of the Maroon War in Jamaica.

CAPITALISM AND CONFLICT

East India Company ships at Deptford, England, painted 1683.

Maritime trade from Europe to Asia and the Americas required huge investment. A new market in stocks and government-sponsored traders emerged, prepared to wage war in order to protect their interests.

Capitalism, private investment for profit as we understand it now, boomed from the 15th century as opportunities to back international trade increased. Competition between private business owners would become the principal economic system for the Western world.

Lending money with interest gained by the lender had existed on a small scale for centuries. The earning of interest on loans, known as usury, was considered a sin and was banned among Christians and Muslims. It was a practice that Jews were allowed to undertake, however, with certain restrictions imposed upon their activities. Jews often found themselves separated from other communities in the towns and cities in which they lived, sometimes forcibly so. The Jews of 16th-century Venice, Italy, for example, had to return by nightfall to a designated living area of the city called the ghetto.

Larger loans necessitated more than one source of finance. The opening up of the Americas and the exploitation of maritime routes to Asian markets required ships and crews to be financed, an expensive proposition. There were many risks for the investor in maritime trading. Ships could be wrecked, cargoes lost, stolen or ruined. Sea voyages were lengthy; it might be years before a return on any investment was earned – but when it did arrive, the profit margins were potentially huge.

Joint stock companies were created to provide capital for large investments. Individuals could buy stocks from these companies with the risk that their value could go up or down, dependent on the success of the company's ventures. The first joint stock company to be established was the Muscovy Company in England in 1555, for trade with Russia. This was followed by the English East India Company in 1600 and the Dutch East India Company (VOC), founded in 1602. The VOC had government approval and claimed the monopoly on Dutch trading in the East Indies.

ARMED TRADE

In order to protect and boost its shipments, the VOC employed soldiers and warships. With an advantage in fleet size and firepower, the Dutch captured trading routes and ports from the Portuguese, Spanish and British by force. Jakarta, in Java, was seized in 1619, followed by Malacca, in Malaysia, and Ceylon (Sri Lanka). The VOC now controlled highly lucrative spice- and textile-trading routes and was able to provide shareholders with an impressive annual dividend of 18 per cent.

Similar companies hurried to join the dash for cash. Joint stock companies opened in France, Scotland, Brazil, Senegal and Chile. Specialist brokers emerged, to help traders buy and sell stocks, for a commission. More and more enterprising souls found a way to profit from the emerging markets by taking a cut. In England, many of these stockbroking deals were settled in coffeehouses, in part because the traders' rowdy behaviour got them banned from London's Royal Exchange.

In 1530, a stock market opened in Amsterdam. In 16th-century Antwerp, Belgium, a building designed purely for trading was established. The Bourse became a major market for international traders and a symbol of European capitalism.

Competition between armed trading missions led to conflict between the English and Dutch, fighting over the Asian spice routes. England increased the size of its merchant and regular navy but over three wars lost out to the Netherlands. By 1669, the VOC was the richest company in the world, with over 150 merchant ships and 40 warships in its fleet, plus 50,000 employees, and a private army of 10,000 soldiers. This was more than a mere merchant enterprise.

European governments benefitted in allowing companies to expand their territory, while private investors took the financial risks. Both the Dutch and English kingdoms employed companies as privatized empire builders with huge consequences for the nations they traded with (page 166).

ITALIAN BANKERS

In the 14th century, coinage from around the world poured into Italy, providing opportunity for currency traders. Setting up stall in Florence in 1397, Giovanni di Bicci de' Medici came from a line of bankers. By 1420, success had allowed his family business to open branches in Venice, Rome, Pisa, Geneva, Avignon and London. Through meticulous bookkeeping and decentralization of their business, the Medici became the wealthiest family in Florence. Their wealth gave them power, while their investment in the arts helped stimulate the period known as the Renaissance (page 156).

Giovanni, Cosimo and Piero de' Medici, depicted in a 15th-century fresco by Benozzo Gozzoli.

SCIENTIFIC REVOLUTION

As well as a Renaissance in the arts, the 15th century delivered a rebirth in scientific enquiry inspired by Classical studies, advanced through observation and experimentation.

Prior to the 15th century, Greek and Roman ideas about the natural world were accepted as fact. Arabic scholars translated Classical theories and developed them, but it was not until the Renaissance that European minds began to properly test and expand on the original theses. The word 'science' was not in use at the time – the study of the natural world was called natural philosophy – but the period's questioning and revision of assumed learning was later described as a Scientific Revolution.

The work of the Polish astronomer Nicolaus Copernicus (1473–1543) did much to upset the apple cart. Scholars accepted the tenet of the 1st-century Greek astronomer Ptolemy that Earth lay at the centre of the universe and the heavens revolved around it. Copernicus' observations challenged this. In his book *On the Revolution of the Celestial Spheres*, published in the year of his death, Copernicus presented a heliocentric view, in which Earth and the five other known planets of the time orbited the sun. His theory outraged the Church, which decreed that the Ptolemaic arrangement of the cosmos was God's creation.

About 50 years later, in Germany, the astronomer Johannes Kepler (1571–1630) backed Copernicus' arguments. He inherited 40 years' worth of records from the Danish astronomer Tycho Brahe (1546–1601) and used them to calculate that the planets followed elliptical rather than circular orbits around the sun.

The Italian Galileo Galilei (1564–1642) also supported the Copernican view and faced the wrath of the Church head on. A keen mathematician and astronomer, Galileo used the newly invented telescope to observe sunspots and four moons orbiting the planet Jupiter. His published findings added more support to the heliocentric argument.

Galileo demonstrates his telescope in front of the Doge Leonardo Donà, in 1609.

For his troubles, Galileo was brought to trial before the papal court. He was forced to denounce the Copernican position and was placed under house arrest for the rest of his life. Both Galileo and Copernicus' works were placed on the Church's list of banned books (page 141). Despite the efforts of the clergy, the Copernican view of the cosmos would eventually be accepted. Galileo was finally pardoned centuries after his death, by Pope John Paul II in 1992.

THE EXPERIMENTERS

In the same year as Copernicus' volume, the Brussels-born anatomist Andreas Vesalius (1514–64) published his *De humani corporis fabrica* (*On the Fabric of the Human Body*), the result of his studies into human anatomy. Most academics followed the lessons of the 2nd-century CE Roman physician Galen, among others. Galen had made assumptions on how the human body worked based on his dissections of apes. At the University of Padua in Italy, Vesalius carefully studied and recorded the muscles, bones and organs of human corpses and corrected Galen's errors.

Another debunked theory of Galen's was the idea that blood in the human body rose and fell like tides. In 1628, the English royal physician William Harvey discovered that heart valves only opened one way, so that blood circulated in one direction around the body, with veins carrying blood to the heart, and arteries carrying it away.

This new wave of 'natural philosophers' had an enthusiasm for experimenting. Experiments confirmed or invalided theories and led to new discoveries. The English academic Francis Bacon (1561–1626) encouraged scholars to observe nature in this way rather than examine old texts, and to use their observations to come up with working theories.

This Scientific Revolution is considered to have ended with the English physicist Isaac Newton (1643–1727). His gravitational theories, that proposed that bodies in space maintained planetary orbits due to the same force that caused objects to fall to earth, were based on the research of both Galileo and Kepler but were no less groundbreaking. Newton also demonstrated how white light was made up of a spectrum, and his three laws of motion remain part of the school curriculum and applied engineering today.

The Scientific Revolution freed scholars from Classical theorizing and Church dogma and heralded a new age of intellectual investigation. It was but a beginning.

The English physicist Isaac Newton used a prism to disperse white light into a spectrum of colours.

SCIENCE SOCIETIES

Natural philosophers welcomed the opportunities to discuss their findings with peers. The first scientific society to publish details of its meetings was founded in Rome in 1610. The Accademia die Lincei (Academy of Lynxes) boasted Galileo among its members. In England, a group calling itself the 'Invisible College' met in private in London and Oxford. In 1660, it became the Royal Society for the Improvement of Natural Knowledge, today's Royal Society. The Society's alumni include the architect Christopher Wren, Isaac Newton, the naturalist Charles Darwin and the physicist Stephen Hawking. France's Royal Academy of Sciences opened its doors on 1666, and several other countries inaugurated similar institutions in the following years.

The entrance to the port of Marseilles, 1754.

CHAPTER 7
ENLIGHTENMENT AND IDEOLOGY

The movement away from superstition to natural philosophy or science continued into the 18th century. Through experiment, scholars challenged ideas that had been accepted for centuries. New ways of finding order in the natural world followed, while lengthy voyages of discovery revealed new animal and plant species, and led one naturalist to propose a groundbreaking theory of human evolution. Over-taxation, lack of representation and the exploitation of workers led to uprisings in France and the Americas. Republics arose with aspirations of liberty and equality. For Africa and India, such freedoms remained just a dream. European rulers carved up Africa's interior for its resources and labour force, while India was taken over by a British trading company. The Americas saw millions of Europeans arrive, while the mapping of a new continent in the southern hemisphere offered further opportunities for emigration. Migration was aided by advances in steam power and locomotion. These engineering innovations were part of an Industrial Revolution that would change working practices forever.

ENLIGHTENMENT

The late 17th and early 18th centuries saw an age of reason, with scientists and philosophers looking to improve society through investigation, without superstition or prejudice.

Seventeenth-century advances in science (page 158) had seen thinkers test Classical thought and provide new or more accurate ideas on how the natural world functioned. In the 18th century, philosophers seized these ideas and aspired to lead people away from superstitious beliefs to an awakening of inquiry and intellectual debate.

The German philosopher Immanuel Kant (1724–1804) coined the phrase that provided a name for this movement. 'What is Enlightenment?' he asked. His answer was, 'man's release from his self-incurred immaturity'. The challenge he set for scholars seeking enlightenment was to 'dare to know'.

Enlightenment scholars thought that humanity and God were basically good and should embrace life and serve society, and that a benevolent God had created the world to be appreciated by humankind. Isaac Newton was a religious man, yet his theories on optics, mechanics and gravity demonstrated that reason rather than theology could reveal the rules that governed the workings of the universe. While God could be accepted as a creator, the properties of the natural world could be fathomed by humanity.

In the coffee houses of London and the literary salons of Paris, thinkers met and discussed human freedoms, privilege and inequality. Their ideas were published and disseminated widely. Enlightenment ideas were shared between academic societies through the modern postal system, books and newspapers.

Enlightenment thought spread to other countries. In Russia and Austria, the ideas were appropriated

Louis XIV establishes the French Academy of Sciences.

by rulers who claimed to be tolerant to discourse but continued to wield dictatorial powers. The theories on governance and the rights to 'life, liberty and property' propounded by the English philosopher John Locke (1632–1704) influenced the contents of the 1776 Declaration of Independence in America and the French assertion of citizens' rights that motivated the French Revolution (page 169).

SPREAD OF IDEAS

This Enlightenment effort to find order in the natural world was most clearly expressed in the work of the Swedish botanist Carl von Line, known as Linnaeus (1707–78), who categorized Earth's plants and animals. At the same time, the British chemist Joseph Priestley (1733–1804) attempted to unlock the properties of air itself, discovering oxygen, while fellow chemist Joseph Black (1728–99) discovered carbon dioxide. Engineering advances during the period would lead to the Industrial Revolution (page 172).

The Enlightenment was not just a philosophical and scientific movement. Its ideas were applied to history and finance. Edward Gibbons' learned *Decline and Fall of the Roman Empire* (published 1776–89) was the result of his comprehensive gathering of records and opinions of the period. It described a Classical and rational empire replaced by the superstition of Christianity, something the Enlightenment had, in part, sought to reverse.

In finance, the Scottish economist Adam Smith (*c*.1723–90) wrote *The Wealth of Nations* (1776), in which he examined capitalism (page 154) and argued that private wealth and self-interest, along with supply and demand, would deliver a working economy for the benefit of all. His book remains a valued text for free-market advocates.

While, generally, the Enlightenment did not offer much equivalence for women, the feminist philosopher Mary Wollstonecraft was inspired by it to argue in her book *A Vindication of the Rights of Woman* (1792) for women to receive a rational education rather than one dominated by domestic classes.

The Enlightenment conviction that knowledge should come from empiricism would be followed up by the naturalists and scholars who joined voyages of discovery to formulate their own revolutionary theories in the following century.

A FONT OF KNOWLEDGE

The 28-volume *Encyclopédie* was an ambitious, secular effort to record all human knowledge, with theories and practices in philosophy, crafts and sciences. The series of books, published in France from 1751 to 1772, comprised 17 volumes of text, a total of 16,288 pages, plus another 11 books of engravings. The *Encyclopédie* was compiled by editors Denis Diderot (1713–84) and Jean-le-Rond d'Alembert (1717–83), with 150 contributors, including the philosophers Voltaire and Jean-Jacques Rousseau. Subjects covered included philosophy, science, architecture and the arts. It was banned on two occasions by the Church for its anti-Catholic content. Similar, if less monumental, encyclopedias were published around the same time in the Netherlands, Germany, Britain, Italy and Poland.

Illustration of a joiner's workshop from the Encyclopédie, *c.1751.*

NEW EMPIRES

The empires of Egypt, Rome, Persia and the Inca were long gone, but new powers in Europe and Asia were rising in the 18th century, battling over trade and expanding their territories overseas.

Wars in the 17th and 18th centuries were typically waged for commercial rather than religious reasons. The major powers of the day – France, England and the Netherlands – fought often, with the latter two at war three times between 1652 and 1674.

East of Europe, the Ottoman Empire (page 138) had avoided involvement in European wars, but had seen conflict on its borders with Russia. Russia was on its way to becoming one of the three largest empires on Earth. It had looked towards Europe in an effort to modernize under the rule of the tsar Peter the Great (1672–1725). Peter inherited an inefficient system from his predecessors, with an army that exhausted up to 96 per cent of the state's revenue. Through reorganization and new taxes, Peter financed a standing army of 300,000 recruits.

Success in a war against Sweden resulted in Russia's takeover of what are now Estonia and Latvia, giving the country access to the Baltic Sea. Tsar Peter commemorated victory by ordering the building of a new port on the site of a captured Swedish fortress. This involved the extensive use of serfs (page 122). Tens of thousands died erecting the city on marshland. Founded in 1703, Saint Petersburg was intended as a European-style capital.

Under the empress Catherine the Great (r. 1762–96) the Russian Empire expanded its borders even further, incorporating Siberia and a settlement on Kodiak Island in Alaska. The Crimea and Central Ukraine were also claimed, with the Ukrainian language and cultural identity suppressed by the new regime.

THE TAKING OF INDIA

Much of the Indian subcontinent had been ruled by the Muslim Mughals since the 16th century. The Mughal Empire is said to have been founded by Babur, a descendent of both Genghis Khan (page 118) and Timur (page 137) who led his army from Afghanistan to India. (Mughal is Persian for Mongol.) The empire had seen a blossoming of arts and architecture, particularly under the reign of Shah Jahan, who in 1631 ordered the construction of the Taj Mahal in Agra as a memorial to his deceased wife. Relative peace had allowed the empire to thrive, with major international trade in cotton textiles.

Britain was already established as a trading partner in India, via the East India Company, a trading corporation that had formed an army to protect and increase its interests. The British faced competition from France, which had also set up trading posts along the coast. Several wars, notably the Seven Years' War of 1756–63, saw the kingdoms face off in Europe, North America, Africa and India. In India, both Britain and France employed Indian soldiers, called sepoys, to fight their battles. Thousands would die waging war for the Europeans.

Britain's eventual victory in the Seven Years' War led to France losing all its claims on both North America and India. With France out of the game, the British East India Company could execute its plans to dominate Indian trade. Since the death of the emperor Aurangzeb in 1707, the Mughal Empire had been in decline, with regional leaders claiming independence, and some areas conquered by the Hindu Marathas. The company fought against the Marathas and became the protector of the emperor in Delhi, effectively taking over the northern capital. Despite Mughal attempts to reclaim power, the British Crown asserted control over the territories taken by the East India Company in 1858.

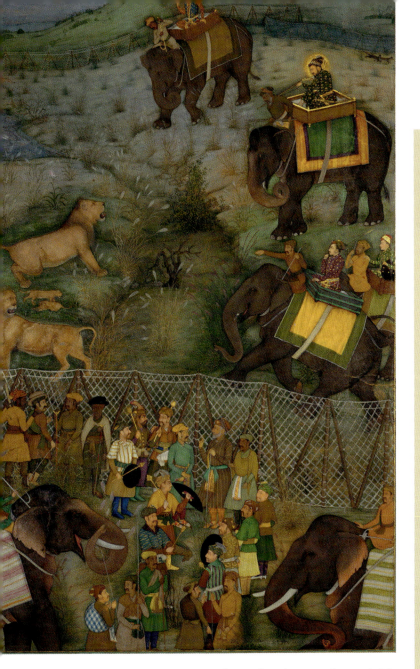

Shan Jahan hunting lions, 1630.

BEHIND CLOSED DOORS

While European countries fought to control trade routes and colonies, one country was enjoying an extended period of peace by cutting itself off from the rest of the world, albeit under a dictator. For centuries, Japan had been controlled by a series of military dictatorships known as shogunates. In 1603, after a long period of civil unrest and regional wars between feuding nobles, Tokugawa Ieyasu (1543–1616) established a new shogunate. From his castle in Edo (modern Tokyo), he exercised his power across the country, with local lords known as daimyos carrying out his commands.

For the next 200 years, the islands cut themselves off from foreign influence. Christianity and business with Western nations was banned. Japanese merchants were prohibited from foreign trade. Apart from a small Dutch-controlled port in Nagasaki, Japan only maintained relations with China and Korea. This Edo Period, or 'the Great Peace', saw society divided into four tiers, from samurai (warriors) to artisans, farmers and merchants, with no possibility of a person being able to change their status. Despite strict military control, Japan enjoyed a great cultural resurgence. Familiar Japanese traditions, such as the tea ceremony, haiku poetry, zen gardens, ceramics and noh theatre, flourished. Japan's isolation came to an end when US warships arrived and demanded the country open its ports in 1854. Trade with Britain, France, the Netherlands and Russia followed.

Shinagawa in the Edo Period, Japanese wood block print.

INSURRECTION AND INDEPENDENCE

Unfair taxes and lack of representation led to revolutions in France and the Americas from the late 18th century. Demand for equality and independence was rising.

Frustration with a lack of representation in government led to popular uprisings in both Europe and the Americas from the late 18th century. North America led the march, preparing a declaration of independence, one that would be mirrored in France and by rebels across the southern half of the Americas. These revolutions led to a swing away from the rule of hereditary kings and queens towards republics, with the common people given the opportunity to choose their leaders based on merit.

Wars between Britain and France from 1754–63 had resulted in North America wholly coming under British rule (the union of England with Scotland in 1707 had created a new state: the United Kingdom of Britain). To help cover the costs of the conflict, Britain threatened to raise taxes in its 13 American colonies, something that, unsurprisingly, did not go down well. Though the government backtracked and ultimately imposed only relatively low taxes on the colonists, the episode brought home to the Americans that they had

little or no say over Britain's policy-making, despite the taxes they paid the government in far away London. The colonists were also frustrated by an order from Britain not to extend their settlements west of the Appalachian Mountains. Grievances took a long time to be answered; it could take four months for a transatlantic communication to receive a response.

Finally, demanding there be 'no taxation without representation' in Britain's government, the Americans rebelled and began to boycott British goods. In one high-profile protest, in December 1773 a group of colonists disguised as Native Americans boarded ships in Boston Harbor and threw 342 chests of taxed East India Company tea overboard. In response to the so-called Boston Tea Party, the British introduced stricter measures and prohibitions on taxes and trade.

UNITED STATES

War finally broke out in 1775, when British forces tried to seize an arms cache in Concord, a small town outside Boston. They were held at bay by local militia. Led by a new commander, George Washington, the American troops were trained to fight as an army. On 4 July 1776, a committee of colonial leaders met in Philadelphia and

The Boston Tea Party.

The taking of the Bastille, 14 July 1789, by Jean-Baptiste Lallemand.

signed a document, the Declaration of Independence, expressing their aims (see panel on page 171). Not all Americans supported the fight for independence, however. Many remained loyal to the British and found themselves in conflict with their neighbours.

Both the Americans and the British made gains, with the British taking New York. In 1778, the French, who had been ousted from North America by the British, sided with the colonists. The war was effectively over by October 1781, when the British forces surrendered at Yorktown, Virginia, after an 18-day siege. American independence was officially agreed by treaty on 3 September 1783. George Washington was elected as the first president of the new United States. Four years later, a constitution was agreed in Philadelphia, followed by a Bill of Rights. While only 13 in number at this point, the United States of America was born.

Around 100,000 Americans who had remained loyal to Britain chose to leave the United States after the War of Independence, relocating to England, the West Indies or Canada, where what was previously a majority French-speaking country became one dominated by English speakers.

BIRTH OF A REPUBLIC

By the 1780s, France had lost much of its stake in both India and North America at a great cost (page 166). The burden of paying the country's debt was placed on the shoulders of the middle-class bourgeoisie and peasants. Despite almost 40 per cent of French land being owned by royalty and the clergy, the upper class avoided paying tax. Two years of poor harvests left many people struggling to eat. Attempts by King Louis XVI to reform the economy came to nothing. In 1789, the Third Estate, part of the legislative assembly representing the general public, broke away from the French parliament to form a new, separate National Assembly.

Parisians, frustrated with the king and his lack of reforms, stormed the city's Bastille prison to claim its weaponry. The revolt extended into the countryside, with peasants attacking the homes of their landlords. Hundreds of women marched 32 km (20 mi) from Paris to the king's palace at Versailles, enraged at the rising cost of bread. The National Assembly voted to end the feudalist system and published a declaration of its aims (see panel on page 171), including a new division of the country, army reform and the sale of church land.

The king and queen attempted to flee France in 1791, but they were arrested and returned to Paris as prisoners. In late 1792, France was declared a republic, and in January 1793 King Louis XVI was put to death using the guillotine, the new execution device of the revolution. With the threat of foreign invasion, revolutionary armies were recruited. Attempts at conscription were resisted in Brittany and the Vendée (western France) and revolutionary and counter-revolutionary forces fought across the country. Under the revolutionary committee leader Maximilien Robespierre, a Reign of Terror began, with a tribunal delivering instant justice to those who opposed its aims. More than 20,000 'counter-revolutionaries' were executed within ten months.

Sanity was restored in 1794. Robespierre was removed from power and executed. A less-violent administration came to power. Then, following two annulled elections, General Napoleon Bonaparte organized a coup and took power. He was crowned Emperor of France in 1804.

Both the United States and France had discarded monarchical rule in favour of a republic. Their aims were similar, in providing accountability of government and freedom for all. Central and South America were next to rise up, sharing the United States' objective of freeing themselves from the 'mother country'.

LATIN LIBERATION

Spain was in disarray at the beginning of the 19th century following war with Napoleon Bonaparte, when the Spanish king was taken hostage. Military forces in Spanish America tried to take advantage by claiming local control. The seeds of an independence movement were growing.

In 1810, in Mexico, American-born Spaniards sought to break the shackles of Spanish rule. Led by the radical priest Miguel Hidalgo y Costilla, an 80,000-strong army swept across the country, removing wealthy European landowners from their homes. Hidalgo was captured and killed in 1811, but his dream of Mexican independence was realized ten years later.

Two years after the death of Hidalgo, the aristocrat Simón Bolívar, known as *El Liberator* ('the Liberator'), led rebels against Spanish forces in Venezuela. His eventual success led to him being named president of an area encompassing Venezuela, Colombia, Panama and Ecuador. In 1817, in the south, a former Spanish general named José de San Martín led 5,000 soldiers from Argentina across the Andean mountains to attack loyalist forces in Chile. He then helped free Peru from Spanish rule.

Brazil gained its independence due to events in Europe. To escape capture by Napoleon Bonaparte, the Portuguese royal court fled to Rio de Janeiro in 1808. When the king returned to Portugal in 1821, his son Pedro was left in charge of Brazil and, by public demand, declared it independent a year later, with himself as emperor.

A banner carried by followers of Miguel Hidalgo showing the Virgin of Guadalupe, c.1810.

A portrait of Simón Bolívar.

DECLARATIONS

Both the North American colonists and the French Revolutionaries provided documents stating their aims. The American Declaration of Independence was compiled and signed by a five-man committee including Benjamin Franklin, and future presidents Thomas Jefferson and John Adams. It declared that 'We hold these truths to be self-evident, that all men are created equal, that they are endowed by their Creator with certain unalienable Rights, that among these are Life, Liberty and the pursuit of Happiness'. The declaration glossed over the rights of the enslaved. Thomas Jefferson held 200 enslaved workers on his lands. Only seven were freed. It would be another half century before this injustice was set right.

France's National Assembly, aiming to replace the royal regime of Louis XVI, published its Declaration of the Rights of Man and the Citizen in 1789. Inspired by the Enlightenment writings of John Locke and Jean-Jacques Rousseau (page 162), the declaration stated that all 'men are born and remain free with equal rights', and that it was the duty of a government to protect its citizens and their rights. The document was used as the basis of many other countries' constitutions and the United Nations' 1948 Declaration of Human Rights.

The American Declaration of Independence.

INDUSTRIAL REVOLUTION

The steam engine and the mechanization of industry turned formerly agricultural societies into cultures based around large urban developments.

New technology, fossil fuels and a thriving economy were the driving forces behind industrial progress in Europe and the United States from the late 18th century. An Industrial Revolution saw workers relocate from the fields to the cities and large factories accelerating the advance of urbanization.

Britain was best placed to take advantage of new factory technology, with vast seams of coal available, a booming economy, a large empire and international trade links. What it lacked was the ability to smelt iron in any great quantity. Iron production had required the burning of charcoal. Britain had limited timber, making charcoal an expensive resource. In 1709, an ironmaster named Abraham Darby began using coke, a derivative of coal, to smelt iron. His son and grandson, who shared his name, improved on the quality and quantity of production until their home in Shropshire, England, was producing more iron than anywhere else in the world. Iron was used to build frameworks for large factories, bridges and tracks for the steam railways from the early 19th century. The Iron Bridge built over the Severn river between 1777–79 became a symbol for the Industrial Revolution which the iron industry made possible.

Manchester from Kersal Moor *by Edward Goodall after an 1857 work by William Wyld.*

English cotton mill, from around 1835.

Powering the Industrial Revolution was the steam engine. Invented by the French engineer Denis Papin in 1682, it was repurposed by the British engineer Thomas Savery in 1698 for use in pumping water from mines. In 1712, Thomas Newcomen, a British ironmonger by trade, improved the technology to design an atmospheric steam engine for use in deep mine shafts. The Scottish inventor James Watt refined the steam engine further in 1776, and set up an engine-manufacturing business with Matthew Boulton. This led to the steam engine's widespread use in factories and mills, and for powering new steamships and locomotives (see panel on page 175).

FROM FARM TO FACTORY

One of the industries to benefit most from steam-powered mechanization was textile manufacture. The invention of mechanized power looms hugely increased production. The city of Manchester, at the heart of Britain's Lancashire textile industry, grew tenfold within the last 25 years of the 18th century, to accommodate new factories and workers. By 1784, Britain was producing over 7,000 tonnes (6,890 tons) of spun cotton, most of which was sourced from the United States, employing vast numbers of enslaved labourers as cotton pickers.

In 1707, unable to compete with high-quality and cheap Indian imports, Britain placed an embargo on Indian cotton. The Industrial Revolution had now turned the British production of cotton goods into a world-beater. India, once a hugely successful exporter of cotton textiles, saw its industry decline and workers returning to agriculture.

As a whole, Britain's population doubled in the first half of the 19th century. It was supported by new, higher-yielding crops and more efficient farming methods, such as the mechanical seed drill. In turn, the reduced need for farmers freed the workforce to take jobs in factories. The 1851 British census report showed that more Britons were living in cities than outside of them, making Britain one of the first countries to become urbanized.

The move to mechanization was not wholly welcomed. Weavers in the lace industry of the British Midlands found themselves unemployed as machines replaced their skills. From 1811, a group called the Luddites began smashing the machinery and factories they saw as the enemies of manual labour. The British government ordered their arrest. The gradual replacement of skilled workers with technology continues to the present day.

URBAN LIVING

With increased factory production came the need to improve transportation to markets. Road and waterway routes were improved and expanded. The invention of the steam-powered locomotive in 1804 (see panel) provided a new, faster and more economical vehicle. Rail transport demanded more iron for tracks. In 1830, there were just a few dozen kilometres of track in England. Ten years later, there were 37,000 km (23,000 mi), with Britain producing 1,134,000 tonnes (1,116,090 tons) of iron and 44 million tonnes (43.3 million tons) of coal annually.

British businesses existed mostly on a small scale prior to the Industrial Revolution, with workshops sited near rivers. The rivers moved water wheels for power and provided a medium for transporting goods. The use of steam engines to power machinery allowed factories to be built in towns and cities. Where once workers laboured in small, rural cottage industries, now they joined large teams where machinery was sited. Urban living and factory work did not improve the worker's lot, however. Many factories were noisy, dark and dirty places to work and wages were low. The speed of the Industrial Revolution, and lack of funding, meant workers had to squeeze into old, existing buildings, and endure cramped, often unsanitary conditions. Cheap child workers were also employed, crawling under dangerous machinery and cleaning fast-moving mechanisms with their tiny hands.

Gas lamps began lighting up factories from the early 19th century, replacing candles and oil lamps. Gas was produced in furnaces from coal, then purified before use, to be burnt behind glass. The invention of the gas lamp allowed factories to stay open for longer. The extended hours of operation meant factory owners could employ more than one shift of workers. Instead of one worker toiling for up to 14 hours a day, two workers might work a 12-hour shift each in a factory that never closed. Outside of the workplace, gas lighting provided better-lit streets in cities and towns.

Gas lamps in Paris, 1850s.

SPREAD OF INDUSTRY

Beyond Britain, the Industrial Revolution was a little slower to take off. The textile industry of the future Czech Republic took advantage of mechanization from the start of the 19th century. Belgium founded numerous mills and iron foundries within reach of its coal mines in the south from the 1820s. Industrialization spread in France from about 1815.

The Blackstone River joining Worcester, Massachusetts, to Providence, Rhode Island, is considered the birthplace of the Industrial Revolution in the United States, with over 1,000 mills opened along its banks from 1790. Vast distances across North America were criss-crossed in the 19th century, with 48,200 km (30,000 mi) of railroad track laid by 1860.

While industrialization created booming economies and established a wealthy class of non-aristocratic proprietors, factory conditions and increased urban living would lead to demands for better sanitation and protection for workers, including the formation of workers' unions.

RAIL NETWORKS

The steam-driven railway was first demonstrated in 1804 by the engineer Richard Trevithick to carry a 10-ton load of coal from the Penydarren Ironworks to the Glamorganshire Canal, in Wales. The potential of the technology to carry passengers was realized in 1825 with the opening of a rail line between Stockton and Darlington in England's North East. By 1850, 10,000 km (6,215 mi) of iron track had been laid across Britain. 'Iron horse' locomotives could reach speeds of 65 kph (40 mph).

Belgium became a hub for pan-European rail transport after completing its first cross-country line in 1835, by which time most Western European countries had a rail network in progress. By the beginning of the 20th century it was possible to cross Eurasia by steam-driven locomotive on epic routes such as the Orient Express and the Trans-Siberian Railway.

American-designed locomotives began to link the east coast of the United States with the Midwest by the 1840s. By 1869, the east and west coasts were united by the joining of the Union Pacific and Central Pacific lines. The British takeover of India (page 166) led to an extensive rail-building programme, with passenger trains running from 1845. North Africa saw its first railways in the 1850s and in the south by 1862. Within decades, countries were bisected by tracks. The speed and cost of transporting materials was cut in half. Rail transport helped drive the success of the Industrial Revolution and open up markets for trade and tourism.

Robert Stephenson's Rocket, *the 1829 winning design for a steam-powered engine to run on the Liverpool–Manchester railway.*

SOCIALISM AND COMMUNISM

Industrialization delivered huge profits to factory owners, but the workers who toiled for hours in poor conditions saw little gain. New political movements sought to create a better balance.

Modern socialism, the idea that the means of wealth production should be community-owned, sprang from the Industrial Revolution (page 172), which had benefitted factory owners at the expense of workers. Large factories with machinery, operated by low-paid workers, provided great profits for the proprietors, who could keep production running for longer and increase output. The system created a new middle class of clerks, foremen and engineers, who could afford to live comfortably. In contrast, non-managerial factory workers often faced long hours in unhealthy working conditions, with poor housing to return to. The situation did not go unnoticed. The issue of child labour, in particular, was addressed in 1833 and 1844 with government acts that banned the employment of children under the age of nine and insisted on some schooling.

Socialist solutions to this inequality included taxation of the wealthy to fund social support for the poor, and the common ownership of land. Collective ownership of property was suggested by the early

Robert Owen's plan for a co-operative community in New Harmony, USA.

Protest against the deportation of the Tolpuddle Martyrs in London, 1834.

19th-century Welsh industrialist Robert Owen, who envisioned utopian socialism, an ideal society where safe housing, child care and schooling were provided for workers. He put these ideals into practice by building a model community for his workers around his cotton mill in New Lanark, Scotland. He guaranteed his workers an eight-hour working day (his aim was to encourage eight hours of labour, eight hours of recreation and eight hours of rest), plus sick pay. In 1825, he set about building a community called New Harmony, in Indiana, USA, with communal facilities, including a library, drama club and school. The town gained a thousand residents but proved to be an economic failure.

UNIONISM

With large groups of workers placed in factories, collective bargaining for better wages and conditions became possible through trade or labour unions. While workers' strikes had taken place in the past, trade unions were outlawed in Britain until 1825. When they were permitted, there were strict limitations on what they could do. In 1834, a group of farmhands working in Tolpuddle, near Dorchester, Dorset, attempted a strike and downed tools to protest at their wages being cut. There was no negotiation. They were arrested and shipped to Australia. For their sacrifice in support of workers' rights, they were called the Tolpuddle Martyrs. (After major protests they were allowed to return home two years later.)

Fee-paying unions arrived in the 1830s with the Amalgamated Society of Engineers, Machinists, Millwrights and Patternmakers, who, for an annual fee from workers, negotiated with bosses and administered sick pay, pensions and burial benefits. After several attempts to place working-class representatives in existing parliamentary parties, the unions launched their own political organization, the Scottish Labour Party.

Unionism in France was far more problematic. An 1834 Combination Law banned associations with more than five members. Strikes did take place, but not all succeeded in their aims. Some protests led to violent confrontations. It was 1864 before France had unions in place. Germany followed five years later. By the end of the century, most European countries had a functioning labour movement.

Influential labour unions formed in the United States, too, while in Australia action by building workers' unions managed to win a reduction of daily working hours in 1856, down to eight from 12 or even 14 hours, an arrangement soon followed by other industries.

THE COMMUNIST MANIFESTO

The cotton mills in and around Manchester were the heart of the British Industrial Revolution. In 1842, it seemed the perfect place for Friedrich Engels, the son of a wealthy German mill owner, to be sent to learn the trade. But Engels was more interested in the plight of the workers than his father's business. In 1845, he published his investigations in *The Condition of the Working Class in England*. The book cast a light on the inequalities between the factory workers and their bosses, and the squalid living conditions of the labour force.

Engels knew and supported another writer interested in the proletariat. Karl Marx was a history and philosophy graduate and editor of political newspapers. With his wages from the cotton-mill industry, Engels supported Marx while they both worked on ideas that would introduce a new and hugely influential political philosophy: communism. In

Karl Marx.

The Communist Manifesto (1848), the pair described a series of class struggles that would ultimately end the capitalist system (page 154), with the abolition of private land and business ownership, and the fair distribution of trade profits. Its famous call to action read, 'Workers of all lands unite! You have nothing to lose but your chains! You have a world to win!'

Marx believed a communist society would only come to fruition through a violent uprising. This would prove prophetic for those countries that adopted this system of governance over the next century. *The Communist Manifesto* did not create great waves on its publication but Engels continued to support Marx as he began work on his next project, *Das Capital*. The three-volume work, which furthered Marx's criticism of capitalism, raised interest in Germany, Russia and France.

Marx's perception of capitalism as doomed did not prove to be the case, but his theories had a huge impact on societies in Europe and Asia. His political ideas inspired revolutionary movements around the world and influenced the communist regimes that took power in Russia and China in the 20th century, though both would eventually adopt a capitalist economy.

COMMUNARDS

Following defeat against Germany in the Franco-Prussian War of 1870–71, the National Guard, who had defended Paris, took control of the capital. Among the soldiers were many who agreed with socialist, communist, feminist and anarchist thought. During their power grab they attempted to introduce a string of policies that could be considered socialist. These included a minimum wage, the separation of Church and state and the abolition of child labour. The Paris Commune, as it is called, was removed from power by the French National Army after just two months. Five to seven thousand Communards were killed in the fighting or executed. Thousands more supporters were sent to penal colonies.

Communard barricade at the Rue des Amandiers, Paris, 1871.

MODERN MIGRATION

The second half of the 19th century saw mass migration across the oceans, mostly for economic reasons. People left their homelands for work opportunities and for cheap land abroad.

In the second half of the 19th century thanks to a greater supply of food, the population in Europe had risen from around 110 million to 350 million, putting pressure on the labour market and housing. Many rural workers had relocated to take employment in city factories during the Industrial Revolution (page 172). Now, people were looking beyond their country's borders for land and work opportunities.

The advent of steamship travel and the opening up of foreign countries to immigration persuaded many people to find a new life abroad. Cheaper, faster sailings also allowed produce to cross oceans and be sold cheaply. European farmers' prices were undercut by imports from the Americas and Australia, compelling more people to head to where work was plentiful and land was cheap. The most popular destination for a fresh start was the United States, which by the early 20th century had amassed a population of more than 100 million people.

Between 1815 and 1914, around 60 million Europeans left home, over half of them making their way to North America, including 5 million from Britain. A further 10 million, mostly from Spain, Portugal and Italy, headed to South America. Russia also saw a large movement of its population, with 4–5 million people migrating east to Siberia as it became part of the expanding Russian Empire.

One of the greatest exoduses was from Ireland. The country had suffered a terrible famine during the 1840s, resulting in about 1 million deaths. Another 2 million left the country, leaving Ireland with a much-reduced population. The United States took in more than 3 million Irish between 1848 and 1921.

Immigrants arriving in New York City, 1887.

A Chinese dragon for a parade in Los Angeles, c.1900.

Since the very first settler crossings in the early 17th century, North America had been regarded as a destination offering freedom from religious and political persecution. At the expense of Native Americans, it also offered vast tracts of land for farming. The arrival of the railroad had opened up the continent and the US Congress agreed the Homeland Act in 1862, which allowed settlers to fence off land for farming in the Midwest. More than 1 million Germans relocated to the United States within the next decade. Millions more followed. Short of farming land at home, hundreds of thousands of Scandinavians sailed to the New World, too.

CULTURAL DIVERSITY

While Europeans arrived on the east coast of the United States, migrants from Asia arrived on the west coast. Many Chinese based themselves in California, following news of a gold rush. Chinese restaurants were already well established in California by 1850. An economic slump in the 1870s resulted in European immigrants and Chinese competing for the same jobs. There was a rise in tension and racial discrimination; Americans blamed the Chinese immigrants for bringing down wages. In 1882, the US Congress passed a law ending Chinese immigration. Restrictions lasted for almost a century.

Many people emigrated for work opportunities. Tens of millions of Indian workers sought employment in the mines, and on plantations in the British colonies of Malaysia, Ceylon, Burma, Trinidad and South Africa. A possible 15 million Chinese toiled in Malayan tin mines and rubber plantations or helped lay the track for the Pacific Coast Railroad in the United States.

People also departed their homelands to escape religious persecution. More than 2.5 million Jews left Eastern Europe to settle in America. Most took residence in cities, where they retained much of their cultural identity. Emigrants often lived close together and held onto their language and culture. Thirty thousand Germans moved to an area described as Over-the-Rhine in 1848, creating a singular Germanic neighbourhood in Ohio. The mass migrations of the late 19th century not only provided a willing workforce for foreign factories and fields, they also added diversity to the countries that became new homelands.

STATUE OF LIBERTY

Designed in France as a gift to the American republic, then assembled in New York City in 1886, the Statue of Liberty was one of the first sights immigrants saw when they arrived in North America; it was placed on Bedloe's Island beside the immigration centre on Ellis Island. A plaque on its pedestal quotes the poem 'The New Colossus' by Emma Lazarus, suggesting a welcome for the tide of hopeful arrivals: 'Give me your tired, your poor, your huddled masses yearning to breathe free, the wretched refuse of your teeming shore.'

DIVISION OF AFRICA

In the late 19th century, European powers set their sights on the interior of Africa. They divided the continent between them, regardless of the wishes of the native people.

The coast of Africa was dotted with European trading posts at the end of the 19th century, providing elephant ivory, palm oil, cocoa, tin and tea for European markets. The slave trade (page 152) had been outlawed by Britain in 1833 and the United States in 1865, but Africans were still being sold by the Arabic Swahili people and the Portuguese.

North Africa and its coastline were familiar to Europeans, but the heart of the continent was only beginning to be mapped. The use of quinine in combatting malaria allowed intrepid European explorers to investigate inland. The 1850s and 1860s saw Richard Burton, James Grant and John Speke survey the African interior and chart the courses of the Nile, Niger, Congo and Zambezi rivers. The Scottish missionary David Livingstone, attempting to locate the source of the Nile, was tracked down by the American journalist Henry Morton Stanley in 1871, generating much publicity. European nations were becoming aware of what Africa offered and they wanted a slice.

In 1875, parts of Africa were already under European control. France claimed Algeria, Portugal controlled Angola, while what would become South Africa was fought over by Britain and the Boers, who were Afrikaners of Dutch origin. The centre of the territory was in disarray, in part due to Shaka, the king of the Zulus, leading an army to expand a kingdom that would become KwaZulu-Natal (see panel). The country was vulnerable to exploitation.

In 1884, the German Chancellor Otto von Bismarck led a conference between European leaders to divide what had not already been claimed of Africa. No African leaders were invited or considered. The European nations claimed areas they already had a stake in or negotiated for control with local rulers. Germany grabbed Togo, Cameroon, and southwest Africa; France and Britain shared West Africa; Portugal took Mozambique; Belgium took the Congo, with help from Henry Morton Stanley, who secured the land on behalf of the Belgian king. Within just 20 years, Africa's many kingdoms were absorbed into 40 states, 36 of them European-controlled. From 10 per cent in 1870, almost all of the continent was in European hands by 1914, with only Ethiopia and Liberia remaining independent.

The Berlin Conference of 1884–85 saw European powers make claims on almost all of Africa.

DIAMONDS AND RUBBER

Some lands were taken by bargaining with local leaders; some were taken by force. The result was that Africa's resources were exported for profit while Africans were exploited as workers in mines or plantations. The southern Cape had a similar climate to Europe, enabling farmers to plant the same crops as in their home nations and raise the livestock they were familiar with. The most fertile land was reserved for the new rulers. Africans were moved aside, taxed and given little say in how their land was run.

The British entrepreneur Cecil Rhodes acquired all the diamond mines in southern Africa and had ambitions to build a white-ruled land from the Cape to Egypt, with a train line linking south to north. This failed to come to pass due to rival European territorial claims, but he did make his mark on the map by naming the country of Rhodesia after himself.

Just as the East India Company had operated as traders with an army, Rhodes' British South Africa Company employed troops to get its way. His soldiers were armed with the Maxim gun, a newly invented mounted machine gun that could fire 500 rounds a minute and mow down fields of spear-carrying natives, as it did with the central African Matabele tribe.

King Leopold II of Belgium was quick to build a railway through his newly acquired state. Africans were put to work laying the tracks. From a workforce of 2,000, an average of 150 labourers died each month. Huge profits were made for Belgium from the sale of wild rubber, with 6,000 tonnes (5,905 tons) exported by the beginning of the 20th century. Rubber was increasingly in demand following the invention of the pneumatic tyre for bicycles and motor cars. Companies operating in the Congo used force to compel villagers to collect the rubber from wild vines. Reports of human-rights abuses reached Europe in the 1890s and the Congo was taken from King Leopold's hands in 1908 and turned into a Belgian colony. Conditions for workers improved somewhat as a result.

African resistance against colonial rule was violently crushed by the new European rulers, but it

Rubber tapping in the Congo Free State.

would not be beaten. The 20th century would see resistance movements erupt in Namibia and German East Africa. Self-rule would, in time, return.

ZULU RESISTANCE

European designs on Africa faced much resistance from the armies of the Zulu kingdom. Led by Shaka, the Zulu inhabited southeastern Africa and could raise a disciplined army of 10–15,000 men. Shaka led his soldiers to take neighbouring Nguri villages, building a large territory in the south and along the coast. Under Shaka and his successors, the Zulu army's warriors, carrying just spears and shields, were capable of inflicting major defeats on the British and the Boers. Ultimately, though, they were no match for the firepower of large European armies.

A photograph of Zulu warriors depicted in 1875.

WOMEN'S EMANCIPATION

Women were not permitted to take part in government elections in the late 19th century. It took years of protest and pressure to bring about equality.

Traditionally, men left home to work in fields or factories while their wives juggled household management and child rearing. In rural communities, women shared farm work or supplemented the home income by weaving or knitting. Unmarried women would also take jobs, often as domestic servants. Generally, though, it was the man who collected wages and a woman's labour, paid or unpaid, was overlooked. Women typically married in their mid-20s, usually to a man some years older who could prove his ability to earn enough to support a family.

The Industrial Revolution (page 172) led to many families relocating to cities, moving into often cramped conditions. Men, women and even children commuted to work in the factories. Mechanization meant nimble fingers were more in demand than physical strength, but women were nevertheless paid less than their male co-workers (children even less). The lower rate for women affected male workers, who found their wages pushed down or their jobs taken by cheaper female staff.

Public outcry over the exploitation of children led to new laws being introduced, restricting child labour until the age of 12 or 13. Compulsory free education was implemented. While this improved the lot of the young, it meant parents had more responsibility for their early care and could not expect their children to bring in extra income. From about 1870, the birth rate fell in urbanized Western countries as families decided to have fewer children.

In the late 19th century, new employment opportunities in office and shop work became available for women. Around 174,000 female shop assistants were employed in Germany by 1907 and, thanks in part to the introduction of the typewriter, women could apply for 146,000 jobs as office clerks in Britain. While women were gaining a higher profile in the workplace, they were disregarded when it came to politics.

Early 20th-century workers in a spinning mill in Ghent, Belgium.

SUFFRAGE

Votes for Women demonstration in Hyde Park, London, 1908.

Women had been active in protests for decades, including the 1789 march over bread prices in France (page 169) and in temperance movements on both sides of the Atlantic. An early attempt to debate equality for women took place at the 1848 Women's Rights Convention in Seneca Falls, New York, where more than 300 women and men met to discuss women's legal rights and how to bring about change.

A suffrage movement, seeking the vote for women, along with equal rights and pay, materialized in France in 1876. Led by Hubertine Auclert, the movement prompted many large marches and protests, raising 6,000 supporters, but failed to change government policy. German and Russian feminist movements were similarly thwarted. The British suffragettes (see panel) gained much more public support due to or despite their occasionally violent demonstrations, but they failed to get much sympathy from government.

The British colony of New Zealand allowed women to vote in elections from 1893, followed by the Cook Islands and South Australia. In Europe, the first state to introduce women's suffrage was Finland in 1907. The result was the election of 19 women to parliament. Finland's move was followed by Norway, Denmark, Russia, Germany and Poland.

Having proved themselves throughout World War I as more than able to manage jobs usually given to men, women (over 30 years old) were finally given the vote in Britain in 1918. (The age limit was changed to 21 and above in 1928.) The US Congress provided a legal right for women to vote in 1920. Among the last Western countries to give women the vote was France, in 1944.

SUFFRAGETTES

In early 20th-century Britain, demands that women be allowed to vote in government elections were continually blocked. Frustrated at the lack of equality, women began a series of protests and gained a lot of support. Even so, their aims were ignored by those in power. The women, who became known as the suffragettes, tried more disruptive methods, including vandalism, chaining themselves to railings and leaving messages in acid on golf courses. Many, including their leader, Emmeline Pankhurst (1858–1928), were arrested, which led to more publicity for their cause. One protestor, Emily Wilding Davison, died after being trampled by a horse when she tried to interrupt the running of the 1913 Derby.

RAF bombers on a mission in September 1942.

CHAPTER 8

WORLD WARS, NEW FRONTIERS

The dawn of the 20th century saw two major dynasties toppled, in Russia and China. Both would eventually be replaced by communist regimes. Borders crumbled across Europe as countries united to battle other allied nations for supremacy or liberty. The conflicts spread to European colonies, turning battles on a continent into world wars that impacted citizens as well as soldiers, and introduced devastating new weapons to the planet.

The world wars seriously weakened the European powers, militarily and financially. Unable to support empires, and facing organized protests, they withdrew from their colonies and supported independence movements.

The postwar world order saw two major superpowers face off – the democratic, capitalist United States and the Union of Soviet Socialist Republics. Their Cold War involved military shows of strength, political disputes and espionage. The rivals backed foreign regimes to prevent each other gaining dominance. The propaganda battle extended beyond Earth, too, as the first space flights launched and the race was on to reach the moon.

More down-to-earth breakthroughs saw human life expectancy extended by vaccines and improved healthcare, successful civil-rights movements and new major players stepping on to the world stage – the oil-rich Gulf states.

THE FALL OF DYNASTIES

The onset of the 20th century saw the end of two major dynasties in Eurasia, as revolution in Russia removed the Romanovs from power and civil unrest turned China into a republic.

The House of Romanov led Russia as virtual autocrats for 300 years and survived several wars and revolutions. Under Peter the Great and Catherine the Great, in particular, Russia had grown in scale to become an empire extending from Siberia to the Black Sea (page 166), with a new capital, St Petersburg, raised from swamplands. But Russia had also generated mass poverty. The country was slow to adopt industrialization. Eighty per cent of the population lived as peasants, most working the land.

Inspired by the words of Karl Marx (page 178), the workers began mobilizing. The Russian Social Democratic Labour Party formed in 1898. In 1902, the party split into two factions – the Bolsheviks, led by Vladimir Ilyich Lenin (1870–1924), who believed change would only come through violent revolution, and the more moderate Mensheviks.

Protests over pay and working conditions erupted in Petrograd (the renamed St Petersburg) in 1905. A crowd of 150,000 marched to petition Tsar Nicholas II at his Winter Palace, but many were brutally cut down by the Imperial Guard. Despite the threat of reprisals, protests continued, and the tsar even faced mutinies from his navy. The tsar gave in to pressure and introduced a new constitution and an elected parliament, called the Duma, over which he retained much control. His grip was weakened, however, during World War I (page 190). Losses on the battlefield against Germany were followed by inflation and food shortages. In 1917, Nicholas II was forced to abdicate.

With the rallying call of 'peace, land and bread', Lenin's army of Bolsheviks took advantage of a weakened government and, with huge support from impoverished workers, took power in a bloodless coup in Petrograd in 1917. Lenin announced plans to hand Church- and aristocracy-owned land and private industry over to the people. Nicholas II and his family were removed from house arrest and shot in 1918.

Following a civil war, Lenin's Bolsheviks became the Communist Party. They banned rival political parties and renamed the country the Union of Soviet Socialist Republics (USSR) in 1922, having joined forces with the neighbouring states of Byelorussia (as Belarus was then called), Transcaucasia (modern Armenia, Azerbaijan and Georgia) and Ukraine. Other countries in the region would be brought into the USSR over the next decades. Lenin survived for just two more years.

His successor, Joseph Stalin, would successfully force through the mass industrialization of the country and introduced large-scale collectivized farms – an ultimately disastrous policy that led to widespread starvation. Stalin ruled through fear; any opposition was crushed. Millions of people were executed or sent to labour camps during his regime.

The May Day celebration in Isaakievskii Square, St Petersburg, 1917.

THE LAST EMPEROR

China's Qing Dynasty had been in power since 1644. It had pushed back against attacks by Imperial Russia and survived several internal rebellions. Improved agricultural practices over the centuries and disease prevention led to a huge population rise.

Trade with Britain was strong in the 18th century, with tea a major export, in exchange for silver. The British also imported opium from India. Its soporific and highly addictive qualities led to it becoming popular in China. When the Chinese government banned its import this led to two wars with Britain. Overwhelmed by Britain's more powerful navy, China was forced to continue trading in the drug and had to relinquish the island of Hong Kong as compensation. In the mid-19th century, the dynasty was seriously threatened by the Taiping Rebellion, a civil war with a rival Chinese state. Over 14 years of conflict, between 20 and 30 million people died.

The end of the 19th century saw a much-weakened China. The Qing dynasty lost the Sino-Japanese War of 1895, ceding Taiwan and much of Korea to Japan. The British, French, Russians, Germans and Italians between them controlled more than 80 of China's ports with 99-year leases. The Boxer Rebellion in 1900 saw peasants rise up against foreign interference. The rebellion was crushed but the end was in sight for the Qing.

The dynasty tried modernizing its education system, industry, military and laws, but it was too little too late. In 1911, the Nationalist Party of China led by the Western-educated Sun Yat-sen led an uprising, aided by Qing soldiers, and the dynasty was forced to accept defeat. China became a republic. The last emperor, Puyi, aged just six, formally gave up the throne in 1912, ending more than 1,000 years of dynastic rule in China.

Aisin-Gioro Puyi (1906–67), right, was the last emperor of China. He gave up the throne aged six, in 1912.

THE EMPRESS DOWAGER

For 47 years, from 1861 China was effectively ruled by women. Empress Dowager Cixi was a former concubine and the mother of the imperial heir, who was aged just five when he took the throne (which he held until 1875, when he died aged 19). She took part in a coup to ensure that she and the previous emperor's widow, Ci'an, became regents. On Ci'an's death in 1881, Cixi became sole ruler and remained the power behind the throne until her death. In 1898, she prevented her nephew, the emperor Guangxi, from pursuing a reform programme and had his supporters executed, but she would later initiate her own modernizing scheme. Cixi died in 1908, just one day after the emperor Guangxi, whom she is suspected of having poisoned. The empress dowager's reputation has since swung between that of a scheming tyrant and one of a wrongly maligned woman who sought to defend China against foreign influence.

WORLD WARS

The first half of the 20th century saw major conflict spread from Europe across the world. The two world wars spawned new lethal technological and chemical weapons along with an extreme nationalist ideology.

European powers had established colonies and extended their empires across the globe. When conflict broke out in Europe, these territories and other allies were drawn in and local battles became world wars. With new, deadly technology and ideologues involved, the results were catastrophic, with millions of citizens and troops killed, cities razed and the genocide of ethnic groups. Huge sacrifices were made in defence of freedom.

Towards the end of the 19th century, two large alliances had formed in Europe. Germany, twinned with Austria-Hungary, was gaining both industrial and military strength. France, Britain and Russia forged a union and made preparations for potential German hostility. A spark was lit in 1914.

On 28 June, Archduke Franz Ferdinand, heir to the throne of Austria-Hungary, was assassinated alongside his wife by a Serbian nationalist in Sarajevo, Bosnia. Austria-Hungary accused the Serbian government of involvement and, with German support, demanded that Serbia root out anti-Austrian terrorists. Serbia made compromises but it was not enough. A month after the assassination, Austria-Hungary declared war on Serbia. Allies took sides. Russia backed Serbia; Germany declared war on Russia, then its ally, France. When Belgium became threatened by the advances of the Germany army, Britain was compelled to give support. Within five weeks of the archduke's assassination, six European countries were facing each other across the battlefield. This was the beginning of the Great War, a conflict expected to end within weeks. It lasted four years.

For much of the war, the British/French/Belgian alliance and the Germans were bogged down in trenches along a Western Front that stretched from Switzerland to the English Channel. Advances came at a huge cost of life. In 1916, on the first day of the Battle of the Somme, in France, 57,470 British soldiers were killed or injured. The battle resulted in 750,000 French and German casualties.

In the east, the German assault on Russia was more dynamic, with substantial advances and retreats. In late 1914, the Ottoman Empire allied with Germany, followed by Bulgaria in 1915. The war spread to the European colonies, with Britain and France occupying German-ruled territory in Africa and the Pacific. Britain was joined by troops from the empire, including Indians, Australians, New Zealanders, South Africans

British soldiers in a trench during the Great War.

Women working in a munitions factory during World War II.

and Irish. Japan took over German colonies in China and the western Pacific. After German threats against its shipping, the United States joined the war in April 1917. While conflicts had crossed continents before, notably the Seven Years War (1756–63) between Britain and France, no war had taken place on such an international scale.

The conflict also introduced new ways of waging war, including poison gas deployed by the Germans. Such was the revulsion at its use that chemical weapons were later banned in the Geneva Convention of 1925. (All sides honoured this pledge on the battlefield in World War II, though not in the Nazi extermination camps.) An armoured caterpillar-tracked vehicle called a tank was also tested in the field, along with airships and aeroplanes for aerial reconnaissance and bombardment. In the oceans, submarines threatened shipping.

British poison gas casualties awaiting treatment after an attack in April 1918.

Russia's Bolshevik regime (page 188) signed a peace treaty with Germany in March 1918, allowing Germany to focus all of its attention on the Western Front. But poor supply lines and massive resistance from the British, French and US forced Germany to retreat to Belgium. Austro-Hungarian losses to Italy led to that state's withdrawal from the conflict. A German naval mutiny was the last straw for the beleaguered German Kaiser Wilhelm II. His abdication was followed by the signing of an armistice by the new government. The war ended on 11 November 1918.

THE HOME FRONT

During World War I, while men were sent into battle abroad, women took on their roles back home, as assembly workers in munitions factories, as drivers, journalists and managers. After the war, it was difficult to persuade women to relinquish the jobs they had proven more than able to accomplish. In 1918, women in Britain were finally given the right to vote in elections (page 184). In World War II, 640,000 women were recruited to the British Royal Naval Service and Auxiliary Air Force, and tens of thousands became Land Girls, living and working on farms.

REPARATIONS

Food and fuel shortages in Germany contributed to its defeat in the Great War, which we now call World War I. Reparations pushed the country towards further strife. A treaty signed in Versailles in June 1919 forced Germany to accept responsibility for the conflict, to pay huge war damages and hand over all of its overseas possessions, including Tanganyika (Tanzania), Southwest Africa (Namibia) and several Pacific islands. The treaty led to the map of Europe being redrawn. The union of Germany and Austria was disallowed; France reclaimed Alsace-Lorraine; Poland gained part of West Prussia; Czechoslovakia and Yugoslavia were born; Poland regained independence; Germany's ally, the Ottoman Empire, forfeited land which became Syria, Lebanon, Palestine and Iraq. To foster worldwide peace, the League of Nations was founded in 1920. This intergovernmental organization was eventually replaced by the United Nations.

Germany's army, having not surrendered on the battlefield, felt betrayed by the Treaty of Versailles. In 1921, Adolf Hitler, the leader of the National Socialist Party, sought to take advantage of his country's discontent by attempting a coup. His early efforts to lead anti-government rallies drew little support; the German economy was in recovery and all seemed well. Then, in 1929, America's stock markets crashed, leading to an international financial depression. US banks called in their loans to Germany, almost bankrupting the country. Economic collapse and weak government led German voters to back a party that offered scapegoats, simple solutions and promised the return of national pride. By January 1933, Hitler's National Socialist (Nazi) Party had taken the most seats in the German parliament and Adolf Hitler had been appointed chancellor.

Months later, Germany's parliament building, the Reichstag, was set on fire. Hitler used it as a pretext to ban opposition parties. Following the death of the German president Paul von Hindenburg a year later, Hitler claimed dictatorial powers. The unemployed were forced to work on large infrastructure projects, and the economy recovered. Life had improved for many Germans but they were now ruled by a nationalist government led by a *führer* with ruthless ambition and a racist ideology, spreading messages of hate against Jews and communists.

British soldiers, Catania, Sicily, August 1943.

WORLD WAR II

In 1936, fascist-run Italy and Japan signed pacts with Germany. The League of Nations failed to act when Hitler began rearming and broke the Treaty of Versailles by annexing Austria in 1938. Germany invaded Czechoslovakia in early 1939, then Poland in September. Having sworn to defend Poland's independence, Britain and France were moved to declare war on Germany, but it was too late for Poland; Hitler had struck a non-aggression pact with Soviet General Secretary Stalin that divided the country between Germany and the USSR.

The 20 years following World War I had resulted in many advances in military technology. Soldiers could communicate more easily via radio. Vehicles were faster and more capable. In 1944, rocket-powered missiles could be fired from the Continent to Britain. Hitler's army was able to take over several countries before a strong defence could be mustered. Poland's

A colourized photo of two German soldiers during the Battle of Stalingrad.

air force was destroyed on the first day of the invasion, its army defeated in just five weeks.

Within three months, German forces had overrun Scandinavia, Belgium, the Netherlands and France, and was demanding that Britain surrender. Britain refused and a wave of air raids was ordered. More than 13,000 Londoners died in the Blitz. This was total war. Countries mobilized all the resources they could afford towards their war aims. Both military and civil resources were legitimate targets. Of the 70 to 85 million that would become casualties of the war, the majority were civilians, through military action, starvation, disease, or genocidal programmes.

With his army held at bay by Britain's air defences, Hitler turned his attention east, disregarding his pact with Stalin and crossing into Soviet territory in June 1941. He seriously underestimated the resolve of the Soviet Union.

THE US JOINS THE FIGHT

While the German army entered the USSR, the Japanese struck against the United States, bombing its fleet docked at Pearl Harbor, Hawaii, in a surprise air attack. After providing funds and munitions for Britain, the United States was now drawn into the fight. The US, USSR and Britain agreed a treaty of mutual assistance.

After initial success advancing in the Soviet Union, the German army came to a standstill. Extreme winter weather, a poor supply chain and a determined Soviet response saw the Nazis suffer a huge defeat at Stalingrad in February 1943. It was the largest single battle in world history. One million lives were lost in the six-month struggle, yet this was nothing compared to the estimated 27 million Soviets killed in the war.

After Stalingrad, the Russians pushed back. Italy switched sides to join the Allies. The Americans and the British came ashore in Normandy, France, attacking the Germans from the west. In May 1945, the Soviets reached the German capital, Berlin. Hitler committed suicide and the war in Europe was over.

But it was not the end. The war in Asia continued, with Japan refusing to surrender. In August 1945, the US made the fateful decision to utilize its latest devastating weapon, the atomic bomb. Two explosive devices were detonated above the Japanese cities of Hiroshima and Nagasaki, destroying them in seconds, along with between 129,000 and 226,000 lives. Many more would suffer a slow death due to radiation poisoning over the following decades. Never before had the world witnessed the use of such a cataclysmic weapon in conflict. Days later, the Japanese emperor announced an end to the war.

The two world wars had seen countries rise up against oppression and nationalist ideology, but they had also seen the use of extraordinary weaponry that could wipe out cities from a distance and unimaginable atrocities. In the aftermath, the great powers of Europe were diminished and debt-ridden. They were to be overshadowed from then on by the competing superpowers of the United States and the USSR.

THE HOLOCAUST

In April 1945, US troops liberated the Belsen concentration camp in Germany. The soldiers found 60,000 emaciated prisoners there, along with 13,000 corpses. One of many such camps, Belsen revealed the horror of the Nazis' 'Final Solution', an organized extermination of people they did not consider their equals. Those captured and transported to the camps were mostly Jews, but also Roma, homosexuals and ethnic Poles. There are various estimates of the number of Jews alone killed in the camps. Six million is the most widely accepted figure.

MARCH TO SELF-RULE

After World War II, the colonial territories of Europe began a march towards independence. The days of empire were numbered.

World War II left many European powers weakened and in debt. Britain, in particular, could no longer afford an empire. After Japan's surrender, the colonial territories it had taken from Europe were yielded but many refused to accept the return of European rule. Native Indians and Africans had joined the war effort and felt that they were due recompense. There was no returning to the old ways as second-class citizens in their own country. Independence movements gained ground, seeking to be free from the rule of empire.

The colonial rulers made some compromises, but struggled to relinquish full control of the countries' resources and large workforces. Achieving self-rule required determination from protesters. Many were imprisoned and violence did occur. In some countries

armed insurgency erupted and led to years of war before independence was achieved.

India was promised independence by Britain immediately after World War I, thanks to its support in the conflict. An Indian parliament was created in 1919, providing civil service experience for Indians, but only a small minority of wealthy Indians was able to vote and many governmental departments remained in British hands. The lawyer Mahatma Gandhi led several high-profile passive acts of civil disobedience, demanding self-rule.

After World War II, full independence was finally agreed and the British began their withdrawal. India at the time had a mixed population, including around 65 per cent Hindus and 27 per cent Muslims. Muslim representatives founded the Muslim League and demanded their own separate state. Violent protests followed. The exiting British powers agreed on partition. Mainly Hindu India was separated from two new Muslim-majority states: Pakistan in the west and

Mahatma Gandhi leads a salt march in support of Indian independence from Britain in 1930.

East Pakistan (later renamed Bangladesh) to the east. Following independence in 1947, the partition of India drove 12 million Hindus, Muslims and Sikhs across the three new countries' borders. It was not a peaceful transition. More than 200,000 people died in religious violence in the first months. Kashmir, an area between Pakistan and India, has remained contested ever since.

DECOLONIZATION

Not all European governments were willing to give up access to the resources of a former colonial province. The Dutch invaded Indonesia in 1945 to retain control over rubber and oil exports before agreeing to independence in 1949. Britain's attempt to keep holdings in Malaya's rubber and tin industries upset a peaceful transition to independence in 1948, which took until 1957 to be settled.

Elsewhere in Asia, the surrender of Japan in 1945 provided an opportunity for the Vietnamese nationalist Ho Chi Minh to declare independence for his country from French rule. French troops fought to take back southern Vietnam. An eight-year war led to a division of the country between north and south. It was only a pause in hostilities. With North Vietnam receiving support from the USSR and China, the US feared a communist takeover and sent thousands of its own troops to the region, entangling them in more than a decade of fighting in the Vietnam War.

In North Africa, France had ruled Algeria since 1830. After World War II, demands from the Muslim population for more autonomy led to an uprising and a violent crackdown. War between France and Algeria lasted from 1954–62, when independence was declared.

The borders created by Europe, dividing Africa between 1870 and 1914 (page 182) did not take into consideration the spread of the continent's indigenous peoples. As colonial power was removed, this led to civil wars between rival groups.

South Africa had been independent since 1910 but was kept in white Afrikaner hands, denying black South Africans emancipation for several more decades.

Independence Arch, Accra, Ghana.

Ghana was the first sub-Saharan country to free itself from European rule after World War II. Following an armed struggle against British forces, the country gained independence in 1957. An eight-year insurgency in Kenya preceded self-rule in 1963. By 1968, all British colonies except for Southern Rhodesia had gained independence. By 1977, 50 African countries had self-rule.

A JEWISH HOMELAND

After World War II, Britain and France promised Palestine in the Middle East to both Jews and Arabs. Jews had been seeking a homeland for centuries. The territory was mandated to Britain, which allowed some Jewish migration. This met with resistance from native Palestinians, leading Jewish settlers to form local defence groups. To avoid further conflict, Britain tried to restrict the number of Jewish migrants.

Unable to find a working solution, Britain asked the United Nations for help. The UN agreed to divide the territory, creating the state of Israel in 1948. However, the state was not recognized by Arab countries. Following its inauguration, Israel had to defend itself against several invasions. By the time of a ceasefire, an estimated 700,000 Palestinians had fled or been expelled. Many violent flare-ups and ceasefire agreements have occurred in the region over the years.

COLD WAR

Allies during World War II, the United States and the USSR found themselves at odds for the following decades, with conflicting politics and competition over global dominance.

Towards the end of World War II, in February 1945, when it was clear that Germany would lose the conflict, the leaders of the United States, the Soviet Union and Britain met at Yalta in Crimea to consider the shape of postwar Europe. The trio were awkward bedfellows. Stalin's Union of Soviet Socialist Republics was communist; the regime was autocratic, with dissenters imprisoned or executed in their thousands. Both Prime Minister Churchill's Britain and President Roosevelt's United States were capitalist, with open elections and freedom of speech.

Poland had been divided by Nazi Germany and the Soviet Union at the onset of the war. The Soviet army then annexed Latvia, Estonia, Lithuania, plus parts of Finland and Romania. Stalin insisted on retaining these territories after the war. The USSR then formed an Eastern Bloc of allies, including Albania, Bulgaria, Czechoslovakia and Hungary, formalized in 1955 by the signing of the Warsaw Pact. The United States pushed back. Roosevelt's successor, Harry Truman, promised US money and military aid for Western European countries looking to rebuild and retain democracy.

The front line of the US–USSR conflict was Berlin. The German capital was surrounded by Soviet territory and split into four zones after World War II, administered by the US, USSR, Britain and France. The Western allies planned a West German state incorporating their quarters of Berlin. Stalin rejected this and blocked ground access to Berlin in June 1948. During a year of negotiation, the capital survived thanks to supplies delivered by air, at a rate of more than 1,000 flights a day. In 1949, Germany was split in two, with the Federal Republic in the west and the communist German Democratic Republic in the east. The division

- Soviet Union
- Warsaw Treaty Organization
- Neutral States
- NATO

SOVIET UNION

EUROPE DURING COLD WAR

Map of Western Europe and Eastern Bloc countries at the height of the Cold War. Yugoslavia was communist but not allied with the USSR.

of Berlin was defined in 1961 by the construction of a defended wall through its heart, which prevented East Germans from heading west (see panel).

ARMS RACE

In the face of the Soviet threat of expansion, the US, Canada and ten Western European countries founded the North Atlantic Treaty Organization (NATO), a military alliance that allowed the US to site military bases on European soil. The US and USSR increased their military spend, both investing in nuclear arms after the Soviet Union successfully tested an atomic bomb in 1949. Conflict between the US and the USSR now presented the possibility of worldwide destruction. The arms race was paralleled by a space race (page 200), an attempt to dominate a new frontier of science.

Paranoia about communist infiltration hit a high in the US from 1947, with the Un-American Activities Committee interrogating possible communist sympathizers in the federal government and public life. Just as the USSR used propaganda films and posters to extol the superiority of its regime, communists were portrayed as the enemy in American movies, novels and comic books.

Stalin's successor Khrushchev attempted a thawing of this 'Cold War', though disaster came close in 1962 when Soviet missile bases were discovered close to the US, in communist Cuba. While not engaging the USSR directly, the US fought against Soviet-supported communist armies in Korea from 1950–53, and in North Vietnam from 1964–73. Both sides also used their intelligence services to influence the outcomes of wars and elections in South America, the Middle East, Asia and Africa, to prevent the other gaining further ground.

The Cold War continued through periods of friction and reduced tension for decades until economic and political reforms in the 1980s led to the break-up of the Soviet Union.

THE BERLIN WALL

Once Berlin was split in two in 1949, 3.5 million people dodged the border's immigration control to defect to the west. Without warning, the communist German Democratic Republic erected a guarded barbed-wire fence in 1961 to keep its populace in place, later replaced by a more forbidding 112 km (70 mi) pair of walls either side of a wide 'death strip', dotted with 55,000 landmines. For the 28 years that the wall was in place, 100,000 people attempted to get through, of which only 5,000 succeeded. The western side became covered with graffiti and messages of hope for German reunification.

In 1989, following the dissolution of the Soviet Union, East Germans were once again permitted to cross over. West Berliners began to hack at the concrete barrier. Unusually, they were not prevented from doing so, and souvenir hunters claimed pieces. The first section of wall was removed in December 1989 and Berlin was finally reunited in October 1990.

Fall of the Berlin Wall, 1989.

COMMUNIST CHINA

Postwar China saw a revolution erupt. An army of peasants, inspired by communism, rose up against nationalist rule, but ambitious reforms and targets for the new People's Republic came at a great cost.

Following the end of dynasties in China in 1912 (page 188) it was many years before unity was achieved, with one power taking control of the nation. The new ruling party did not come from the aristocracy or the military, but from the fields. The common factory and field workers were seen as the standard-bearers for a revival that could challenge the world with its output in food and steel. Instead, fear and fervour delivered widespread famine.

After a period of disunity under competing warlords, from the late 1920s the Nationalist Party, the Kuomintang (KMT), began to assert control under Chiang Kai-Shek, who based his capital in Nanjing. The party had backing from the Soviet Union and worked with the recently formed Chinese Communist Party (CCP). After success tackling warlords in the north, Chiang turned against the communists, massacring thousands in Shanghai.

With huge support from the peasantry, the communists amassed a Red Army to take on the KMT for control of China in a civil war that lasted ten years. After one offensive in 1934, the communists began a year-long retreat. The estimated 10,000 km (6,200 mi) trek with more than 80,000 soldiers and workers over tough terrain became mythologized as the Long March. By the time the marchers had established a new base at Yan'an, only 8,000 of the original train had survived. The leader of the march, Mao Zedong, now took control of the Chinese Communist Party.

Hostilities between the KMT and CCP paused in 1937 when the rivals formed a new alliance to repel a Japanese invasion. The compact was limited and fragile, barely even a ceasefire. Once the Japanese had been removed, with help from World War II allies, the KMT and CCP fought once again for control. The

Mao Zedong inspecting the Red Guards in 1967.

communists had gained further rural support thanks to their land reforms and were supplied with Japanese weapons taken by the Soviets, while the KMT army was weakened and dealing with uncontrolled inflation. A third of a million Nationalists surrendered in January 1949. Chiang Kai-Shek and 2 million supporters retreated to the island of Taiwan to establish their Republic of China. On 1 October 1949, Mao Zedong declared the founding of the People's Republic of China.

GRAND AMBITION

Among Mao's first targets for China was an increase in industrial output. Mao would use this as a measure of the country against Western states for years to come, to the detriment of his people. Spurning urbanization, Mao focused on agriculture, creating large, collectivized farms. A strategy he called The Great Leap Forward took this drive even further, placing workers in communes. Mao predicted this would lead China to surpass the output of Britain within 15 years. Instead, the result was a breakdown in family bonds, and famine. Local leaders would proclaim unrealistic production achievements then export food to the USSR that was needed to feed farm workers in China. Birds were exterminated to stop them eating seed, prompting a rise in crop-attacking insects. Cooking pots were melted down to achieve targets for steel production; the results were unusable. Between 1959 and 1962, 15–45 million Chinese died.

Mao tried reinvigorating the country with his next great project, the Cultural Revolution. This was an attempt to expunge old customs and culture, and purge the country of 'bourgeois' influence. Young Red Guards were inspired to burn books and hound intellectuals, teachers and even parents who failed to show rigorous communist spirit. Professionals were removed from their skilled jobs and forced to take up manual labour. Regular purges in government also saw formerly trusted allies of Mao accused of disloyalty and removed before they could threaten the leader's grip on power.

Following the death of Mao in 1976, the People's Republic of China slowly opened up to the rest of the world. New leaders confronted the mistakes of past regimes and introduced elements of a free market that would see China become one of the richest and most influential economic powers of the 21st century (page 212).

LITTLE RED BOOK

The best-selling, non-religious book of all time is *Quotations of Chairman Mao*. Known colloquially as Mao's 'little red book', the volume was an essential accessory for his followers, often raised aloft during rallies as a display of loyalty. The book was first published in 1964 as a teaching tool for the People's Liberation Army (the Red Army), before being revised and distributed to the general public in 1966. In an attempt to put the book in the hands of 99 per cent of the Chinese population, hundreds of new printing houses were built. Estimates of the number of published copies are between 6.5 million and, according to one calculation, 'billions'.

Demonstration in Tiananmen Square during the Cultural Revolution in 1967, Beijing, China.

THE SPACE RACE

The competition between the two superpowers of the 20th century saw them scramble to be the first into orbit and to land on the moon.

The United States and the Soviet Union were in the midst of a Cold War (page 196) in the years after World War II. Through propaganda and covert operations they wrestled for supremacy in military power and influence. Another field of competition was scientific progress and, in particular, the conquest of space. The rivalry provided great impetus for both governments to invest in scientific and engineering development.

Rocket technology had been developed during World War II by Wernher von Braun (1912–77). Under the direction of the Nazis, he had overseen the production of the V-2 (Vengeance) rockets, ballistic missiles that could be fired from Continental soil to deliver a warhead to Britain's cities, 320 km (200 mi) away. After the war, von Braun was recruited by the US Army to work on its ballistic missile programme.

The US revealed its plans to launch an artificial satellite into Earth orbit in July 1955. The Soviet Union expressed a similar ambition days later. The launch pistol for the so-called Space Race had been fired. The Soviets were the first to succeed, when they sent the first artificial satellite, *Sputnik I*, into orbit in October 1957. US radio was able to receive the beeping signal of *Sputnik* as it passed over the country for 22 days. A month later, *Sputnik II* was in orbit, carrying Laika, a dog, as the first Earth-orbiting passenger. The revelation that the Soviets were technologically ahead of the US and sending craft high above US airspace created anxiety for the Americans. Not only were the Soviets taking the lead in space exploration, they conceivably possessed the technology to launch a nuclear missile into orbit. The US had to respond.

The National Aeronautics and Space Administration (NASA) was established in October 1958 with an early goal of sending a man into orbit. Once again, the Soviets beat the Americans to the punch, when, in April 1961, cosmonaut Yuri Gagarin completed a single Earth orbit in the spacecraft *Vostok I*. The US managed the same feat three weeks later, but it was already looking further afield.

US President John F. Kennedy announced the Apollo space programme in 1961 with the clear intention to land a man on the moon and bring him home safely before the end of the decade. Von Braun was key to this endeavour, with his design of the largest and most powerful heavy-lift vehicle ever to launch. At 111 m (363 ft) the *Saturn V* rocket was taller than the Statue of Liberty (page 181).

LUNAR LANDING

After several successful NASA missions sending astronauts into Earth and lunar orbit, two men landed on the moon via a lunar module on 20 July 1969. Five further missions repeated the achievement and completed additional studies of Earth's satellite. After the US achieved the extraordinary goal of putting the first man on the moon, the USSR's own secret moon-landing programme was cancelled. (Its existence was only revealed in 1990.)

Edwin 'Buzz' Aldrin leaves the lunar module to walk on the moon's surface, 1969.

The USSR refocused its attention on *Salyut*, which would become the first working space station to orbit Earth in 1971, as well as the first landing of probes on Mars (*Mars 3* in 1971) and Venus (*Venera 8* in 1972). In 1972, enmity between the two superpowers was put aside for a joint Apollo-Soyuz Test Project, which managed to complete the docking of US and USSR spacecraft in July 1975. Cooperation between scientific institutions would continue; after the Cold War, in 2000, 15 nations helped construct and share use of the International Space Station (see panel). The Space Race was over.

While the competition had succeeded in its aims, many questioned the use of funds for such a grandstanding effort. Should the investment have gone towards improving housing, education or reducing world hunger? Cost aside, the Space Race was a rare example, outside wartime, of a large collective enterprise leading towards a major scientific advance. Its achievements, taking humankind to new frontiers beyond Earth, provided major milestones in human history.

INTERNATIONAL SPACE STATION

Following an agreement between the US and Russia to work together on their space programmes, plans for an International Space Station were announced in 1993. The first section of the modular station was launched into Earth orbit in 1998. Part of a collaboration between five space agencies from the US, Russia, Japan, Europe and Canada, the station operates as a laboratory for scientific research and observation, and is able to support six working astronauts. More than 250 astronauts and cosmonauts have stayed on the ISS, along with a small number of paying space tourists. The movement of the ISS through the night sky can be tracked and seen from the ground.

The International Space Station, photographed by crew members aboard a Soyuz spacecraft, 2018.

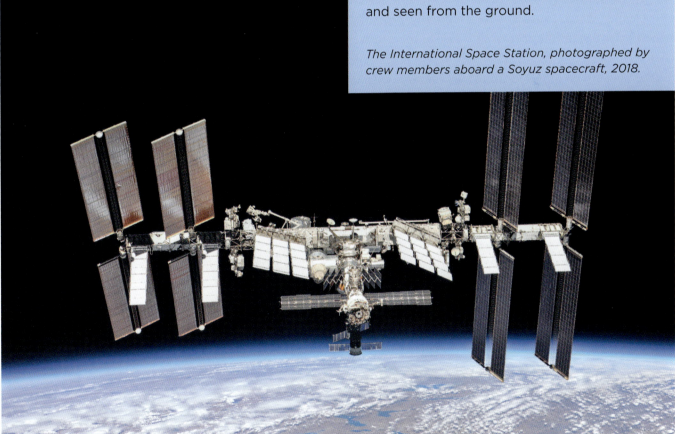

HEALTH IMPROVEMENTS

People living in the 20th century could expect to live much longer and healthier lives than their predecessors a century earlier thanks to major improvements in public health.

Life expectancy at the beginning of the 20th century in the UK was 48 years for males and 52 for females. Within 80 years, this had been raised to 71 and 77 respectively, figures that were matched by other industrialized countries of the time. The improvement was due to a multitude of factors – social improvements, better sanitation, medicine, vaccinations and improved communication between international experts.

Urbanization in the 19th century had pushed families into crowded cities, where aged public sewers became overwhelmed by a swelling population. Waste ended up in rivers, where people bathed and laundered clothes. Better waste management, new sewers and cleaner water sources were eventually provided, which helped stem the spread of water-borne diseases such as cholera.

For those who suffered illness and injury, time in hospital was made safer. Simple solutions in health treatment, including the improved cleanliness of wards, with staff washing hands between operations, had a measurable positive effect. Operations on damaged or diseased parts of the body were eased in the early 19th century following the use of anaesthetics, which allowed surgeons to work more slowly. Surgical tools were regularly sterilized with carbolic acid. Protective masks, gloves and aprons were brought into use. The employment of X-rays from the 1930s helped in diagnosis and locating broken bones.

Among new effective drugs being prescribed were quinine, from cinchona tree bark, for malaria; aspirin, from willow bark, for pain relief, from 1897; and Salvarsan to combat syphilis, from 1910.

VACCINATION

Smallpox, which had caused tremendous devastation among the native people of the Americas in the 17th century (page 147) was still a major problem in the 18th century, with an estimated 10 per cent of the human population dying from it (and with even higher mortality rates in towns and cities). In the late 18th century it was noticed that milkmaids who caught the

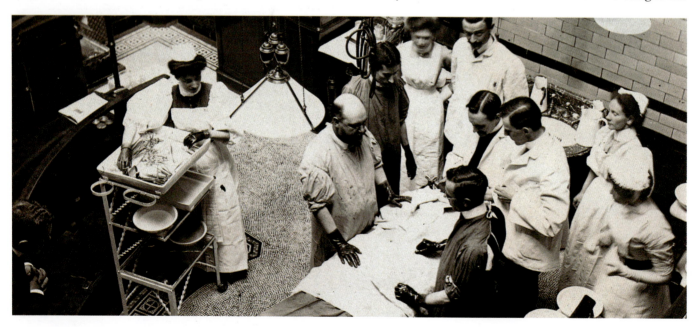

Operating theater, Charing Cross Teaching Hospital, London, late 19th century.

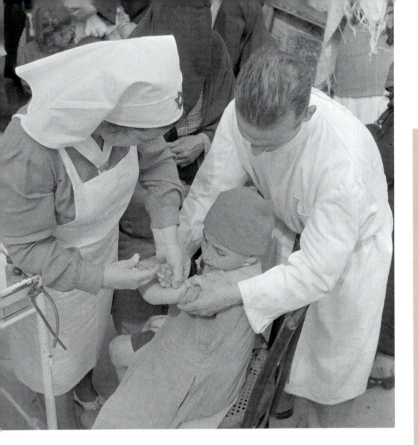

Influenza vaccine being administered in New York.

ANTIBIOTICS

A major health breakthrough occurred in 1928 when the Scottish biologist Alexander Fleming (1881–1955) observed the properties of a mould-inhibiting bacteria on a culture plate. The mould was penicillium. The agent, penicillin, was synthesized for use as an antibiotic in 1942 for the Allied armed forces in the last year of World War II, then more universally soon after. New antibiotics continue to be developed – which is necessary, as new infections often come about or old ones mutate and develop resistance.

Sir Alexander Fleming, who discovered penicillin.

mild disease cowpox avoided the deadlier smallpox. A vaccine based on the lesser disease was introduced in the 1790s through the work of the British physician Edward Jenner. Later vaccines included one to prevent rabies in the 1880s and the infectious disease typhoid in 1897.

Military casualties during World War I (page 190) were large but far fewer than the millions who died immediately after the conflict due to the spread of influenza (Spanish flu). Diseases did not respect borders; an international solution to the spread of viruses was needed. The foundation of the World Health Organization (WHO) in 1948 provided better communication about health issues and led to major vaccination programmes against tuberculosis and smallpox, which was finally officially eradicated in 1979. Mass immunization programmes in the late 20th century also reduced the instances of common childhood diseases including polio, mumps and measles.

The benefits of improved health systems and vaccinations were not universal, though. For the developing world, access to quality healthcare and medicines was scarce. Interventions by the WHO and international charity organizations have attempted to improve the balance.

CIVIL RIGHTS

Achieving racial equality and integration was a slow process in the United States from the 1950s, while in South Africa segregation was protected by law until the 1990s.

The American Declaration of Independence of 1776 (page 168) stated that 'all men are created equal', yet it was ratified at a time when slaves were employed in American plantations, even by those that signed the declaration. When slavery was abolished on the continent in 1865, there was little equality for black people. They were given citizenship four years later, followed by the right to vote (for males) in 1870, but there was resistance to integration from many whites and attempts in some southern states to restrict black rights. Between 1910 and 1970, almost 7 million African-Americans moved to northern and western states for better conditions.

During World War II, black soldiers fought for the US in separate units, though mixed training took place; segregation within the military ended in 1948. Black men and women were representing their

Civil rights march from Selma to Montgomery, Alabama, USA, 1965.

country and giving up their lives for the United States, yet, even in the 1950s, in the southern states, there was still segregation. Signs beside railroad waiting rooms or drinking fountains read 'Whites Only' or 'Coloreds Only'. African-Americans were expected to give up their seats to white people on buses. So-called Jim Crow laws allowed for segregation, with separate facilities, including schools, restaurants and hospitals. These were often poorly funded and of a lower standard than those offered to white people.

A civil-rights movement began campaigning from 1954, aiming to end racial discrimination through non-violent protest such as marches and boycotts (see panel). The National Association for the Advancement of Colored People (NAACP), founded in 1909, took the cases of children excluded from schools to court and won. While the NAACP had some success, ending segregation was a slow process, and protesters faced intimidation and violence. In 1963, more than 200,000

African-Americans, with white supporters, marched through Washington to the Lincoln Memorial, where they heard a speech by the preacher Martin Luther King Jr. King adopted the non-violent protest methods of Mahatma Gandhi (page 194).

Through a series of legal challenges, the campaign managed to secure its aims, ending segregation. The Civil Rights Act of 1964 formally outlawed discrimination based on race, colour, religion or sex. While, in law, African-Americans were equal, often they found themselves in low-paid work, and living in poor conditions in the inner cities, segregated by wealth and housing, but it was progress. African-Americans had more opportunities and could dream of one day becoming president.

THE END OF APARTHEID

In South Africa, during World War II, large numbers of non-white workers had arrived in the cities to relieve labour shortages in industry. Postwar, there was concern from the white minority about the possibility they would lose power. The ruling National Party introduced a series of laws that prioritized white people for work opportunities and housing. Apartheid (an Afrikaner word meaning 'separateness') was an institutionalized system established in 1948 that denied black Africans to right to vote and segregated them from the ruling white minority. Four tiers of racial groups were determined – White, Indian, Coloured and Black – with mixed marriage banned and different rules applied to each.

Eighty per cent of the land was set aside for the white minority. Three and a half million black Africans were evicted from their homes between 1960 and 1983 and settled in segregated districts. There was resistance to the policies, but uprisings from the black community were severely dealt with. Many protesters were killed by police, and thousands arrested.

International opposition to apartheid included major economic sanctions, forcing the South African government to make some reforms, but it was not enough. Apartheid was finally ended in 1991. Nelson Mandela, the leader of the banned opposition party the African National Congress (ANC) was released from prison after 27 years. Following multiracial elections, Mandela became the first black president of South Africa in 1994. The anniversary of the election is celebrated every year as Freedom Day.

ACTS OF RESISTANCE

One of the most effective non-violent protests used by the American civil-rights movement was the boycott. In a famous incident in December 1956, department store worker Rosa Parks refused to give up her public bus seat in the 'colored' section to a white person. She was arrested for her act of resistance. On the day of her trial, members of the NAACP handed out leaflets calling for a boycott of the bus company. The boycott ended up lasting for 381 days. Within the year, bus segregation was ruled unconstitutional. Rosa Parks' action and the ensuing boycott inspired further effective protests.

Rosa Parks re-enacts her public bus protest in Alabama, USA, 1956.

OIL DEPENDENCE

International reliance on oil from the Gulf states led to major economic disruption when an embargo was placed in the 1970s. Governments sought to reduce the wasteful use of resources and investigate alternative energy.

In the mid-20th century the US economy was buoyant thanks to a huge consumer-spending boom. Americans were filling their homes with new technology, such as TVs, washing machines, vacuum cleaners and refrigerators, while driving the latest luxury cars. Jobs were plentiful and wages were high. After the austerity of World War II, Americans were keen to spend.

The boom relied on cheap and available fuel for transport and electricity. The United States' oil fields in Texas and Southern California supplied the country's needs for a time but, as car ownership and fuel usage rose dramatically from the 1950s, there was a need to import oil. By 1972, more than 80 per cent of US oil imports came from the Gulf states. The countries that controlled the market and the price of oil now had influence on world economies and politics.

Oil had been discovered in the Middle East in 1908. Saudi Arabia gave permission for the US company Standard Oil to prospect in 1933. It discovered the largest reserves in the world. Large-scale production began after World War II and the Arab states became hugely rich and powerful. Iran, Iraq, Venezuela, Kuwait and Saudi Arabia formed the Organization of Petroleum Exporting Countries (OPEC) in 1960. When they placed an embargo on sales to Western powers, it had massive implications.

In October 1973, Egypt and Syria attacked Israel to reclaim territory lost during a war six years earlier. They were supported by Soviet military intelligence. The United States intervened by airlifting arms and supplies to Israel. It became a Cold War (page 196) battle by proxy. The Arab oil producers responded by placing an embargo on oil exports to Israeli-supporting nations, including the US. Over six months, the embargo caused the price of oil to rocket by 300 per cent. Such was the importance of oil in the international economy, the embargo and a decrease in oil production caused a global recession. Industrial output decreased while inflation increased.

THE RISE OF ARAB NATIONS

Americans had got used to low fuel prices for decades. Now, they had to reduce their reliance on cars. Some gas stations ran out of fuel. The US and European countries imposed a degree of fuel rationing. The famous lights of New York City's Times Square were switched off. The embargo was described as an 'Oil Crisis'. After ignoring US overtures to end the embargo, Saudi Arabia finally lifted the restriction in March 1974.

The embargo did little to change the situation in Israel, but it proved the oil-rich nations could engineer great disturbances in the international economy. Governments began to court the oil-rich Arab countries and pay more attention to their grievances over Israeli territorial claims.

Oregon introduces a system of odd and even numbers for fuel purchases during the Oil Crisis, 1974.

An oil refinery in Jordan.

The Oil Crisis led to several other long-term changes. Consumers began a switch from large 'gas-guzzling' automobiles to more fuel-efficient models. New, slower speed limits were introduced to reduce fuel consumption. The crisis also spurred interest in alternative energy sources (see panel).

Reduction in oil use was prompted by the Oil Crisis, but soon concerns about pollution and global warming would influence decisions about usage, including the introduction of unleaded fuel. These responses anticipated 21st-century efforts to reduce reliance on fossil fuels.

ALTERNATIVE ENERGY

The Oil Crisis of 1973 focused minds on seeking alternative energy sources to oil. Wind power had been used for centuries, in mills to grind grains. Denmark and the US led the way in developing large-scale wind generators for electricity from the 1970s. Solar power was in its infancy, used on satellites, but it was prohibitively expensive for domestic use until the 1990s.

A working nuclear reactor was built in the United States in 1942 as part of the military's top-secret programme for designing an atomic bomb. Nuclear power plants, supplying electricity to national grids, began operation in the USSR in 1954, and Britain from 1956. The Oil Crisis compelled France and Japan to invest heavily in nuclear power. Concerns over safety and the storage of nuclear waste slowed the adoption. Accidents at nuclear power plants in Chernobyl, Ukraine, in 1986, and Fukushima, Japan, in 2011, only increased anxieties. Despite these concerns, nuclear power is now being promoted as a renewable energy source and an alternative to fossil fuels.

TOURISM

Leisure travel was once the preserve of the wealthy few. In the 20th century it became an industry and the primary income for several countries.

Travel for leisure rather than trade, politics or religious pilgrimage was something only the wealthy could afford for centuries. From 1670, the Grand Tour, a lengthy exploration of the historic sights of Italy and Germany, was seen as a rite of passage for young, rich Europeans. Typically, these wealthy tourists would travel with a tutor for several months, as an education, buying up paintings and antiquities to show off on their return home.

The age of the train and steamship allowed cheaper and faster domestic and international travel. Cruise ships became affordable for middle-class travellers between England and Greece from 1844. The British businessman Thomas Cook set up a travel agency arranging rail excursions before branching out into foreign tours for small groups from 1855. This was the beginning of mass tourism. Popular destinations included the European coastal resorts of Heiligendamm beside the Baltic Sea, Ostend in Belgium, Boulogne-sur-Mer and Deauville in France, and Taormina in Sicily. Health was one reason to venture abroad, for the cleaner air of coasts or mountains, or for spa treatments in areas boasting hot springs.

The American businessman George Westinghouse is credited with the introduction of paid holidays for his workforce in the late 19th century, with half-day Saturdays. Westinghouse believed that the chance to rest and recuperate would improve productivity in his factories. The weekend became a feature of the working week in many countries from the 1940s. Paid holidays allowed families to take longer-distance breaks from home.

BUDGET TRAVEL

From the 1980s, the cheaper fares of budget airlines encouraged people to take more short breaks abroad. In Europe, former Soviet Bloc cities became attractive destinations. Specialist holidays tempted visitors for sports, arts and cooking classes and, in the 21st century, for those with many millions to spare even space tourism was an option (see panel).

Tourism became an increasing source of revenue for many countries and allowed people from different cultures to mix and better understand each other's way of life. By the early 21st century, over 1 trillion US dollars was being spent on tourism per year, with almost half of that spent in Europe. Tourists contributed over a quarter of the annual income for island destinations such as Aruba, the Maldives and the Seychelles, while the hospitality industry worldwide was employing hundreds of millions of people.

While providing income to countries that lack large industry or major exports, tourism also has its downside.

British gentlemen on the Grand Tour.

The increase in air traffic adds to the amount of carbon that enters the atmosphere. Overcrowding during busy seasons puts stress on infrastructure and accommodation. Some scenic locations have seen degradation due to unsympathetic building work. Private investment in luxury tourist destinations can lead to the exclusion of locals or the diversion of resources, such as water, to maintain appearances.

The natural environment is much of the attraction for holidays. Large numbers of visitors can put pressure on the environment and local amenities, and create extra waste. Sustainable tourism grew in response to mass tourism and a growing awareness of environmental issues in the 1960s and 70s. Extremely popular destinations such as Venice, Italy, and the Inca Trail hiking route in Peru introduced tourist taxes or placed limits on the number of visitors. While tourists put pressure on locations, historical sites became profitable and worth preserving. The Forum in Rome is one such site that was left to decay and exploited for building materials before it was excavated at the end of the 19th century and turned into a hugely popular and lucrative monument.

A balance continues to be sought between satisfying a desire to travel and 'broaden the mind' with protection of the environment so that it retains its allure for both residents and visitors.

SPACE TOURISM

The 21st century and the involvement of private enterprise in space travel led to the onset of space tourism. Several companies began offering flights to experience zero gravity and witness the curvature of the planet from space. Successful 10-minute passenger flights have crossed the Kármán Line, 100 km (62 mi) up, the zone regarded as the official boundary between Earth's atmosphere and outer space. The International Space Station (page 200) also became a destination for the ultra-rich, paying $20–25 million dollars for a week aboard the orbiting station. So far, seven paying astronauts have visited the ISS.

Large cruise ship docks in Venice, Italy.

Skyscrapers rise above the Shanghai skyline at night.

CHAPTER 9
THE MODERN WORLD

The late 20th century invention of microprocessing power, smartphone technology and the Internet now allows friends, family and colleagues to instantly communicate between continents via messages, email and video calls, and to tap into the shared knowledge of humankind. With such capacity at hand people are becoming inseparable from their devices.

This connectivity comes at a pivotal time in history, as humanity needs to work together to resolve issues that affect the entire planet. Only through united international effort can problems such as inequality, pandemics, overpopulation and climate change be mitigated. The detrimental effects of human civilization on Earth have been hard to ignore over recent decades. Such has been our impact that the era of human influence has been given its own name – the Anthropocene.

Changes have also come to the workplace. Robots and artificial intelligence are taking greater roles. Repetitive and dangerous jobs can now be done by machines. Trained humans could find themselves competing with tech for employment. And, if there is no work to be done, there is always retail therapy. This is the modern world we live in.

RISE OF THE EAST

Cheap labour and new technology fired up Asia's 'Tiger economies' in the late 20th century, while a radical change in direction led to China's rise as a major world market and financial power.

The dynamic so-called 'Tiger economies' of Asia rose from the turmoil of the Second World War. With cheap labour and the skilled production of electronics and automobiles, these countries became commercial powerhouses within decades. Soon to follow was China, dropping the communist policies of Mao to chase profit. The country would evolve into one of the world's most powerful economies.

During the Cold War (page 196), fears that other Asian countries would follow China, Vietnam and North Korea's march to form communist administrations led the United States to offer substantial economic support to neighbouring countries that shared its market-driven ideology.

Japan was blocked from maintaining armed forces after the Second World War. With support from the US and access to its markets, the country was able to focus on its recovery and on rebuilding its economy. Booming coal, steel and energy production was followed by a focus on hi-tech electronics and fuel-efficient cars. Exports in automobiles, cameras and computers helped Japan become the world's second-largest economy (after the US) by the 1990s, with a highly educated and skilled workforce.

Similarly successful economies emerged in South Korea, Taiwan, Singapore and Hong Kong. They were described as 'Tiger economies' for the speed of their growth. With cheap labour costs, South Korea and Taiwan generated a thriving export market for their consumer electronics. Singapore and Hong Kong became important international financial centres.

Hong Kong viewed from Victoria Peak.

COMMERCIAL CHINA

In 1978, Mao's successor, Deng Xiaoping (1904–97) sought to reverse many of Mao's programmes (page 198), allowing private ownership and profit-making while maintaining an iron grip on political power. Marxist slogans were replaced with new mantras such as 'to get rich is glorious'.

Foreign companies were tempted by tax breaks to invest in the country and employ Chinese labour. This provided China with the currency to buy new technology. The once closed-off country joined the World Bank and International Monetary Fund. Cheap Chinese goods flooded Western stores, making it difficult for competitors to price match. Between 1979 and 2002, China's gross domestic product grew at an annual rate of 9.3 per cent, faster than any other country.

The move to a more free-market economy was not followed by a freer political system, as was demonstrated by the brutal massacre of young demonstrators in Tiananmen Square in 1989. The event is censored from Chinese history books and any attempt to commemorate it is banned.

In 1997, a long-standing agreement provided for the transfer of Hong Kong from Britain to China, followed by Macao from Portugal two years later. China now benefitted from the expertise and experience of the Tiger economies.

As had happened in Europe during the Industrial Revolution (page 172), vast numbers of rural workers relocated to cities to take jobs in factories. This was the largest human migration in history, with 150 million people relocating to cities. Urbanization resulted in the equivalent of one major city being constructed every year. The rush to industrialization came at a cost to the environment, though, with polluted rivers, unregulated logging and the capital city of Beijing plagued by regular smog.

China's financial success has led to the country investing heavily abroad, buying property and companies. The One Belt One Road initiative launched by General Secretary Xi Jinping (1953–) in 2013 involved investment in infrastructure in nearly 150 countries.

The intention is to build a modern-day equivalent of the Silk Routes (page 108) and ease international trade, while also giving China greater influence abroad.

The prospering Asian economies suffered financial crises in the 1990s and 2000s, but returned to growth in the 21st century. The once-dominant Western states are now dependent on investment from the buoyant markets in the East.

THREE GORGES DAM

To provide power for the burgeoning nation, China began work on a new hydroelectric dam at the Yangtze river's scenic Three Gorges in 1994. The dam, the world's largest power station, cost about 203 billion yuan ($31 billion) to construct and began full operation in 2012. Thirteen cities and 140 towns were flooded due to the increase in water levels, with 1.24 million residents relocated. The resulting changes to the river's behaviour raised the risk of landslides but reduced the occurrence of major floods downriver which had, in the past, been responsible for millions of deaths. The dam is not only a major source of electrical power for the country, but its ambition and scale symbolize the capacity of the new industrial China.

Aerial view of Three Gorges Dam at night.

INFORMATION TECHNOLOGY

The invention of computer microchips and the Internet changed society significantly. Information technology pervades modern life, controlling human infrastructure and financial and social interactions.

In the 21st century, computing technology is at the heart of most homes and businesses, and in the hands of billions via the smartphone. The Internet keeps people in touch and provides access to more information than one person could possibly absorb. Internet-linked phones and desktop computers allow people to communicate around the globe in an instant and answer queries at the push of a button.

The progress of computer technology and its integration into society has been phenomenal. The computers of the 1950s were colossal machines that filled rooms and stored data on magnetic tape. They were only affordable for large businesses. The invention of the transistor in 1957 and the integrated circuit a year later greatly improved the reliability of the computer and reduced the size of the machines considerably. In 1961, there were just 4,000 computers in operation around the world. Ten years later there were 150,000, found mostly in research labs and universities.

Microchips, tiny integrated circuits housed on a wafer of semiconducting silicon, were first conceived

Central processing unit within a desktop PC.

in 1958. The invention eventually allowed billions of electronic transistors at a microscopic scale to be placed on a chip the size of a fingernail. The development of the silicon chip reduced the size and the price of computing, but it was the creation of the intuitive graphical interface and the development of gaming and its massive popularity that led to the household adoption of PCs.

HOME COMPUTERS

Computer gaming in arcades had been popular since the 1970s, with addictive titles such as Space Invaders and Asteroids. Once home computers became fast enough, with quality graphics and controllers, the market in gaming machines was born. The global gaming industry is now worth over $300 billion.

The use of punchcards or the laborious typing-in of commands on early computers was replaced by the use of a mouse to click and drag icons on a screen and to position a cursor for text inputs. The breakthrough interface was Windows, developed by Microsoft, a company set up by home-computer enthusiasts Bill Gates and Paul Allen in 1975. Supported by a suite of software, Windows dominated the market from its launch in late 1985. The operating system did not require knowledge of a computer language in order to use it. Today, touchscreens and voice commands have taken the intuitive use of computers to another level. A spoken command to a smart speaker can activate an internet query and provide a response in a second.

RUNNING THE WORLD

The ability of microprocessors to understand complex systems and react instantly to changes has led to their use in controlling infrastructure, including the regulation of transport networks, and as automatic pilots in aeroplanes.

Vehicles now incorporate electronic circuits that measure speed and fuel usage, and alert the driver to malfunctions and hazards. Drivers follow satnav guid-

Transistor Count

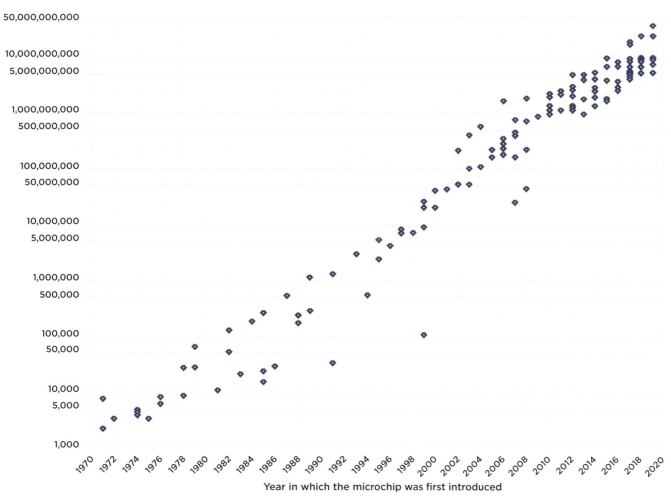

Year in which the microchip was first introduced

The increasing speed of computers was predicted in Moore's Law in 1965, which now estimates that the number of components that could be placed on a computer chip (essentially, the processing power) would double every two years. The law has held up well in the 50-plus years since its conception.

ance systems to get from A to B. The development of driverless cars sees artificial intelligence control every aspect of a journey.

As well as their use in computers and smartphones, microchips are included in credit cards to automatically approve and deduct payments, and swipe cards to allow secure access to buildings. Most bank transactions involve digital records rather than physically moving cash from branch to branch. In the United States alone, 99 per cent of the country's $3 trillion worth of financial transactions are digital. People have put their trust in remote computers and invisible calculations to protect their money and provide safe passage.

A contactless card payment.

WORLD WIDE WEB

The birth of the Internet was a pivotal moment in human history. It provided a gateway to knowledge, an easy shopping experience, a way of communicating instantly and globally through social media, and influenced elections.

The World Wide Web was developed by British engineer Tim Berners-Lee in 1989, as a collaboration tool for researchers at CERN, the European Organization for Nuclear Research in Switzerland. The WWW used onscreen hyperlinks to jump to files on a network of computers. The web software was released in 1991; web browsers launched two years later. By the early 2020s, the Internet had grown to include 1.25 billion webpages, containing about 175 zettabytes of data (1 ZB equals 1 trillion GB), accessed by an average 4.95 billion people a day, almost 60 per cent of the world's population.

Internet access is now considered almost as vital as access to clean water and electricity. The move to online storage has reshaped the way we live and work, with files saved in the Cloud (on remote computer servers accessed from online devices) and less reliance on physical office space. Shopping online pushed many high-street stores into bankruptcy, as they were unable to compete with online pricing and wider product ranges.

SMARTPHONES

The 21st century has made it possible for people to carry a personal computer in the palm of their hand. The average smartphone carries more processing power than the computer that helped guide astronauts to the moon in the late 1960s. So much of modern life revolves around the use of applications on the phone, from calls, messages and emails, to internet browsing, music, videos and games, weather reports and maps. Quality in-built audio players, cameras and video recorders have removed the need to carry separate devices. People have become dependent on the information they can access via a smartphone.

Newspaper sales plummeted as readers turned to more up-to-date and free news online. The sharing of music files online forced record companies to reassess their sales strategies. The advent of popular digital music players and smartphones (see panel) compelled the same companies to offer digital formats. Digital and streaming media has replaced many physical formats.

The first web server, 1989.

With the Internet came email. Invented in 1971, the system allows people to send messages, documents, images and videos to contacts securely. In the 21st century we are now just as likely to communicate via email, messaging apps and social media as through direct contact or phone calls.

Internet communication is not just between humans, but between devices, too. In what is described as the Internet of Things (IoT), microprocessors in household appliances, such as refrigerators, can store data and order food deliveries on behalf of the owner.

The Internet is not wholly unrestricted. Censorship exists in some countries, but news gets shared widely, and appeals for international help are answered. The Internet provides a mixture of scholarly research and information as well as provocative opinions and misleading reports. Without checks, spurious claims can become widespread and accepted, and influence elections and the democratic process. Calls for regulation of content persist, balanced by a demand for freedom of speech. The Internet has proved a force for good and bad, but life without it now seems barely imaginable.

CYBERATTACKS

The ubiquity of information technology inevitably led to its abuse for criminal or vindictive activity. Internet users have to be alert to attempts by strangers to access passwords to monitor private computer use, raid bank accounts or install malicious software on to a machine. Large corporations spend fortunes protecting the security of their systems. Many major cyberattacks have targeted stock exchanges and other financial institutions. One of the largest-recorded data breaches took place in 2013, when a cyberattack against the US tech company Yahoo led to the account information of more than 3 billion users being compromised. Cyberwarfare involves agents attempting to uncover military secrets, disrupt military systems and infrastructure, and spread information or misinformation to opponents. Governments now recruit software experts to defend their country from cyberattacks. Malware codenamed Stuxnet is believed to have been deliberately employed as a cyber weapon by the US and Israel to cause damage to Iran's nuclear programme in 2010. The United States Cyber Command has been in operation for over a decade as part of the US Department of Defense.

The seal of the United States Cyber Command. Personal, business, military websites and computer networks require protection from potential cyberattack.

ROBOTS AND AI

Robots and artificial intelligence (AI) are being employed in offices and factories. Will the increase in workplace technology lead to new roles for human workers or do we face a future of mass unemployment?

Robots have been used in industry since 1961, when the programmable robot arm Unimate joined the General Motors assembly line at a plant in New Jersey, USA. Based on a patented design by US inventor George Devol and developed with Joseph Engelberger, Unimate took on dangerous tasks, including the welding of die-cast automobile parts. The revolutionary machine became a celebrity of sorts, with appearances on chat shows, demonstrating its ability to play golf and conduct a band. Unimate fascinated the general public, but labour unions expressed concern about it causing job losses. Regardless, Unimate delivered increased productivity – double the rate of any other automotive plant. Within two years, 450 robot arms were operating in General Motors plants. Rival car manufacturers ordered the technology. The automobile industry was the first to adopt large-scale robotic manufacture and remains the largest employer.

These types of robots, doing repetitive, sometimes hazardous work, have not resulted in a great loss of human employment. Indeed, they have resulted in new roles for people, in the design, construction and repair of robots. The improved performance of robot-led factories (robots do not need lunch breaks or sleep) has kept product prices low, and has bred more opportunities in sales, marketing and distribution.

There are now more than 3 million industrial robots in operation worldwide, particularly in car and electronics production. The electric car manufacturer Tesla uses 160 industrial robots working in sync to build 400 cars a week. In South Korea, over 900 robots are employed for every 10,000 workers.

REPLACEMENT SERVICE

Robots are able to take on highly skilled operations, even surgery. The Da Vinci surgical system is guided by a human surgeon but it is able to wield a scalpel more precisely, to fractions of a millimetre. More common are robotic workers and automated machines replacing lower-skilled workers. Amazon warehouses use armies of Kiva Systems robots, guided by barcodes

Industrial robots constructing car bodies on an automobile assembly line.

on the floor to aisles where they can find and deliver palettes of products to packers.

ATMs, self-service supermarket tills, and transport ticket machines are examples of technology replacing staff in the service industries. Touchscreen ordering and payment may appeal to businesses and some consumers, but the personal touch and small talk is hard for technology to replace. The ability to engage in a more personal way, imitating human interaction, is the domain of AI (artificial intelligence).

ARTIFICIAL INTELLIGENCE

Artificial intelligence is the technological development of comprehension and decision making normally requiring human involvement. AI applications can now comfortably map faces and recognize speech, access the Internet and provide answers in seconds. AI can control cars, taking in information on location and environment to safely steer passengers to their destination, monitor financial transactions, or play sophisticated games, such as chess, to the highest level. AI has replaced customer services to some extent, with auto-replies to online questions and even phone calls. The AI used in smart speakers and Apple's voice assistant, Siri, are constantly improving. Human operators are becoming a backup only when virtual customer services fail to provide satisfactory answers.

If a job can be learned and is routine, an algorithm will be able to master it. Even creative roles are at risk of being taken on as technology improves (see panel). Estimates of the number of existing jobs that may be replaced with automation within the next 20 years are 47–80 per cent. For many people, losing or giving up work is a difficult process. One's job often defines a person. If humans are to be removed from the workplace, they will need to find satisfying and stimulating activities to occupy their time as well as the resources so that they can afford to do so.

CREATIVE COMPUTERS

Computers lack imagination (at least for now!) but they can study and duplicate techniques to produce art and music. In 2009, the first album by Emily Howell was released to mixed reviews – but Howell did not exist. She was a pseudonym for the computer programmer David Cope, and was an evolution of his composing program Experiments in Musical Intelligence (Emmy). The program had been fed examples of classical music and produced its own compositions. Cope input his criticism, guiding the program to compose something to appeal to his personal taste. While composed by a program, Emily Howell's music is played by humans and can trigger emotional responses from listeners. Similarly, impressionistic and abstract artwork is being generated by AI with some success, even prompting sales at auction for hundreds of thousands of dollars. Human artists use computers as tools for expressing their ideas, but can computers create artistic works that express and elicit genuine feelings? Art is as much about the human flaws of the creator. If these elements are removed from the process, is the art diminished? The debate over the value of AI-generated art continues.

The painting shown on the smartphone, Théâtre D'opéra Spatial, was created by an AI and won the Colorado State Fair's annual art competition in 2022.

CONSUMERISM

Consumerist culture and easy credit has turned shopping into a leisure activity where visiting the mall is 'retail therapy'. Capitalism needs a constant flow of consumers, but is it sustainable?

To keep capitalist economies thriving, the population is encouraged to shop for more than necessity's sake.

Consumerism demands fashions constantly change, and technology needs a regular upgrade. With a credit card at the ready, there's no need to be left behind.

The postwar years of the 20th century were a time of austerity and rationing for Europe, as money was tight and basic goods were scarce. In Britain, households were provided with ration cards that could be exchanged for a weekly allowance of one egg per adult, 50 g (2 oz) of butter and 225 g (8 oz) of sugar, among other food essentials. This system continued until 1954. In contrast, the United States enjoyed a postwar boom, with job security, higher wages and new wares to procure. These were promoted widely on one of the most in-demand products of the period – the television.

Henry Ford, who developed assembly-line production for his Model T motor car in 1913, was aware that he needed to pay good wages and sell his automobiles at a fair price to make his industry sustainable. The workers needed to be able to afford the product. Higher wages allowed most US families to afford cars by the 1940s. A decade later, industry needed to sell cars to those same people, regardless of whether or not their old car was failing. Desire replaced need, as advertising tempted owners to swap their antiquated models with new, improved vehicles. This concept extended across all markets. And, if a new product seemed unaffordable, easy credit was available, with credit cards issued by most banks from the 1960s.

Planned obsolescence was another way to develop a perpetual market. This meant the production of goods with a shorter lifespan, so that they need replacing within years rather than decades. Cheap products were considered disposable and not worth repairing. The drive to constantly replace led to more waste.

High-street fashion sale. This year's chic replaces last year's dated styles.

SIMPLE LIVING

The simple living movement began in response to growing consumerism and materialism. Simple living, as the name suggests, involves reducing your possessions to the bare minimum and making them last as long as possible, through repair. Choosing to live in a more frugal and minimalist way may be for religious reasons or personal taste. Some people prefer not to be surrounded with 'clutter'. The move to simpler living may also be an ethical decision, seeking to reduce the amount of waste left behind and to shrink one's carbon footprint. Other ways of reducing one's impact on the environment include buying eco-friendly products that are sustainably sourced, and purchasing local, seasonal produce.

ADVERTISING TARGETS

From the latter part of the last century, with the emergence of the department store and the shopping mall, shopping was sold as a leisure activity, not a chore. Retail therapy promises the joy of browsing and rewarding oneself with a new purchase. On-site food courts and cinemas help keep the customer satisfied.

Ever more resourceful and targeted advertising brings in shoppers. The algorithms of websites track your visits, record your preferences and recommend more products to click on and buy in an instant. Peer pressure, desire to emulate the wealthy, celebrity endorsements, product placement and social media influencers all play a part in the constant drive to push sales.

Religious holidays have become sales festivals. Events such as Black Friday, Cyber Monday and the Boxing Day sales promise huge discounts and lure eager customers. The fast churn of new products replacing old is great for business but not for energy consumption and the overuse of resources. As landfill sites fill up with last year's models, humanity needs to ask itself a serious question: do we really need this?

CULTURE AS COMMODITY

Culture, too, has become part of consumerism. Art and music are sold as a lifestyle accessory. Major art exhibitions are described as blockbusters, must-see events, like a concert or movie. The art is exploited for T-shirts, bags and souvenirs in the gift shop. Everything has a price. Art has long been commodified, collected not just for its aesthetic value but also for its worth as an investment. In the 21st century, the NFT (non-fungible token) format took this to another level, with investors buying the equivalent of a digital certificate that listed them as the sole owner of a computer-generated image. No physical artwork existed that could be framed and exhibited. From the mid-20th century, popular music was dominated by sales charts which influenced radio playlists and availability. This element of competition was not necessarily the best way of inspiring originality, with a limited choice of commercial fare achieving the most success. The Internet has now made it easier to circumnavigate music marketing, to discover and share new music, with artists able to reach consumers directly. Despite the commercialization of art and music, there is much joy and inspiration to be gained from exposure to culture. The need to express ourselves, not for commercial gain, is a human trait. Art, literature and music can evoke moods, new ways of seeing and spur the imagination.

PANDEMICS

In a fast-moving world of international travel and trade, epidemics can spread across borders in days. Worldwide health organizations have to be alert to contain them and share treatments.

The Columbian Exchange of the 1600s (page 146) saw imported European diseases wipe out a huge percentage of the American population. From the 18th century, arrivals in Australia brought similar ruination, delivering smallpox to the Aboriginal people (page 164). In a connected world of international trade and long-haul holidays, local epidemics can escalate swiftly into pandemics, affecting many nations. Improvements in healthcare and vaccinations (page 202) help stem the spread, but viruses adapt and new threats evolve, as recent history has reminded us.

The deadliest of all pandemics occurred in the 14th century when the Black Death (page 124) took between 75 and 200 million lives in Eurasia and North Africa. The post-First World War spread of influenza was responsible for up to 50 million deaths across North America and Europe, many more than those who died in the war itself. While both the bubonic plague and influenza viruses still exist, they are now controlled by antibiotics and vaccination programmes. Smallpox has been eradicated.

Of recent pandemics, HIV/AIDS (Acquired Immunodeficiency Syndrome) was a virus condition that spread from the 1980s via sexual contact and contaminated blood. Symptoms took weeks to appear, leading to further infections. HIV destroys the human immune system, making carriers susceptible to diseases that they might otherwise shrug off. About 25 million lives were lost to it. It took two years for scientists to identify the cause, and a decade for medicines to be developed to slow its progress. Outside of Africa, HIV is now under control and people with the virus can receive antiretroviral treatment and live normal lives.

Further epidemics, notably the respiratory disease SARS from 2003–4, bird flu in 2005, swine flu from 2009–10, and Ebola in 2014 have also been contained.

LIFE AFTER COVID

Having coped with the outbreak of SARS (Severe acute respiratory syndrome), the populations of Asian countries were used to following health guidance and wearing protective face masks in public. When a new strain, COVID-19, was detected in Wuhan, China, in 2019, a compliant population followed scientific advice and prevented many deaths. Western countries underestimated how contagious the virus could be and were slower to respond. The COVID virus caused different symptoms in different people, many similar to flu. While, for the majority of people, COVID just left

Anti-Vaxxer demonstration in Los Angeles.

Disinfection of a subway in Rio de Janeiro, Brazil, during the COVID-19 pandemic.

them feeling ill and weak for several days, in the worst cases people suffered severe breathing problems and required hospital care. By early 2023, the international death toll from COVID was more than 6.8 million.

A major international vaccination programme greatly reduced the risk of severe symptoms and succeeded in bringing down the death rate. International health organizations remain alert to the spread of old and new diseases, with medical teams poised to control outbreaks by quarantining individuals with symptoms and tracing others that have been in contact with the affected person. Pharmaceutical teams are also quick to respond by testing antidotes and offering vaccinations. As with influenza, humanity will likely have to live with waves of COVID variants, and regular immunization. History has warned us to be prepared for future pandemics.

MISINFORMATION

While governments and news organizations worked hard to share information aimed to reduce the spread of COVID and recommend the uptake of vaccinations, misinformation also spread, particularly via the Internet and social media. The origin of the virus was questioned and the advice of scientists was ignored in preference for conspiracy theories and rumour. Many felt that rules on wearing face masks in public and showing proof of vaccination were an infringement of their personal rights. There was reluctance to follow government guidance and protest marches were organized in many cities.

EQUALITY

The fight for equal recognition and opportunity continues into the 21st century, with LGBTQ+ rights and acceptance of non-binary genders a new battleground.

The 20th century had seen huge steps forward in providing equality for women and people of all races. Women have the right to vote in the vast majority of countries in the world, while government acts have made it a crime to discriminate on the grounds of race. Yet, in the 21st century, there is still much to do. In some countries, women are prevented from exercising their voting rights by their husbands, and being able to gain public office is another matter.

Prejudice still exists, preventing women and people of colour being offered the jobs and gaining the promotions they are qualified for. This barrier against reaching the highest positions is referred to as a glass ceiling. There have been many welcome exceptions, though, with the first African American US president in 2009 and, in 2022, 27 countries in the world could boast female leaders.

While almost everyone has the right to vote, not everyone has the same opportunities in life. Children from poorer backgrounds are more likely to attend poorly funded schools, and lack the backing to attend university. They are then more likely to be employed in low-skilled work, prolonging a cycle that perpetuates inequality and social immobility. The gap between rich and poor shows no sign of shrinking. Figures from 2022 estimated that the richest 10 per cent of the world population own 76 per cent of the wealth, with approximately 500 million people subsisting on an income of less than $5.50 a day.

Initiatives to reduce the wealth gap include better provision of public education and job-related training, a minimum wage, and a taxation system that demands the rich pay a higher proportion of their earnings than the poor. Further to this is the proposal that everyone should receive a basic income to cover their essential needs, regardless of their means, as a way to end poverty. This idea has gained traction in the 21st century; a proposal to introduce a basic income was put forward in a referendum in Switzerland in 2016 but was defeated.

GENDER RIGHTS

Equality for all extends to people in non-heterosexual relationships and those who do not identify as male or female. Same-sex marriage only became legally recognized in 2001, with the Netherlands being the first country to allow it. By 2023, 34 of the world's 195 countries permitted same-sex marriage, with many others offering civil unions with similar legal rights. In contrast, homosexual relationships were criminalized in 67 countries.

More countries are also allowing people to decide their gender identity and have it legally recognized. In 2022, 16 countries, including the United States, Australia, Germany and India, allow their citizens to choose 'X' as their passport gender designation.

The Yogyakarta Principles, a human rights document published in 2007 (and revised in 2017), was intended to clarify how the law should respect a person's gender identity: it is to be determined by the person according to their personal feelings and experience, and understood with no legal demand for medical procedures. Acceptance of the principles has met resistance in the United Nations but it remains a guiding standard.

In 2018, in opposition to a US government proposal to legally define gender as a binary condition determined at birth and based on genitalia, more than 2,600 scientists signed an open letter describing the plan as 'inconsistent not only with science, but also with ethical practices, human rights, and basic dignity'. Freedom to choose one's gender identity, one's sexual partner and to have equality and protection under law continues to be an aspiration.

RAINBOW COLOURS

The rainbow flag has been adopted as a symbol for the LGBTQ+ (lesbian, gay, bisexual, transgender, queer+) movement. It first gained use in 1978 and has been employed to represent pride, solidarity with the movement for recognition and equal rights, and as a sign of a queer-friendly location. The US White House was lit in the colours of the rainbow flag in 2015 after legislation approved same-sex marriages in every US state.

LGBTQ+ supporters on a Pride parade in Amsterdam.

THE ANTHROPOCENE

Human impact on planet Earth has been so profound that a whole new geological epoch has been proposed to encompass the period of our influence.

The Anthropocene is the name for a proposed geological epoch to cover the period of Earth history when humanity has greatly impacted on the planet's geology and ecosystems. The name comes from the ancient Greek for 'human' and 'new'. The epoch would follow the Holocene, which

The last known thylacine, or Tasmanian tiger, photographed at Berlin Zoo, 1933.

began 11,650 years ago after the last Glacial period (page 28). Proposed dates for the beginning of the Anthropocene range from the Agricultural Revolution (page 34), 12–15,000 years ago, the Industrial Revolution (page 172) and the detonation of the first atomic bomb in 1945 (page 193).

Regardless of whether or not the Anthropocene is accepted as a geological event or epoch, there is no disagreement that humanity has had a pronounced influence on Earth and its ecology. One measurable effect is the dying out of flora and fauna. Some experts describe this period as Earth's sixth major extinction, following the catastrophes of the prehistoric era. Extinctions have occurred naturally through Earth history from climate or habitat change, reproductive problems, or, in the case of the Cretaceous-Paleogene extinction that wiped out the dinosaurs 66 million years ago, very likely though extraterrestrial collision.

Estimates vary, but it may be that species of plants and animals are dying out at a rate a thousand times faster than they naturally would, due to human intervention – and at a rate that has been accelerating since

the 19th century. Reports suggest an average fall of 68 per cent in vertebrate populations over the last 50 years alone. The causes of extinction include over-harvesting, which not only affects the species collected but the creatures that feed on it; habitat loss, where the homes of plants and animals are destroyed for materials or land for raising livestock and building; invasive species, where plants or animals are brought into an area and predate or compete with the local species; pollution, which affects the health of animals and their environment; and global climate change (page 242). Humanity now has to actively protect species from the effects of our increasing numbers and way of life.

At the same time, humanity has domesticated many species for food and bred them in such numbers that they far outnumber wild species. It is estimated that there are currently 1.5 billion cows, the same number of pigs, and half a billion sheep being raised as livestock. The domestic chicken is now the most abundant species of bird on the planet, with possibly 50 billion bred for consumption each year.

SHAPING THE LANDSCAPE

The effects described do not only affect the species that we share the planet with. They shape the continents, too. Global warming, a consequence of humanity's use of fossil fuels and agricultural practices, is melting the ice caps at such a rate that ocean water levels are expected to rise by between 30 cm (1 ft) and 2 m (6.6 ft) by 2100. This will see low-lying atolls, such as the Maldives, become uninhabitable, and countries with large populations living in coastal areas (Bangladesh, Vietnam, China, Philippines) facing major flooding.

Cities and dams have significantly changed the paths of rivers and the delivery of sediment to farmlands. Quarries and mines have reshaped the landscape and redistributed the metals and minerals of the earth. Crop fields now claim 20 per cent of the planet's land mass. Should future generations cut into the rocks to examine the last few centuries of human life they would find layers of slow-to-decay refuse, particularly plastics. The seas now feature mid-ocean gyres of garbage and microplastics. These waste products left in the oceans to form layers in sedimentary rock have been dubbed 'technofossils'.

Even more long term are the by-products of the nuclear energy industry. Radioactive waste has to be buried deep underground, with high-level nuclear waste needing to be safely stored for a hard-to-fathom million years according to some agencies.

The notion of an Anthropocene epoch exists to remind humanity of its impact on the planet. It is a call to action for us to do what we can to protect the environment we share (page 228).

A layer of industrial sediment deposited in a cemented beach in Biscay, Spain.

ENVIRONMENTALISM

The destructive impact of industrialization and commercial activity on Earth led to the founding of campaign groups and protest movements to raise ecological awareness and reduce environmental degradation.

Concerns about humanity's impact on Earth's ecosystem led to the environmentalist movement. Through dissemination and protests, environmentalists continue to raise awareness of the issues affecting the healthy future of our planet.

The effects of the Industrial Revolution (page 172) in the 19th century prompted action to stem pollution and waste from factories. Concerns about hydrochloric acid gas entering the atmosphere during the production of soda ash, for the glass, textile and paper industries, led to the first modern pollution law being introduced by the British parliament in 1863. The Alkali Act ordered inspectors to supervise emissions from factories. The first Act led to several more laws curbing industrial pollution.

1898 saw the formation of the British Coal Smoke Abatement Society, an early non-governmental organization which helped push a Clean Air Act through British parliament in 1956. The Act was in direct response to a Great London Smog in 1952 which caused thousands of people to die due to air pollution. The act offered incentives to households to switch from coal to gas fires, and power stations were moved outside of heavily populated cities.

The Russian anarchist and environmental activist Peter Kropotkin (1842–1921) was one of the first significant figures to raise the issue of climate change (page 242). In a series of books he described the consequences of hunting, the destruction of animal habitats and major deforestation. He noted that Swiss and Siberian glaciers had begun melting following European industrialization, a sign that Earth was getting warmer as a result of human activity. His work was republished in the 1970s and became an influence on the period's environmentalist movement.

In the United States, Yellowstone was inaugurated as the country's first national park in 1872, in order to protect the land from commercial interests and provide public access. In 1970, the United States Environmental Protection Agency was formed. One of its first acts was to restrict the widespread agricultural use of the harmful pesticide DDT.

Grand Prismatic Spring in Yellowstone National Park.

The Extinction Rebellion protest in London on 19 April 2019.

PROTEST MOVEMENTS

Government actions on environmental issues have often been the result of pressure from well-organized protest movements. Friends of the Earth was formed in California in 1969, and Greenpeace in Canada, in 1972, as independent campaigning groups. Both continue to document acts that harm wildlife and blight the environment.

Political parties with an environmental agenda launched in the 1970s. There are now almost 90 countries with active Green parties running for office. The Green Party in Germany has proved popular enough to enter government in a coalition on more than one occasion.

Direct action taken to protect environments and raise awareness includes protesters occupying trees in threatened forests, and tunnelling below roadworks. Greenpeace uses ships to disrupt damaging fishing practices, whaling, nuclear tests and the dumping of toxic waste into the oceans.

Extinction Rebellion is a recent international environmental protest group, established in the UK in 2018, whose members have used non-violent civil disobedience to draw attention to climate change and ecological collapse. Protests have included blocking bridges and gluing members to roads. Protestors' actions have seen them come into conflict with the police and face court actions, but their proactive and headline-grabbing methods have encouraged a new generation of environmentalists to get involved.

Awareness that action needs to be taken has resulted in several international agreements on curbing climate change. The Kyoto Protocol of 1997 was the first legally binding climate treaty. Coming into force in 2005, it required developed countries (but not including China and India) to reduce their emissions by 5 per cent on 1990 levels. The Paris Agreement of 2015 went a step further and demanded countries set emissions targets to prevent a 2°C (3.6°F), and preferably 1.5°C (2.7°F), increase in the global average temperature above pre-industrial levels.

Annual UN conferences, known as COPs, see government leaders convene to address the climate issue, though attempts to persuade countries to commit to phasing out the use of fossil fuels remains an unachieved goal.

EARTH DAY

First observed in the USA in 1970, Earth Day is an international event, celebrated in 192 countries, aimed at raising awareness of environmental issues. On 22 April each year, people are encouraged to take action for the planet, including turning off their house lights for an hour. On its 50th anniversary, Earth Day 2020 saw more than 100 million people get involved in what has been described as the largest online mass mobilization in history.

MIGRANT WORKERS AND REFUGEES

People leave their countries for work or to flee war and persecution. Many need help and support. How we treat those in need of a safe haven is a measure of our humanity.

People migrate for various reasons but mostly for a better life. Some relocate for work, some to be safe from harm. Climate change (page 242) is likely to be a major reason for migration in the coming years.

Migration has always played a part in human history, from the initial explorations of *Homo sapiens* (page 26) from Africa to Australasia and the tip of South America, the flood of people fleeing the nomadic armies of Central Asia (page 104), to the millions of Europeans who sailed to the Americas seeking land and opportunity (page 180). In the 21st century, people still seek work abroad or sanctuary from violent regimes. Some receive a welcome, others a refusal. Many offer skills, friendship and a cultural exchange that can enhance a nation.

The UN's International Labour Organization estimated that there were 169 million migrants working across the world in 2019. The developed world demands labour and it cannot always be serviced by its citizens. Major building projects or seasonal work need foreign workers to fulfil roles. For migrant workers this can mean better wages than at home.

Many workers arrive through legal means, receiving work permits for limited periods and returning home after the job concludes. These include skilled workers in healthcare, engineering and architecture. The Philippines alone supplies about a million workers to other countries every year. The money sent home from foreign workers is substantial. In 2019, this remittance was estimated to be worth about 175 billion US dollars.

Some migrants take enormous risks to cross land or sea borders illegally, often with the help of criminal gangs. North America and Europe are inviting destinations for desperate migrants. In the US, there may be more than 10 million undocumented migrant workers. Without work permits, they are at risk of exploitation and being forced to endure unsafe working conditions.

ESCAPING PERSECUTION

Refugees are people crossing borders to escape conflict or persecution. 2021 saw 89.3 million people forced to flee their homes due to conflict, violence, fear of persecution and human rights violations. Of these, 27.1 million were refugees, a number growing year on year.

Some may claim asylum in the country they arrive in; countries are legally bound to investigate such a claim. If the asylum seeker is found to have a good claim that they would be at risk by returning home, then they would be allowed to stay.

Rohingya refugees walk along a flooded road in Bangladesh, September 2017.

The refugee camp at Dadaab, Kenya, in 2011. At its peak the camp contained more than 230,000 inhabitants before it was closed by the Kenyan government in 2021.

As of 2022, there are around 700 refugee camps in the world. These are set up by governments and aid agencies to receive and accommodate large numbers of refugees. They are meant to be temporary, while administration work is completed and resettlement arrangements are made, or in hope that the political situation that caused an exodus is quickly resolved. The camps hosting Palestinian refugees removed from Israel have been running for 70 years. There are now over five million registered Palestinian refugees in Middle Eastern countries.

Most refugees would gladly return to their home countries if safety was assured or permanent peace was restored. In 2021, more than 400,000 refugees did so. Helping bring peace to nations is the most effective way to end a refugee crisis.

Refugees can offer much to their new home countries and deserve a welcome from their hosts. A good measure of society is how well it treats those most in need, and that includes those in need of a safe home.

CLIMATE MIGRATION

Worsening climate change (page 242) is expected to result in major migration. Agriculture that relies on predictable rainfall will suffer, with Asia, Central and South America, sub-Saharan Africa, the Middle East and North Africa likely to be most affected. Millions of people are already forced to leave their homes due to floods, storms and drought. Estimates suggest about 200 million people will be displaced due to climate change by the mid-21st century. Some may flee due to conflict over resources. Mitigating climate change is the best solution to this situation, but a major movement of people is to be expected.

OVERPOPULATION

The world's population is increasing by about 83 million every year, with an equivalent demand on the limited resources of the planet. Can we, and should we, stabilize numbers? If so, how?

Over the last 100 years, the human population has been increasing at an exponential rate. Can Earth's resources cope with the extra numbers, and should we be doing something to keep the population at a sustainable level?

At the beginning of the 19th century there were about 1 billion people on Earth. By 1900, this figure was 1.65 billion. In 2023, there was an estimated 8 billion, with numbers expected to rise to 11.2 billion by 2100. The reasons for such growth include better medical care and nutrition. Improved agricultural practices have made it possible to feed more mouths. People are living for longer: an average 73.4 years, compared to less than half that 100 years ago.

Crowded shopping centre in Osaka, Japan.

Not only has the number of people on the planet risen, but people are consuming much more than they used to. Eating more meat means more livestock needs to be bred. Livestock demands more space than the equivalent amount of protein produced in fields of beans or cereals. In 2014, the Worldwide Fund for Nature estimated that we would need the equivalent of one and a half Earths to satisfy humanity's current consumption rate, or four Earths if everyone used up resources at the level of the United States.

To cope with greater numbers on Earth, people will have to reduce their impact on the planet, consider having fewer children, giving up car ownership, taking fewer flights and eating a more plant-based diet.

LIMITING NUMBERS

Methods aimed at stabilizing the number of people being born include better family-planning advice, with good access to contraception, improving the status of women to help them find roles other than being a mother, and reducing infant mortality so that families don't feel the need to compensate with larger families.

Some attempts to reduce the fertility rate have not had the desired result, while some religious groups forbid the use of contraception and encourage large families. China's One-Child Policy introduced in 1979 (with looser quotas allowed in following years) resulted in the population skewing slightly more towards males. India initiated a family-planning programme from 1965. The country's birth rate is dropping but, following current trends, India will still gain about 1 million more people a month and exceed China's population in 2023, with more than 1.4 billion people.

Fertility rates have been dropping in many countries, such as Japan, with couples deciding to have fewer or no children, to prioritize careers or due to lack of funds. This puts pressure on the country's economy, with an aged population receiving less support from younger taxpayers (see panel). Contrastingly, birth rates continue to rise in the least-developed countries, where food shortages can be a problem.

Scientists do not agree on a maximum figure for Earth's population, the planet's 'carrying capacity'. Estimates range from 500 million (a fraction of the current world population) to 1 trillion. A lot depends on how much each person consumes. While management of Earth's resources can be improved, hard decisions may need to be taken to allow the human population to live in comfort without hunger or further detriment to the environment.

AVERAGE AGE

With people living for longer, the average age for the human population has increased. Just 50 years ago, the global median age was 20 years. Today it is 30, with 10 per cent of the population over the age of 65, living in what used to be considered retirement age. The numbers are also the result of lower infant mortality rates. In 1950, 1 in 5 children born was not expected to reach their fifth birthday. Today the rate is 1 in 20. For the first time in history there are now more people on Earth over the age of 64 than under 5. To be able to fund an older population, retirement ages will have to be raised higher than today's average of 60–67.

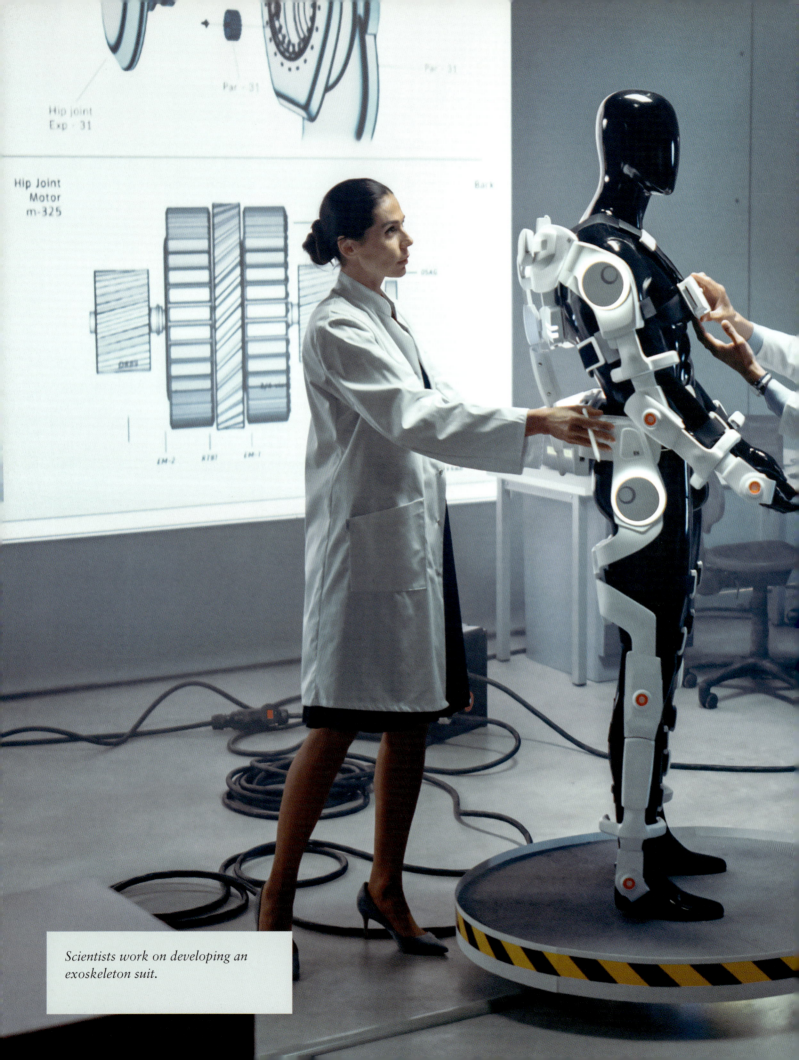

Hip joint
Exp - 31

Par - 31

Hip Joint
Motor
m-325

Back

Scientists work on developing an
exoskeleton suit.

CHAPTER 10

DESIGNING THE FUTURE

What lies ahead for the human race?

Faced with a fast-rising population living for longer, agriculture needs to get smarter, using technology and new methods to grow food for millions more. Continuing climate change will make this more difficult, with unpredictable and extreme weather forecast. A switch from fossil fuels to renewable energy sources could prove our salvation.

Humankind's ability to communicate is one of our greatest assets. We are more connected than ever though the Internet but it is getting harder to sift fact from misinformation. With truth and compassion, we can work together and overcome the greatest of problems and thrive for many more centuries.

In the coming years we can expect a return to the moon. A permanent base will follow. Within the next two decades, the first human astronaut could step on to the surface of Mars. Going further may be beyond the capabilities of the human body. It may be time to venture beyond *Homo sapiens*. With genetic engineering, bionic implants and neural interfaces at our disposal we could replace ourselves with upgraded models. The next stage in evolution could be a digital version of humanity that could last for thousands of years: artificial intelligence.

FUTURE FOOD AND FARMING

To cope with a growing population, farming methods many need to incorporate new technologies, including more automation and GM crops, while helping protect the natural ecosystem.

The move from hunting and foraging to agriculture about 10,000 years ago (page 34) changed humanity's relationship with the world and began a process that reshaped the landscape. As the planet's population grew to number billions, farming methods had to adapt to feed the extra hungry mouths. The 1960s saw a Green Revolution, when new high-yielding and disease-resistant strains of wheat and rice were combined with modern fertilizers to boost food production and prevent famine in the developing world. Agricultural practices continue to progress as land for cultivation and water resources become more limited, while climate change means unpredictable seasons, with periods of drought or floods.

In the late 19th century almost half of US workers were employed in agriculture. By the year 2000, fewer

Autonomous tractor at work in a crop field.

than 2 per cent were. Similar reductions in the farming labour force were seen in Europe, but food output continued to rise. The difference was machinery. Farmers could buy or hire vehicles to plough, plant and harvest in a fraction of the time it took people and horse-drawn tools. In the 21st century, autonomous tractors, drones, soil monitors and irrigation systems can be deployed. Intelligent soil sensors can determine when to water and use just the right amount of fertilizer, eliminating wasteful spreading over entire fields.

Dairy farming has also become mechanized, with cattle able to make their own way to the dairy where they are plugged in for milking. The identity, health and location of each cow can be monitored using electronic ear tags.

Only in the harvesting of delicate fruit and vegetables is large-scale human labour still required on the farm.

NEW CROPS

Farmers have much to consider – animal welfare, sustainability, carbon emissions and protecting the natural ecosystem. Agriculture is the largest contributor

of the greenhouse gases methane and nitrous oxide into the atmosphere and a major consumer of clean water through the raising of livestock. Of particular concern is soil health. A healthy soil regulates the flow of water, filters pollutants and provides support for plant growth. To improve soil fertility and prevent erosion, non-harvested cover crops are planted to grow over winter. An active network of micro-organisms in soil helps plants absorb nutrients. In the future, it may be possible to reduce the use of agro-chemicals as fertilizer by seeding the soil with micro-organisms.

Biologists continue to seek better yielding crops. Since the 1980s, genetically modified (GM) strains (page 240) have been tested and adopted, particularly corn and soya beans, in the quest for hardy, tasty and pest-resistant options. Their use has raised fears about the effect of GM crops on the natural ecosystem, should cross-breeding occur but, so far, they have provided a safe and more productive option for growers.

Agriculture is adapting to new trends and consumer concerns about animal husbandry. Some people are changing their diet for health and environmental reasons, choosing to eat less meat. New meat-production methods are being explored which may even entice vegetarians. Cultured meat is grown in laboratory conditions using tissue engineering, without the exploitation of animals. The technology has been demonstrated, with the world's first cultured hamburger served in 2013. In 2020, Singapore was the first country to approve the sale of lab-grown meat for consumption, with the US Food and Drug Administration following suit in 2022. Work continues to make it a viable alternative to the exploitation of livestock.

Other sources of sustainable future food include algae, which can be farmed in aquaculture sites to provide fishmeal. Insects could also provide sustainable food for future generations. They are high in protein and multiply quickly, though consumers may have to ignore their natural aversion to eating bugs.

VERTICAL FARMS

Indoor vertical farms are one way of alleviating the demand for land. They can also provide a local source for fresh food in an urban environment. In a vertical farm, food – soft fruit and salads – are grown over different levels, often without soil and using LED lights rather than sunlight. Growing systems include hydroponics, aquaponics and aeroponics, where mineral nutrients are provided through a water-based solution or mist. While having the potential to provide a wide variety of crops on less ground, vertical farms are expensive to set up and run, and use much more energy than arable land. Greater efficiency and the use of renewable energy may eventually make vertical farms sustainable. They also have the potential to supply food for future human settlements on the moon or Mars.

Organic vegetables grown using aquaponic or hydroponic methods.

LIVING FOR LONGER

People are generally living longer than they ever did due to better healthcare and nutrition. Is there a limit to how long we can extend life, and should we?

The world's population is booming (page 232) not just because of the birthrate but because more people are surviving to reach old age. For someone living in the Iron Age (roughly 1200 BCE–100 CE, page 66) to live longer than 26 years was above average due to a high infant mortality rate. Thanks to better healthcare and nutrition, in the 2020s more people can expect to live for an average 71 years (male) and 76 years (female). These figures, of course, differ greatly depending on where one lives, economic circumstances and lifestyle.

The current considered limit for the human lifespan is 125 years, but science could push that figure higher. The body ages due to gradual damage to cells, tissues and organs, and greater age brings more likelihood of suffering cardiovascular disease and cancer. Drugs aimed at reducing dying cells and cutting age-related diseases are in development. Different diets and even reducing food intake may play a part in extending life. More radical approaches include genetic alterations and cybernetic implants.

Cybernetics involves the replacement of body parts with mechanical ones. People are regaining hearing and sight thanks to cochlear and retinal implants. Bionic limb replacements are already part of modern medical solutions, with electrode arrays implanted into the brain allowing the user to control robotic limbs. The system also has the potential to relay the sensation of touch.

Bionic replacement parts are already part of medical science.

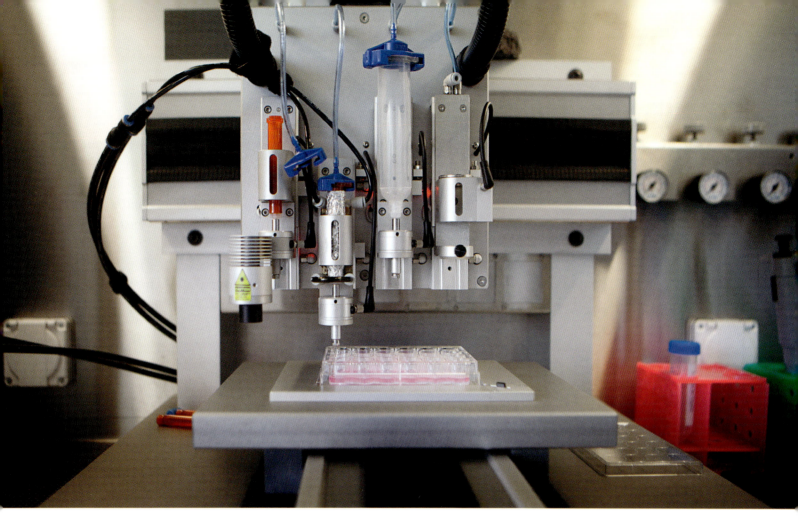

A bioprinter used to produce human tissues.

ETERNAL LIFE

Nanotechnology could provide microscopic cell-repair machines for medical use. Cloning and stem-cell research offers the possibility of growing healthy replacement organs or even bodies in the lab. The concept has been proven in trials, with successful implants of bio-engineered bladders placed in a patient. New organs and tissues could conceivably be 3D bio-printed. In 2002, a US bio-tech company revealed they had managed to 3D-print and transplant a replacement outer ear.

All of the options for life extension are expensive. Several Silicon Valley company founders have invested heavily in the research. A fortune has been spent by the Google Ventures company Calico since 2013 to study the biology of ageing. Altos Labs is a biotech company exploring the possibility of reprogramming genes to persuade mature cells to become immature stem cells, which can then be modified into any other kind of cell.

Of course, any success in extending life does not guarantee it can't be cut short by accident, and one has to consider the quality of life as much as its length. It is in the nature of humanity to seek solutions and, if ageing and even death is considered as a physical problem, resolving it will continue to occupy minds.

DIGITAL IMMORTALITY

The human body may not stand up to the test of time, but machinery may allow a kind of digital immortality. The possibility of downloading one's mind, memory and personality patterns is currently beyond the ability of science but it has its advocates. Should it be possible to store the brain patterns of a person on a microchip, could they not then be uploaded into a new body, such as a clone or android, or even a number of bodies?

GENETIC ENGINEERING

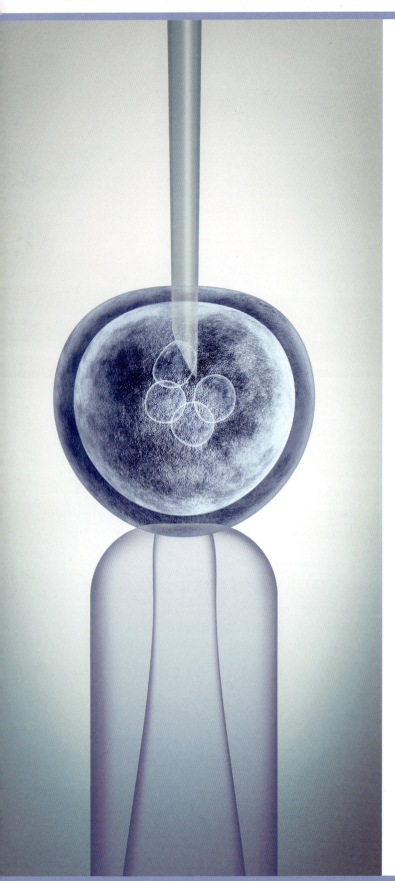

Being able to manipulate genes has given humanity the power to alter the nature of plants and animals. From pest-resistant fruit to bringing extinct animals back to life, is anything off-limits?

Genes are essentially the program files for the human body, instructing it on how it should grow and how it should deal with problems such as injuries and disease. In recent decades knowledge of how genes, or our DNA, works has increased apace, with the complete mapping of the human genome (see panel) in 2022 and the use of genetic profiles in understanding the health of individuals. Genetic engineering allows scientists to work with these building blocks.

Humanity has been altering the makeup of plants and animals for millennia, through the selective sowing and breeding of domesticated crops and livestock. The Aztecs turned the unpromising wild grass teosinte into multiple varieties of the staple food corn. The submissive descendants of wolves now share our homes. Genetic engineering provides humanity with even greater control over species.

The technology was demonstrated for the first time with a genetically modified (GM) bacterium in 1973. Since then many GM crops (page 236) have been designed to shrug off pests and diseases and produce higher yields and new flavours. As well as improving or changing the taste of plants, beneficial minerals and vitamins can be added. The first GM food, a tomato altered to have a longer shelf life, went on sale in 1994. In the future, if geneticists can increase a plant's ability to photosynthesize, crops could be manufactured to grow much faster.

Gene research with a fertilized human egg embryo.

BACK FROM THE DEAD

In 2012, the CRISPR (clustered regularly interspaced short palindromic repeats) system was introduced. This allows selective and easier changes to be made to the complete set of genes, or genome, of almost any organism.

Among the work being undertaken by genetic engineers is modifying the genome of mosquitoes to make them less likely to spread malaria, and developing bacterium that can produce insulin. The science of genetic engineering offers the prospect of helping cure genetic diseases, including Parkinson's, via gene therapy.

For a price, you can now take a genetic test to identify mutations in your genes that may cause a future genetic disorder, or order a complete genome sequencing for a lot less than the billions spent over decades to map the very first human genome.

Control of DNA also brings up the prospect of resurrecting extinct species. Bringing the woolly mammoth back to life using a genome extracted from a frozen specimen has been posited. Attempts are now underway to raise a thylacine, the Tasmanian marsupial that died out in captivity in 1936. Scientists hope to edit stem cells of a similar marsupial to produce an embryo that is 99.9 per cent the same as the original creature and eventually release it into the wild.

THE HUMAN GENOME

In 2022, after 32 years of research, scientists at the Human Genome Project announced that they had sequenced the complete human genome, the DNA blueprint of a human being. By comparing different DNA, scientists will be able to better understand how a person's body reacts against disease. Knowledge of genome sequencing also allows experts to locate mutations that cause genetic disorders.

A researcher prepares a sample of DNA for sequencing for the human genome project.

CLIMATE CHANGE

Our use of fossil fuels and increasing consumption is changing Earth's climate in ways that will seriously impact life on the planet. What can we do to slow down the process and how can we adapt to what is to come?

Earth's climate has seen many changes. Over millions of years the temperature and atmosphere of the planet fluctuated, wiping out species of dinosaurs, then allowing others to flourish. Ice ages saw continents freeze and sea levels drop, providing a route for early humans to migrate to what would later become isolated lands. These changes were determined by natural events, such as volcanic activity and variations in earth's orbit around the sun.

The climate change we face today is different. It is mostly caused by our own actions, the burning of fossil fuels and the removal of forests. Greenhouse gases, such as carbon dioxide (CO_2), are necessary to keep the planet comfortably warm but they are entering the atmosphere at a greater pace. Levels of CO_2 are now 30 per cent higher than a century ago, at amounts unseen on Earth for about 4.1 million years, during the Pliocene. Humanity has never experienced these volumes before.

Receding glaciers are a sign that Earth's temperature is rising.

The consequence is a warmer world. Rises of a few degrees may seem subtle, but it's enough to cause the ice at the poles and millennia-old glaciers to retreat. By 2050, we are likely to see ice-free summers in the Arctic. The Arctic tundra retains much methane, another greenhouse gas, that could be released should its permafrost melt.

Melting ice means sea levels have been rising by about 3 mm (0.1 in) a year since the early 1990s. Low-lying islands will begin to disappear underwater. A fifth of the population of the Marshall Islands in the Pacific Ocean have left, concerned that their home will be swamped before long. Bangladesh could lose 10 per cent of its land within a few decades, forcing up to 18 million people to relocate.

The oceans are warming, too, and becoming more acidic, causing coral reefs to expel the algae living in their tissues and turn white. Weather patterns are becoming less predictable and more extreme.

SAVING THE PLANET

It is no longer just an issue of how to stop or reverse climate change; climate change is here. We have to mitigate the problem. An international agreement initiated in Paris in 2015 (page 229) set a limit on the global temperature rise above 19th-century pre-industrial levels. This maximum temperature is expected to be hit by the mid-2030s. Avoiding a higher temperature is to be achieved by countries setting limits on their carbon emissions.

The most obvious way to reduce emissions is to use fewer carbon-based fuels, like oil and coal. This may mean fewer journeys by car or air, improved home insulation and the use of more efficient technology, such as LED lighting. Using renewable energy (page 244), including solar or wind, to generate power helps.

Electric cars are slowly replacing gas-guzzling vehicles. Several automobile manufacturers, including Ford, General Motors and Volvo, have committed themselves to phasing out the production of fossil-fuel vehicles by 2040 or sooner. 2021 saw a total of 16.5 million electric cars in use but, with a billion motor vehicles in the world, there is still a way to go.

Planting more trees, while protecting those we have, will also help. Forests, oceans and soil are carbon sinks, where carbon dioxide is naturally absorbed and stored. Forests absorb 2.4 billion tonnes (2.36 billion tons) of carbon dioxide a year.

There are also technological innovations that could be used to cut the amount of carbon dioxide in the atmosphere. Direct Air Capture (DAC) would see companies take CO_2 from the air and use it for fuel or even to add bubbles to soft drinks. More extreme technological solutions, such as adding alkaline to the oceans, tampering with clouds, and even blocking sunlight are being explored, but it is hoped that none of these will prove necessary.

Climate change is happening now and it is already affecting the environment and triggering extreme weather conditions. Keeping the planet habitable or otherwise, after millennia of adverse human action, is likely to be the most significant act for humanity in the coming years.

THE OZONE LAYER

The depletion of the ozone layer was the major environmental talking point of the 1980s. While it is still of concern, the response to the issue proved that global action is possible and effective against major ecological problems. The ozone layer is a region in Earth's stratosphere that shields the planet from harmful ultraviolet rays from the sun that can cause skin cancer. The use of chlorofluorocarbons (CFCs) in aerosols and refrigeration was identified as a major cause of the ozone layer's depletion. Action in 1987 led to CFCs being phased out. Since 2000, the ozone hole has shown good signs of recovery.

RENEWABLE ENERGY

What are the options for replacing fossil fuels, and can they completely replace coal, gas and oil?

The exploitation of fossil fuels (coal, oil, gas) powered the Industrial Revolution (page 172) but, by releasing greenhouse gases into the atmosphere, it delivered human-made climate change (page 242). Humanity has to find alternatives to maintain a healthy and habitable planet for future generations.

Renewable energy is energy sourced from mostly sustainable sources that are not exhausted by use. Examples are solar, wind, hydropower and geothermal energy. Bioenergy, which uses organic materials, is considered renewable but is not entirely sustainable. In 2020, renewable sources accounted for 29 per cent of global electricity generation, with 256 gigawatts of power produced over that year.

The first functional solar cell was invented in 1954. Since then, the efficiency of the cells in converting sunlight into electricity has risen from 6 per cent to 47 per cent. Over the last 70 years, more efficient designs have coincided with a reduction in costs to make it possible for more households to add panels to the roofs of their homes and benefit from a cleaner source of power. Solar power now generates about 2 per cent of the world's electricity. In Australia, where much sunny weather is guaranteed, more than 30 per cent of households have installed rooftop photovoltaic panels.

Solar photovoltaic cells are also available in small, portable versions, for use on mobile homes, while pocket-sized models can recharge a smartphone. Solar panels seem obtrusive, particularly when they are arranged in quantity on large solar farms but, in the future, they are expected to work using thinner and transparent layers, as photovoltaic glass in windows. Solar filaments woven into fabrics would allow the wearer to generate solar power on the move.

WIND, WATER, WOOD

Wind farms made up of towering, three-bladed turbines have become a familiar sight on open land and offshore. China is taking the lead in new wind-turbine installation, establishing more capacity in 2021 than the rest of the world combined over five years. The UK, well-located for wind-power generation, boasts the largest offshore wind farm, sited off England's east coast. These installations are part of the countries' expressed aim of reaching net zero emissions within decades, but increasing demand for energy means progress towards this target is somewhat hampered.

Hydropower, which converts the kinetic energy of river flow or tides to generate electricity, is extremely productive but requires huge investment in infrastructure, which has an impact on the environment. The largest power station in the world is China's Three Gorges Dam which can generate about 100 Terawatt-hours (TWh) a year.

Solar panels installed on the roofs of private houses.

Blue Lagoon with Svartsengi geothermal energy plant, Iceland.

Bioenergy is a more controversial option. While its source is renewable, it requires the planting and harvesting of sugar and oil-producing plants and forests on land that could be providing food, or habitats for wildlife. Burning biofuels also adds pollutants to the atmosphere. Sources for bioenergy include wood residues, methane gas produced by rotting food waste, or alcohols from fermented sugar and starch plants.

Geothermal energy is provided by thermal energy inside the earth and tends to be exploited in countries, such as Iceland, with high volcanic or hot-spring activity.

Concern over climate change and pollution, along with more efficient technology, has led to the rising use of renewable energy. Conflicts with countries that possess and export large resources of oil and gas – Russia's invasion of Ukraine in 2022 is a recent example – have provided further reasons for countries to invest in renewables, to ensure they retain energy security. A switch to using nothing but renewably sourced energy is viable but it requires commitment from governments.

FUSION FUTURE

Nuclear power stations do not release climate-changing gases but they do produce radioactive waste as a by-product of nuclear fission, which splits heavy atoms, such as uranium, into lighter elements. An alternative is nuclear fusion, the process by which the sun generates light and heat, by turning light atoms, such as hydrogen, into heavier atoms, like helium, under enormous heat and pressure. In 2020, a team at Korea's Superconducting Tokamak Advanced Research lab managed to maintain their 'artificial sun' at 100 million°C (180 million°F) and the conditions for creating energy for 30 seconds. In 2022, researchers at the US National Ignition Facility in California announced they had used high-powered lasers to spark a fusion ignition that delivered an energy gain, another step forward in developing clean fusion power. Nonetheless, nuclear fusion is a long way from being sustained on earth. Should it be mastered, it promises to deliver an almost endless source of power without any waste.

THE ONLINE WORLD

Over half the population of the world are regularly using the Internet as work and social lives revolve around it. Could humanity get any more connected?

In 2022, approximately 5.03 billion people used the Internet, more than 63 per cent of the global population. This number is only expected to grow. Over a typical 12 months the figure jumps by about 180 million. The average user spends almost seven hours online a day.

Most people use a smartphone to access the Internet, for work, entertainment or to connect with friends through social media. Approximately 4.7 billion people have social media accounts. Facebook alone has 2.96 billion users, more than the populations of the two most populous countries, China and India, combined.

Social media has become the medium for cataloguing lives. It has also played a part in the organization of protests and provided a platform for the reporting of injustice. The Arab Spring of 2011 saw many people drawn together via social media to take to the streets in protest against authoritarian regimes. In 2021, right-wing protestors stormed Capitol Hill in Washington DC, spurred on by social media.

The medium has proved important for candidates in election campaigns hoping to reach supporters, but

the unpoliced nature of the Internet means that much misinformation is shared and once-trusted print, TV and internet sites find themselves accused of bias by online opposition. Fake news and conspiracy theories find eager devotees. Sometimes truth struggles to be heard.

Despite its flaws, the Internet provides much of value – broad knowledge and scholarly insight, a place for people to unite with those of shared tastes or experience, a direct-market store and a repository of seemingly endless entertainment and distraction.

DIRECT CONNECTIONS

In the near future, the use of neural interfaces could connect humans directly with the Internet without the need for touchscreens or vocal commands. As with a desktop browser, the contents of libraries, the output of webcams and the calculating power of supercomputers would be at one's disposal. The proposed cortical modem would require much getting used to, as the user would have to switch between the evidence of their eyes and input from the Internet. There is also the risk of malware reaching the brain just as it threatens any online computer.

Virtual Reality (VR) has been around for decades. Early models required the user to don a clunky headset and wired gloves. After finding a market in gaming, VR tech took off in leaps and bounds, with affordable consumer VR headsets becoming available in the 2010s. The technology is now sophisticated enough that doctors can examine patients and supervise trainees from afar.

AR, augmented reality, does not require a computer-generated environment but provides images and information overlays on top of the existing landscape. Early examples, such as Google Glass, connected with the Internet to project mapping and descriptive text on to the lenses of a pair of spectacles. Similar tech can be used with smartphone apps and games, placing animated characters in the phone's camera view.

Fast internet connections have reduced the need to work in an office. Online video conferencing connects teams for virtual meetings.

In 2021, the company that owns the social-media giant Facebook announced a new name, Meta, and an intention to focus on a virtual platform, the Metaverse, which would utilize headsets that incorporate both VR and AR technology. The aim of the Metaverse is to provide an online environment for work meetings, educational visits to VR locations, e-commerce and entertainment. Just as almost

Use of VR headsets by the US Army.

every business has its own website or shop, success for the Metaverse would mean every business needing to have a VR presence, too.

YOU ARE THE PRODUCT

Most websites are free to access. Though many run adverts, the product they gain most from is the user. Data is everything. Knowledge of the user's preferences is valuable for website controllers wanting to find a direct market for promotions or information. The smart algorithms and cookies built into websites can build a picture of visitor preferences. Soon goods you never knew you wanted will appear to tempt you. Opinions you might share will attract campaigners seeking your vote on issues you care about. Much of your personal information is being gathered without you being aware of it.

The accumulation of information on human behaviour is a vast resource described as Big Data, and it can be analyzed by artificial intelligence (page 218) and used to predict business, health, crime and political trends. With this information available, AI can be used to make major decisions on our behalf. But could we allow it to run our lives? AI using facial recognition algorithms and recruitment data has proven to be flawed due to biases introduced by human creators or limited sources. Can we trust AI's

impartiality, and is a machine's lack of human empathy a benefit or handicap? The ethics of using artificial intelligence in decision-making remains a hot topic.

CRYPTOCURRENCY

Cryptocurrency was invented in 1983 but took off in the 21st century. This digital form of currency does not rely on a central bank and is not controlled by any government, which is part of its appeal. Records of its ownership and worth are kept online in a computer database. Despite its lack of physical form, the process of maintaining cryptocurrency requires vast computing power, consuming electricity on the scale of a country such as Sweden. The validity of a crypto coin is provided by an encrypted record called a blockchain which registers every transaction. Relatively little cryptocurrency is spent on physical items. It is kept as an investment and, in that regard, it has proved risky. The values of various cryptocurrencies have undergone dramatic rises and falls. Instances of hacking have also led to the loss and theft of huge amounts of the digital currency and, if a user forgets the password to their digital wallet, they are locked out of it forever.

EXPLORING NEW WORLDS

Fifty years after the last astronaut stepped on the lunar surface, plans for crewed missions to the moon are underway, with Mars on the horizon. Where next for humankind?

Humankind last stepped foot on another world in December 1972, when the final Apollo mission delivered US astronauts Eugene Cernan and Harrison Schmitt to the moon. Having proved it possible to send astronauts to Earth's satellite, and gathered rock specimens, NASA ended the Apollo program. In the 2020s, the age of private space travel, voyages to the moon and beyond are once again being planned.

In 2022, NASA successfully launched its new Artemis rocket and placed an Orion capsule in lunar orbit. NASA plans to send a four-person crew to the moon using such a system in 2025, including the first female and first person of colour to walk on the lunar surface. The mission could provide the groundwork for a permanent space station in lunar orbit, followed by a base camp on the moon's south pole for teams of astronauts to work a week at a time. China and Russia have also planned a joint programme for an orbiting lunar station and moonbase.

The moon has no atmosphere, nothing to breathe and nothing to block harmful radiation from the sun. Day to night surface temperatures range from 120 to −153°C (248 to −243°F). If humans were to begin a life there they would need to bring almost everything with them. The moon has water, an estimated 600 million tonnes (590 million tons) as ice in the shade of craters around the moon's poles. This could provide water for a moon-based crew and for plants grown as food and oxygen suppliers. The water could also provide for liquid oxygen as rocket propellant.

One benefit of a moonbase would be as a launch-pad to missions even further afield and, in that respect, Mars is high on the agenda.

The launch of Artemis I, NASA's moon-capable Space Launch System rocket on the launchpad at Kennedy Space Center, 2022.

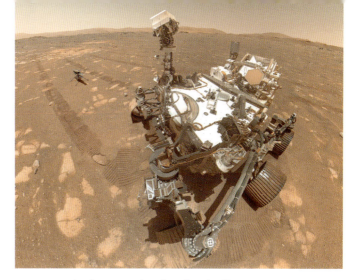

A photograph taken by the Perseverance rover on the surface of Mars in 2021, showing the Ingenuity helicopter behind it.

THE RED PLANET

Mars seems an obvious next target for a landing after the moon but, even with the 21st century's efficient rocket technology, there are limits to what chemical fuels can do. A one-way journey to the Red Planet would take about nine months, depending on Mars' position in orbit. Astronauts would then have to stay for around 16 months until another nine-month journey window was possible. As well as a major step in human exploration, examining Mars could provide answers on how climate change affects planets and reveal whether life in any form once lived on the world.

The tech billionaire Elon Musk announced ambitions to place a million people on Mars within 100 years, using his company's SpaceX rocket. He won't be short of volunteers. When the non-profit Mars One Foundation asked for potential colonists for a one-way trip to Mars in 2013, it received more than 200,000 applications. Tests have been run to see how humans might deal with small-group isolation. In 2010, as part of the MARS-500 mission, six Russian men were placed in a facility in a Moscow car park for 520 days to simulate being on a Mars mission. They managed to avoid conflicts and worked well together, though they became more lethargic in the latter months.

Mars is marginally more welcoming than the moon. It is also thought to have water ice buried underneath the surface. It has an atmosphere, 95 per cent carbon dioxide, toxic to humans. Landings are very tricky. There is little atmospheric pressure, only 38 per cent of the gravity of Earth, and it's a chilly −85 to −5°C (−121 to 23°F). Large dust storms also occur.

Robotic missions would likely be sent first, to supply the materials needed to build safe shelters for astronauts. Current expectations are that a NASA-crewed Mars mission could occur in the late 2030s or early 2040s. China also plans crewed missions, one every two years from 2033.

For Mars, more than the moon, settling is likely to be a claustrophobic and lonely experience for the first arrivals and probably a one-way trip. Astronauts who have spent weeks in Earth orbit on the International Space Station (page 200) have lost bone density with little gravity to move against. After a nine-month spaceflight, the astronauts would need to build strength to explore the Mars landscape on foot.

Earth's brightest minds will focus on how to expand humankind's reach to other worlds and launch distant colonies, but the hurdles presented and the difficulties in making it possible for the human body to survive and thrive in a hostile environment make it clear that we should expend as much effort protecting the one place in the universe where we already know humankind is at home.

INTERSTELLAR TRAVEL

The limitations of chemically fuelled rockets and the human body prevent us from voyaging deep into space. New power sources, such as ion drives, solar sails and nuclear fusion could send us beyond Mars but, even if scientists were able to create a space vehicle capable of near light speed, it would still take over four years to reach Proxima Centauri, the nearest star beyond our sun. Current technology could get us there in 6,300 years. If it were not possible for the astronauts to be cryogenically frozen for much of the journey, then it would take many generations.

THE FUTURE OF HUMANITY

Where next for humankind? Will *Homo sapiens* adapt through technology to become a new artificial life form? Can we survive the next millennia and provide a safe environment for future generations?

Over the thousands of years since *Homo sapiens* first migrated from Africa the human body has altered little. We have got much smarter and more sophisticated and, thanks to better healthcare and food science, the average human height has risen by 8–9 cm (3–3.5 in) in the last century. How might we evolve over the next centuries?

Transhumanism is the idea of using technology to improve human beings. Methods includes genetic manipulation, pharmaceuticals and machine enhancements. Genetic engineering (page 240) offers up the prospect of our DNA being altered to reduce the risk of genetic disorders, but gene manipulation could also provide enhancements for all. Specific genes could be directed to enlarge certain parts of the brain, improving our cognitive skills, memory and intelligence. Personality could be affected too, stimulating a happier and more generous mood.

Will AI become sentient in the future?

The ability to tamper with the nature of humanity brings with it major moral implications. Even if the process was approved, do we want to create a race of super-intelligent humans to guide or rule a compliant majority of genetically happy people?

There may come a point when people choose to replace body parts for machinery that gives them added strength or speed. Bionic implants are already replacing eyes and missing limbs; exoskeletons are helping people with walking difficulties, or for military exercises.

We may reach a limit to what we can replace in the human body. The next step would be attempting to download a human brain into a machine body. This may be the day we say farewell to *Homo sapiens* and announce the dawn of the next *Homo* species, a genetically superior or artificial version. A cyborg body would not need food, water or air. It would suit long-distance space travel. Artificial intelligence could one day be smart enough to live independently and become the ambassador for Earth in the far reaches of space.

CHALLENGES AHEAD

Whatever physical form humanity takes in the next centuries, we have many challenges to overcome, many of our own making. Human migrations still occur for reasons of war and economic betterment, but now also to escape the damage from climate change. Contagious diseases still threaten humankind, though we now have better means to deal with them. Inequality still exists; corruption and dictatorships still need to be confronted.

Where once we domesticated flora and fauna, now we reconfigure the building blocks of life to create genetically modified foods. The written word is now a digital record shared instantly on social media. Precious metal is still coveted, but coinage is replaced by online transfers. Art old and new can be admired as a jpg file or an immersive 3D experience. All the world's music is available to stream to a handheld device.

Our curiosity has led us to investigate the natural world, reach for the moon and stars, and question what it is to be human. Through art, writing and music we express ourselves and challenge our perceptions; through religion, we have attempted to explain the unknowable; through science we have decoded the human body and peered back in time billions of years. The drive to find answers keeps us moving forward, but development has also introduced catastrophic weapons, pollution and global warming to our planet. The greatest danger to humanity is ourselves, and we must unite to safeguard our future.

We have done it before. Humankind has survived ice ages, wars and plagues. We have built cities and monuments, created images and shared stories that have lasted millennia. We have designed tools for combat but also for cultivation.

Technological progress demonstrates the ingenuity of humankind. But, just as remarkable is our ability to communicate, to work together, empathize and be generous. These are the attributes that should see humanity thrive through and beyond the 21st century. Humankind needs to come together to deal with climate change, conflict and prejudice. With the best of intentions, *Homo sapiens* will continue to do remarkable things and provide the material for many more chapters.

THE SINGULARITY

The singularity is the point at which AI possesses an intelligence beyond our own. There are many theories about what might happen at this point, from the optimistic idea of computers taking control of Earth affairs and solving all our problems, to the dystopian concept of humanity under the metal boot of the machine or considered a nuisance that it needs to be rid of. AI is already playing a major part in our lives. Could it one day convince us that it possesses consciousness?

INDEX

PICTURE CREDITS